THE 9 STEPS TO FINANCIAL FREEDOM

ALSO BY SUZE ORMAN

You've Earned It, Don't Lose It:
Mistakes You Can't Afford to Make When You Retire

The Courage to Be Rich: Creating the Life of
Material and Spiritual Abundance

THE

9 STEPS

TO

FINANCIAL

FREEDOM

**PRACTICAL & SPIRITUAL
STEPS SO YOU CAN
STOP WORRYING**

SUZE ORMAN

THREE RIVERS PRESS • NEW YORK

A Note to the Reader: As of the publication of this book, all of the information is up to date. It is possible that in the upcoming years, laws, especially those pertaining to retirement accounts and estate taxes, may change. In order to remain abreast of current legislation, please go to the NineStep updates section of my website, www.suzeorman.com. On the site you may download important information regarding any new financial laws.

Copyright © 1997, 2000 by Suze Orman

All rights reserved. No part of this book may be reproduced or transmitted in any form or by any means, electronic or mechanical, including photocopying, recording, or by any information storage and retrieval system, without permission in writing from the publisher.

Published by Three Rivers Press, New York, New York. Member of the Crown Publishing Group.

Random House, Inc. New York, Toronto, London, Sydney, Auckland www.randomhouse.com

THREE RIVERS PRESS is a registered trademark and the Three Rivers Press colophon is a trademark of Random House, Inc.

Originally published in hardcover by Crown Publishers in 1997.

Printed in the United States of America

Design by Cynthia Dunne

Library of Congress Cataloging-in-Publication Data
Orman, Suze.
    The 9 steps to financial freedom / Suze Orman.—1st pbk. ed.
    Includes index.
    1. Finance, Personal. I. Title.
  HG179.0755 1997
  332.024—dc21   98-3320

ISBN 0-609-80186-4

Not long ago, I asked my mom whether, when my dad was alive, she had seen him cry a lot. She thought for a second and said, "Well, he only really cried when he watched *Wheel of Fortune.*"

"*Wheel of Fortune?*"

"Yes," she said, "when people would win a lot of money, he would be so happy for them that he would cry." That sums up my dad—to wish for others what he wished for himself. This is true generosity. Dad, I hope you can see me now and are as proud of me as I only wish I could tell you that I am of you. Mom, I will always be there for you, so don't you ever worry, I love you—you are the best.

Contents

Preface ⇥ ix

What Do You Want from
Your Money? ⇥ 1

Step 1: Seeing How Your Past Holds the Key
to Your Financial Future ⇥ 9

Step 2: Facing Your Fears and Creating New
Truths ⇥ 21

Step 3: Being Honest with Yourself ⇥ 35

Step 4: Being Responsible to Those
You Love ⇥ 51

Step 5: Being Respectful of Yourself and
Your Money ⇥ 133

Step 6: Trusting Yourself More Than You
Trust Others ⇥ 231

Step 7: Being Open to Receive All That You
Are Meant to Have ⇥ 303

Step 8: Understanding the Ebb and Flow
of the Money Cycle ⇥ 317

Step 9: Recognizing True Wealth ⇥ 327

Index ⇥ 333

PREFACE

When it comes to money, the question "What are you afraid of?" is a powerful question indeed. I knew that when I wrote *The 9 Steps to Financial Freedom*. After working for years as a Certified Financial Planner® professional*, I had seen over and over with my clients how dramatically fears affect finances—every time. I came to understand that, as much as I knew about money, I also had many fears to overcome. It was a steep learning curve, for me as well as for my clients, probing into the pain and fear and destructive emotions that will swirl around our money for as long as we let them. And eventually, moving beyond that pain, that fear, step by step, into a new realm and reality where financial freedom is truly possible. After taking this journey together, after following the nine steps, it was amazing to see how my clients' money would simply fall into place.

As profoundly as I believed in these nine steps myself, I could not have imagined in my wildest dreams that my book would touch so many lives. In the years since it was first published, I've

*Certified Financial Planner® is a federally registered mark owned by the Certified Financial Planner Board of Standards, Inc.

given up my practice and embarked instead on a mission: to turn people toward their money. I've traveled throughout and beyond America, met and talked to hundreds of people about their money, and received letters from thousands of readers, from Wall Street tycoons to housewives who are slowly but surely working their way out of credit card debt. These letters have reinforced what I knew, in my heart, all along. These nine steps work. They can work for you, just as they've worked for many others. On their own, they can't change your life, but you can change your life, if you take them. You can set yourself on the course to financial freedom.

When I say that I've given up working with clients on a daily basis, however, I don't mean that I've given up working with money: studying it, tracking it, watching new trends, analyzing new laws, assessing which kinds of investments work best for which kinds of investors. I have more time now to monitor money, and I spend a good part of every day doing so. Why? Because you will never be financially free simply by facing your fears and moving beyond them.

Once you turn to your money, you must also take the financial actions necessary to create that freedom, and ensure it. Those financial actions are among the nine steps as well, and they, too, will help you set yourself on the course to financial freedom.

As it happened, *The 9 Steps to Financial Freedom* was published at a revolutionary time in the financial world, a world which in one way or another deeply affected us all. The stock market had risen dramatically, in record-setting ways, and fallen just as dramatically, as always, on a course of its own but with a surge in momentum, as it became more available to more of us. Discount brokers began to appeal to newly savvy investors, who saw that they need not pay such high commissions as they had in the past. Investing over the Internet, not even possible a few years ago, further made the stock market accessible to more and more people. There were more mutual funds than ever before, funds for every niche of investor. Suddenly stock prices began to be broadcast over the television, all day, every day. New money magazines appeared over the past few years, targeted, perhaps for the first time, for people not in the money business but for people who were turning to their money. Not to mention new websites. Suzeorman.com couldn't have existed even a few years ago—but I hope you'll visit it today. It's as if the language of money has pervaded our culture in a new way and is imploring us to listen. Once you turn toward your money, you will want to listen, I can promise you that. And financial freedom will give you the power to hear.

I'll be the first to tell you very sincerely that I love money, and also the first to ask you: Who doesn't love money? You can claim you don't care about money, that you don't understand money, or tell the world that you'll never have any money . . . but why send that message out into the world? You can have money, all the money that you and your loved ones will ever need. You can enjoy financial freedom, regardless of the amount of money you have at this very minute. Financial freedom is within the reach of each and every one of us. When you turn toward your money, and begin to value it, nurture it, and truly respect it for what it can (and cannot) do, you'll see what I mean.

The course to financial freedom is also, I believe, the path to true wealth, which is a state of being, a state of grace, that transcends the bottom line, any bottom line. It's where you know beyond a shadow of a doubt that you and your money have done everything possible to make your loved ones safe and sound. It's where money flows into your life and out of it into the larger world, generously and expansively. It's where your money will sustain you but not define you, nor assign you your true worth.

It's not the goal of this book to teach this kind of wealth, but I remind you of it here, because it's the essential goal of life.

Your future is at hand, and your future is at stake. I hope you'll take this book into your hands and into your heart and embark on the course to financial freedom and true wealth.

What Do
You Want from
Your Money?

WHAT DO YOU want from your money? College tuition for your kids? A bigger house and a new car? Security when you retire?

Wouldn't it be great simply to have enough money so you don't have to worry?

The "enough money" part of that equation is easy. By the time you finish this book you will understand everything you need to know about managing and protecting your money and making it grow. The "so you don't have to worry" part is much more complex. It actually has nothing to do with how much money you have or how little. You can balance your checkbook until you're blue in the face, you can move money every day between your mutual funds, you can double your life insurance, you can buy lottery tickets—and none of it will do you any good until you get beyond the worry and fear. The fear of money, the fear of not having enough, the fear of having enough, the fear of taking action, the fear of inaction.

There isn't a part of our lives that money doesn't touch—it affects our relationships, the way we go about our everyday activities, our ability to make dreams reality, everything. Most of us, I think, have a core of anxiety that we carry around with us, though we may not admit it to ourselves. That is part of money's power over us.

From years as a financial planner I have learned that true financial freedom doesn't depend on how much money you have. Financial freedom is when you have power over your fears and anxieties instead of the other way around. That's why, in this book, we'll address first the fears, then the finances.

Whatever their circumstances—in debt, working, downsized, afraid of becoming downsized, retired, having just inherited money, having just lost money—my clients invariably arrived with a handful of financial papers and a heart full of anxieties. Like most Certified Financial Planner® professionals, I started my practice to help other people with their money, but as time went on, I realized that it was far more than their money (or lack of it) that needed attention. Clients arrived expecting me to ask to see their papers. Instead I asked them first to share their fears.

It's never too soon to begin, and it's never too late, no matter how the bottom-line numbers read today on your particular handful of financial papers. This book presents a nine-step process that will take you back into the past, when your attitudes about money were born and began to grow. It will help you face the present honestly and clear the way for you to create a future you will love.

I know it works. As you read this book you will meet others who have taken the steps toward financial freedom—and finally made possible the lives they dreamed about.

You will also see that if I could do it against all odds, so can you. When I was very young I had already learned that the reason my parents seemed so unhappy wasn't that they didn't love each other; it was that they never had quite enough money even to pay the bills. In our house money meant tension, worry, and sorrow. When I was about thirteen my dad owned his own business, a tiny chicken shack where he sold take-out chicken, ribs, hamburgers, hot dogs, and fries. One day the oil that the chicken was fried in caught fire. In a few minutes the whole place exploded in flames. My dad bolted from the store before the flames could engulf him. This was when my mom and I happened to arrive on the scene, and we all stood outside watching the fire burn away my dad's business.

All of a sudden my dad realized that he had left his money in the metal cash register inside the building, and I watched in disbelief as he ran back into the inferno, in the split second before anyone could stop him. He tried and tried to open the metal register, but the intense heat had already sealed the drawer shut. Knowing that every penny he had was locked in front of him, about to go up into flames, he literally picked up the scalding metal box and carried it outside. When he threw the register on the ground, the skin on his arms and chest came with it.

He had escaped the fire safely once, untouched. Then he voluntarily risked his life and was severely injured. The money was that important. That was when I learned that money is obviously more important than life itself.

From that point on, earning money, lots of money, not only became what drove me professionally, but also became my emotional priority. Money became, for me, not the means to a life rich in all kinds of ways; money became my singular goal.

Years later this kid from the South Side of Chicago was a broker with a huge investment firm. I was rich, richer than I could have imagined. And I realized I was profoundly unhappy; the money hadn't bought or brought me happiness. So if money wasn't the key to happiness, what was? It was then that I began a quest, which has taken me deep into the meaning of life—and the meaning of money.

I don't know if I have discovered the meaning of life, but I have learned a great deal about what money can and cannot do. And it can do a lot. Your money will work for you, and you will always have enough—more than enough—when you give it energy, time, and understanding. I have come to think that money is very much like a person, and it will respond when you treat it as you would a cherished friend—never fearing it, pushing it away, pretending it doesn't exist, or turning away from its needs, never clutching it so hard that it hurts. Sometimes it's fatter, sometimes it's skinnier, sometimes it doesn't feel so good and needs special nurturing. But if you tend it like the living entity it is, then it will flourish, grow, take care of you for as long as you need it, and look after the loved ones you leave behind.

Most of us already know at least some of the steps we could take to free ourselves from money anxieties—we could manage our debt better, arrange for our children's education, strategically plan now for later, protect what we've saved, save more. Yet most of us are paralyzed, too, when it comes to actually taking these steps, however wise they seem, however much we think we really want to take control.

What good will it do you to know what you should do, if you can't do it?

THE NINE STEPS TO FINANCIAL FREEDOM: A PREVIEW

The first steps of this book take you back to discover why you don't do the things you know you should do and bring you beyond that—to where you can take action. These steps will free you to open up a dialogue about money with your parents, your children, and, most important, yourself. The next three steps are the laws of managing money. These laws are must-do's. They cover everything from wills and trusts and what insurance you need (and don't need) to new ways to think about debt and your 401(k) or retirement plan to how to invest and what to invest in. They teach you why you must trust yourself more than you trust anyone else with your money.

The goal of these particular steps is to make you as independent from financial advisers as possible. Over the years, I learned that it was in my clients' best interest for them to take control over their money, not to relinquish it, even to me. If, later on, they choose to entrust their money to someone else, with these steps they would no longer be able to be taken advantage of by an unscrupulous adviser—or by their unwillingness to face up to the facts and figures of their own finances. Once you take these steps, you will discover the exhilaration that comes from wanting to deal with your money, not just having to deal with it.

The last three steps take you beyond the realm of finances, to the wealth that money can't buy.

When it comes to money, freedom starts to happen when what you *do, think,* and *say* are one. You'll never be free if you say that you have more than enough, then act as if and think you don't. You'll never be free if you think you don't have enough, then act as if and say you do. You will have enough when you believe you will and take the actions to express that belief. And you'll have more than enough when you realize that you can be rich at any income because you are more than your money, you are more than your job or title, than the car you drive or the clothing you wear. Your own power and worth are not judged by what money can sell and what money can buy; true freedom cannot be bought or sold at any price. True freedom, true wealth, is that which can never be lost.

SETTING YOUR GOALS

Please ask yourself right now: What is it that I want to get out of reading this book?

Financial freedom is something we're all working for, but each of us has specific things that concern us the most. To achieve complete financial freedom, you'll need to follow all the nine steps. But depending on what your goal is, you'll want to pay special attention to certain sections of the book. So let us begin by deciding on your goals. Here are some examples; feel free to choose new ones or rephrase these in a different way.

⊰ӂ I want to pay off my credit cards and get out from under my debt. (See Step 5.)

⊰ӂ I want to make sure there will be enough money for my child's education. (See Step 6.)

⊰ӂ I want to retire in ten years. (See Step 5.)

⊰ӂ I want to be confident that my family will be provided for if something happens to me. (See Step 4.)

⊰ӂ I want to take a year off and travel. (See Step 5.)

⊰ӂ I want to get a better grasp on my expenses so I'm not always behind paying my bills. (See Step 3.)

⇥ I want to know my mother can afford it if she needs medical care as she gets older. (See Step 4.)

The most important thing to remember is that whatever your goal is, you can make it happen and goal by goal, step by step, you can take charge of your destiny and achieve financial freedom. The power is within you.

STEP 1

SEEING HOW YOUR PAST HOLDS THE KEY TO YOUR FINANCIAL FUTURE

THE ROAD TO financial freedom begins not in a bank or even in a financial planner's office, but in your head. It begins with your thoughts.

And those thoughts, more often than not, stem from our seemingly forgotten past with money. I'll go so far as to say that in my experience, most peoples' biggest problems in life—even those that appear on the surface not to be money related—are directly connected with their early, formative experiences with money.

So the first step toward financial freedom is a step back in time to the earliest moments you can recall when money meant something to you, when you truly understood what it could do. When you began to see that money could create pleasure—ice-cream cones, merry-go-round rides; and also to see that it could create pain—fights between your parents, perhaps, or longings of your own that couldn't be fulfilled because there wasn't enough money or even because there was too much. When you first understood that money was not just a shiny object or something to color on. When you understood that money was *money*. I want you to think back and see that your feelings about money today (fearing it, enjoying it, loving it, hating it) can almost certainly be traced to an incident, possibly forgotten until now, from your past.

SUZANNE'S STORY

Suzanne came to a financial planner for the same reason that brings many people—she didn't want to deal with her money. Her earliest memories about money helped explain why. She had learned that what money buys is nothing compared to what it takes away.

It would have been the very end of first grade. My father said, "How would you like to go live on the Great Lakes?" I didn't even know what *great lakes* meant, but I said no, I wanted to stay in Virginia, where we were. He said too bad, we're moving anyway, but that it would be great because we'd have more money. The moving truck came and that was that. All my friends were waving from the driveway, and I remember just sobbing and sobbing as we drove away. My father kept getting promoted, so we had to move every year, sometimes twice a year, and the reason was always more money. It was so hard in the new schools. My clothes were never right, and kids would laugh at my accent, whatever it was that year. The teachers would teach the subjects in all different ways—old math in one school, new math in another. Plus I had to make new friends each time; by the time I'd made them, it was time to go. It was hard on my mom, too. By about the tenth move, she stopped unpacking half the dishes—what was the point? They'd just have to be packed up again.

Most of us leave a cluttered paper trail marking where our money went behind us, but Suzanne was unlike any other client I'd ever had. She had no debt. She rented a furnished house: no mortgage. She leased her car. She had no savings, no investments. Divorced, with one son, she had come to see me about putting aside money for his education. I saw a woman alone with no money for emergencies, or tomorrow. I could have said to her, "Now, Suzanne, see here, you are forty-three years old and you really must start investing for the future." But clearly she knew that, and clearly knowing it made no difference at all to her, at least on the level that inspires us to take action. Suzanne was still living as if she might have to move the next day—no commitments, no ties, no furniture, no complications to undo if she suddenly had to pull up stakes. She had turned her childhood message around and had come to believe instead that to keep away from pain, you keep away from money.

ANDY'S STORY

If you've lost it all, how can you think you have the power to keep money safe, let alone make it grow?

When I was about eight, my mother gave me ten dollars to go to the bakery to buy bread. My grandparents and cousins were all coming to lunch, and this was a big deal. It was the first time that I got to go all the way by myself—down the block, to the right, then across the street all by myself, and down one more block to the corner. I'd been that way a million times, but never all by myself. And ten dollars! It was an enormous amount of money. Mom told me how much the bread would probably cost and told me to keep the change in my pocket. There was all this trust in me, all this responsibility. And what did I do? Lost it, the ten-dollar bill. When I got to the bakery: no money in my pocket. I had no idea what could have happened to it, no idea. I was late getting home; I looked everywhere. My grandparents and cousins were already there when I got back; everyone was in the kitchen; there was the noise of everybody talking. "Where's the bread, Andy?" my mom said, and I had to say I lost the money. The room grew so quiet. Nobody said anything; they were all just looking at me. I didn't get punished or anything. I think everyone knew how bad I felt, and there wasn't anything anyone could do. We had our lunch with the bread basket on the table but without the bread.

When he and his wife, Leslie, came to see me, Andy said, "I was so overwhelmed by that loss, I think I never wanted to be in control of my money after that." Leslie had never heard his story before, and even Andy had forgotten about it until we did this exercise together. But after Andy told the story, everything started to make more sense for both of them. They had come to me to talk about investing for the future, but the two of them could never agree on the kinds of investments they should make. Most of these disagreements ended up with one or the other of them storming out of the room, to the point where they decided they needed professional help. Leslie wanted to invest aggressively; in their early forties they were young enough, she felt, to take some risks. Andy, on the other hand, was adamant about putting the money into a bank account, where, he said, "it'll be safe." He never understood why investing scared him to death until he made this connection to his past.

CATHERINE'S STORY

I remember when my twin sister and I were seven, and we both asked for bikes for our birthday. I could already ride one, and I wanted to tie a balloon to the back wheel and make it sound like a motorcycle as I sped through the neighborhood. That's what all my friends had done with their bikes. But my parents made a huge deal of it, said that bikes were too expensive, maybe we could just share a bike. Well, I didn't like that idea so much. I wanted my own bike and told them so. They told me—in a very loud voice, I might add—that I was being so selfish, that all I cared about was what I wanted, and that I didn't deserve a bike at all. I didn't know bikes were expensive; everyone else had a bike, and I just wanted a bike. Who knew? The morning of our birthday, there in the driveway were two bikes, one with pink streamers and one with white. I was so excited, I could not stand it. I immediately put a blue balloon on the back tire, and off I went. As I rounded the first corner to go around the block, before I knew it I was flat on the ground with my bike on top of me. I tried to get up, but my arm would not move. I can remember lying there, screaming for my mom to come help me. For the next six weeks I had this big cast on my arm. And all I could think was: This is what happens when you get something you're not supposed to have. After my arm healed, I never really rode my bike again.

When I met her, Catherine was still living her life as if she did not deserve to have anything she wanted. More than anything else, she wanted to buy a house in the town where she was a teacher in a fine private school; she wanted to start a garden. She even had a particular house in mind, she had the money saved for the down payment, but she couldn't bring herself to make an offer. It was as if she felt afraid to take up any space in the world. She didn't know why she felt so paralyzed, until together we went back to her first money memory. For Catherine, the bike episode popped up right away, although she hadn't thought about it in years. She began to see that the seven-year-old she had been had every right in the world to ask for a bike, and that the pain of her broken arm wasn't punishment for her desire.

MONEY MESSAGES

Messages about money are passed down from generation to generation, worn and chipped like the family dishes. Your own memories about money will tell you a lot, if you take that step back and see what those memories taught you about who you were—and whether those memories are still telling you who you are today.

For me, the first message I remember came when I was eight or nine. In the hot Chicago summers, all of us in the neighborhood would go to the Thunderbird Motel to go swimming. It was heaven, jumping into the cold water of that crowded pool, everyone screaming. It cost a dollar to get in. One Saturday, as usual, I said to my mom, "Can I have a dollar to go swimming?" And she said, "Suze, I'm sorry, we don't have it." I said, "But Mom, I need a dollar to go swimming with everyone else," and she said, "Sweetheart, this is very hard for me to say, and we don't want anyone else to know, but I just don't have a dollar to give you."

I could tell that saying this to me made my mom want to cry. I also knew I was not to tell anyone. I felt as if the wind had been knocked out of me. What was I going to tell my friends? I don't remember what I told them, but I do remember this: I suddenly felt I was different from my friends, that I had less than they did, and therefore they wouldn't like me anymore.

I'm not proud of what happened next. Every night when my dad came home from work, he would place his pants over a chair in the dining room right outside their bedroom. He kept his money in the pocket of his pants. At night, after my mom and dad went to sleep, I would sneak into the dining room and take some bills out of his pants pockets. I took this money not to spend on myself or to save, but to buy gifts for my friends. I really thought that if I could show them that I did have money, they would continue to like me.

Interesting, isn't it, that the happy memories of the dozens of times I did go swimming at the Thunderbird Motel pale against the agonizing memory of the one time I couldn't?

Without my knowing it, this memory played itself out well into my adult life. For years, even though I was becoming more and more successful, I felt "less than." Until I could connect the dots—that who I am today is not the same little girl with no money to go swimming at the Thunderbird Motel—this memory defined how I felt about myself.

A few years ago I asked my mom if she remembered that Saturday, and she did; she still remembers the look on my face when she said she didn't have a dollar to give me. Ever since then her biggest fear in life when it comes to me is that I don't have enough money to get what I want and that I am suffering. It doesn't matter how successful I become, she still calls me and asks, "Suze, are you okay? Now, if you need anything, you'd ask, wouldn't you?" It's as if she is still trying to make up for that Saturday.

Now it's your turn to look back.

YOUR EXERCISE

As it was for Suzanne, Andy, Catherine, and me, this is a connect-the-dots exercise, revisiting the past and tracing the memories to where and how they affect your life today, and they do affect your life today.

In childhood we live full force, and when you delve into childhood memories, they are vivid, alive with all the five senses—you can see, touch, taste, smell, and hear them. The smell of cotton candy from the local amusement park, the feel of the wind against your face when you leaned out the car window, the mud squishing through your toes as you ran barefoot in and out of mud puddles, the cold on your face when temperatures dropped below zero, the way your house smelled when your mother was cooking your favorite meal. I am asking you to look back into your childhood and remember everything you can about money, the wonderful things it did and the ways in which it might have scared you.

Remember back to when you were three, twelve, or seventeen, and see what comes up for you. When one money memory feels true, important, and keeps coming back, that's the one we want. Here are some questions to help you remember:

⇥ What were the best presents you recall receiving when you were a child?

⇥ Did your friends have things you didn't?

⇥ Did your mother have to work when others didn't, or not have to work when others did?

⇥ Did you get money every time you went to see your grandparents?

⇥ Were you ashamed to bring your friends home to your house?

⇥ What were the special treats of your childhood? Did you have to be good in order to earn them?

⇥ Did you feel like your friends had nicer clothes than you did? Did your friends' parents have more expensive cars than yours did?

⊰⊱ Did you feel ashamed of having far more than your friends did?

⊰⊱ Did you hear your parents fight about money?

⊰⊱ Did you receive only money as gifts, instead of the personal touch of a handpicked present?

⊰⊱ Did your mother close the windows when she bought something because your father would yell and she didn't want the neighbors to hear? (Mine did.)

⊰⊱ Was shopping for school clothes a ritual you looked forward to every year?

⊰⊱ Did you steal—from piggy banks, your parents' wallets, the dime store?

⊰⊱ Do you remember the very first wallet you ever had? Was it given to you empty, or with a penny in it, or a dollar?

⊰⊱ Did you get less of an allowance than your friends or siblings? Did you have to work for it, or was it given to you as your right? What did you do with it—spend it? save it?

⊰⊱ What is the biggest amount of money you ever saw as a child?

⊰⊱ Did you get money for birthdays? Did someone tell you what to do with it?

⊰⊱ Did your friends go on better vacations than you?

⊰⊱ What did your parents tell you about money that made you feel good? That made you feel bad?

THINK ABOUT YOUR PAST

As you are thinking back to your past, close your eyes. See whatever you can; remember what the scene looked like. Was someone baking cookies? Were you holding a wet bathing suit? What else was happening in the scene? Was someone laughing, arguing, crying, in the next room? With your child's eyes, and with the adult eyes you have now, remember everything you can.

This first step may open the floodgates to many emotions. I've done this exercise with hundreds of people, and most people—even those who grew up in the wealthiest families—recall a painful memory, a memory that leaves them sad still. One woman remembers stealing from a schoolmate's cubbyhole and still feels ashamed. One man remembers his magic Roy Rogers' hat, which was stolen from him when he left it behind in a restaurant; he mourned the loss of his most valuable possession for weeks and never recovered the powers it gave him. One woman received less allowance from her father than her older brother and younger stepbrother did, and her rage at her father's unfairness—and her powerlessness against it—still hurts today. One man still remembers crouching in the back seat of his father's stretch limousine so his friends wouldn't see him. Even now he feels ashamed of his money. Every one of us has such a memory, and every such memory tells at least part of the story of who we are today. If you let it, your memory will reveal the roots of the fears that so strongly rule your financial life today.

After you have spent some time thinking about this, please write down everything about this memory that you can. Do not censor anything. If any of your friends or family members are interested and willing, you might want to invite them to do this exercise with you. If they take you up on your invitation, please be sensitive as everyone re-creates their memories; we want to resolve the pain of the past, not add to it. If you can do it with others, this exercise will not only help you to begin to remove your personal blocks about money, it will also help free you from the taboo that forbids you to talk about your fears about money. You will be amazed at the things everyone remembers. *This is a very important exercise.*

We are all powerless as children, and money looms so powerfully. As we grow up we claim our power in one way after another, taking on jobs, families, commitments, responsibilities.

Yet we don't grow up to claim our financial power until we look money directly in the eye, face our fears, and claim that power back. Each of our memories is different, but they all lead us to similar places, places that are riddled with self-doubt, unworthiness, insecurity, and fear. Fear that has paralyzed us into thinking of all the things we can't do, not all the things we can. No financial advice you get or financial book you read is worth anything unless you can put that advice into action. I've been afraid at times, and you might be afraid now. Let's see what you're afraid of, then do what must be done to put the fears to rest.

STEP 2

FACING YOUR FEARS AND CREATING NEW TRUTHS

IN OUR CULTURE it's okay to talk about therapy we've gone through, marital problems we've had, our deepest intimate secrets—but telling the truth about money, confessing our worries to our children, our parents, our friends, just isn't done. Money is our secret both in private and in public. Imagine going to a dinner party and telling a group of close acquaintances, "I just don't know what to do. My credit card debt has gone up to $17,000, and I don't know how I'll ever get out of it." The room would fall into embarrassed silence. (Most silent of all would be the others in the room weighed down by the secret of their own credit card debt.)

In the most profound sense our money says nothing about us, about whether we're kind, generous of spirit, living our lives well. Yet we need money to live, as surely as we need air to breathe, and this need cuts across all races, both sexes, all income brackets.

Almost all of us have, at some level, fears or anxieties about money—but we rarely admit them to those around us. We may not admit them to ourselves. But because they are holding us back, preventing us from taking control of our financial lives, looking these fears in the eye is an essential step toward freedom. This chapter will show you not just how to confront your fears, but how to replace them with new, positive truths for yourself. Remember the goals you set for yourself when we began? You'll be surprised at how taking this step will free your mind and give you strength to take other action toward those goals.

THE TIME FOR MONEY

Don't you find it strange that you can raise a family, hold down a job, fix things that are broken, and deal with everything that comes up in your life—except your money? I used to hear it from clients every single day: "I'm too busy at work to deal with my money. I just don't have the time." How is it possible that we're all too busy working so hard to earn our money to be able to deal with the money we're working so hard to earn? The answer is that it's not possible. There's plenty of time for work, barbecues, bike rides, reading books (even books about money), seeing friends, talking on the phone, hanging out on the Internet, knitting, golfing, playing baseball, watching

TV . . . time isn't the problem. What prevents you from dealing with your money is not lack of time, but your fear of money.

We saw in the last chapter how powerful our memories of money from childhood are, even today. In this step we will hold these memories up against our fears. Then we will replace the grooves in our brains that our fears have created with strong new messages to ourselves about what we will achieve with our money, beginning now. The sooner you deal with your fears, the more money you will be able to create. With money, when you heal your heart, you help your pocketbook.

FEARS: THE WEEDS IN YOUR FINANCIAL GARDEN

The trouble with fears is that when we keep them inside and refuse to deal with them, they grow, like weeds left alone in a garden. Take the fear of not having enough to cover the bills this month and let it wander around by itself, unchecked. Where will it go? It will become the fear of not having enough in general. Stretch that fear out, and what do you have? The fear of having nothing, of somehow losing everything. Take that fear one step further, and there's the fear of being worthless, being nothing. That's a long way from not quite being able to pay all the bills this one month. Even so, that's a fear too many of us live with, whether we really realize it or not—and we don't have to.

When you hold things in this way, you give them power. The way to control the fear instead is to voice it. Once you say it, you can see it: There's no crocodile under the bed. So some bills will be late this month, it can't be helped, things happen. That's one reason we say time is money. The less time your fear allows you to devote to your money, the less money you will have. Weed out your fears, so you can give your financial garden what it needs to grow.

FACING THE FEAR

In the previous step we looked back at our first experiences with money. I found with my clients over and over again that when they examine their fears, they're connected to those early memories. Understanding your fear often allows you to see what those memories mean. Take Sheila, Mark, and Liz, for example—all paralyzed by their fears.

SHEILA'S STORY

When asked, "What is your greatest fear when it comes to money?" Sheila answered, "That I will lose everything. That I will not be able to hold on to it, and I will lose it all." Had she ever lost money before? "No."

It's not a money memory exactly, but what comes to mind is that I broke my grandmother's lobster platter when I was seven, eight, nine—I can't really remember how old I was. But I do remember what happened. Grandma was telling us—my cousins were there, everyone was there—about how in colonial times poor people would eat lobsters, they were so plentiful. But for us they were a special treat, and we had them only in the summers at her house in Maine. She always served them on this huge platter that was shaped like a lobster, and she loved that platter. Anyway, when the lobsters were done, she piled them onto the platter to be taken into the dining room, and I said, "Can I carry them in?" She said no, I was still too little. But I begged and begged until she said yes. There was a swinging door into the dining room, and—you guessed it. One of my cousins came through the door; bang, the lobsters went everywhere and the platter, Grandma's special platter, broke to pieces. Lobsters and platter everywhere, scattered all over the kitchen floor.

There the memory ended for Sheila, but it was very telling even so: She was afraid that she would lose it, that she couldn't hold on to it. This was her fear. And how was it playing out in her life?

Sheila and her new husband had come to see me about switching some of his assets into her name; they were both in their sixties, and he wanted her to be safe should something happen to him. Here was a new first for me: Sheila didn't want to take any of the money at all. She refused to let him give her anything. But what she was really saying was that she was afraid she would break another platter, so he shouldn't even bother giving her anything to put on it.

MARK'S STORY

"The thought of having a joint checking account with my wife— I just can't do it" was Mark's problem. "It's as if I just don't trust anyone when it comes to my money." I asked Mark if he loved and felt safe with his wife. "Yes, of course." Had she ever given him a reason not to trust her? "No. Never."

The big joke in my family was that I saved everything, just hoarded it all away. I had all these different banks and would move money—we're talking pennies and dimes here—from one to another, counting it and playing with it. I guess I was about nine, and I had twenty-seven dollars in my room saved up in my banks, and I felt so rich. I was thinking I wanted to buy something, and what I wanted to buy was a trampoline. It cost forty dollars, so I kept saving. I added more and more money to the banks, then went to count it up again, to see how much closer I was. And there was only twenty-four dollars! I couldn't believe it. I knew my sister had stolen the money, I just knew it. She denied it. And when I told my parents, they said I had probably counted wrong, how could I accuse my sister of stealing? And she was standing there in the room, smiling. I knew she stole it, and she knew I knew.

Having a joint checking account? When a sister you love steals your money, isn't it possible, too, that she also stole your trust in those you love? I could see Mark's face drop at the possibility.

I was the fourth financial planner Mark had been to see, after he no longer trusted the first, second, and third. Not only did he not trust his wife enough to pool their resources into a joint account, he didn't trust anyone when it came to his money. Coincidence?

LIZ'S STORY

Liz's biggest fear was being audited by the IRS. Had she ever cheated on her income taxes? "Absolutely never." Had she ever been audited before? "No." Had her parents? "No." Had anyone she knew ever been audited? "Not that I know of."

It was Halloween, and we all had bags, for candy, and also cans, to collect for UNICEF. But it was chaos—we were running everywhere, and sometimes the UNICEF money went into the bag instead of the cans. I tripped over a curb and dropped my bag. All the candy and UNICEF money went flying. I recovered what I could but knew a lot was missing. The next morning I went back and found forty-five more cents right where I had fallen. I kept looking, and then I saw a drain. As I looked into it, I could see all these bright shiny pennies, but there wasn't a thing I could do to get them back. I never told anyone to this day that had happened, but you know I still feel just like I did then: as if I had stolen money from UNICEF and if anyone knew, they would put me in jail.

Liz's fear was an IRS audit. Most people fear an IRS audit when they've hidden something from the IRS, and are correct to fear an audit. This was not the case for Liz, who had never remotely tried to steal or hide anything from anyone. But she felt as if she had. Those coins for UNICEF had been collecting interest in the form of fear for long enough.

I asked Sheila to go out and buy a big new platter, the biggest she could find, and to begin using it. I asked Mark to write a letter to his sister, saying he forgave her. Liz wrote a nice-size check to UNICEF right then and there, which she mailed immediately. They had started to connect the dots from their pasts to their fears today. It's a slow process sometimes, this kind of healing, but the relief each expressed to me after doing this step was extraordinary to witness. More important, they were ready to move on, toward financial freedom.

WHAT IS IT YOU'RE AFRAID OF?

Struggling to remember defines so much of our lives—to remember birthdays, dentist appointments, turning off the stove, where we put the keys, when the dry cleaning will be ready, what time the children need to be picked up . . . the rituals and obligations of everyday life.

Find yourself with a money problem, on the other hand, and just try to forget it. You can't. It will be with you day in, day out, at the movies, when you're trying to sleep, always there, never far from center stage of your consciousness. The fear is, very likely, powerful enough to keep you silent, too all-consuming to talk about, too big to take action against.

YOUR EXERCISE

Most of us push away our fears without even knowing it. I am asking you now to step into them instead, pull them closer for a moment. What is it that you're afraid of? If nothing profound comes to mind, just give it time; often we block what we don't want to face. Here, to give you an idea, are some of the other fears that I have heard over the years:

❧ I'm afraid I'm going to be a bag lady.

❧ I'm afraid I won't be able to support my family.

❧ If something goes wrong at work, what other job could I possibly get?

❧ I feel that I can't keep up.

❧ I'm afraid that if my friends find out how much money I have, they won't like me.

❧ I'm afraid that my wife is going to make more money than I am.

❧ I'm afraid because I don't even know the right questions about money to ask.

❧ I'm afraid that my husband will leave me, and then how will I get by?

❧ If my wife dies, who will take care of me?

❧ What if my parents have to go into a nursing home?

❧ I keep having to use my credit card just to cover the bills each month.

◈ How will I ever pay for my children's college expenses?
◈ I'm afraid I'll have to support my ex if we break up.
◈ I am afraid I will lose everything I have.

Now take your fear and write it down. As you read it back to yourself, go back to the piece of paper on which you wrote your childhood memory, the one you recovered in the last chapter. Do you see an obvious connection? You might not at first. Give it time. You've opened your memories of money, long forgotten, and you've faced the fears long held inside you. The connections will come, too.

NEW TRUTHS

The mind gives us thousands of ways to say no, but there's only one way to say yes, and that's from the heart. It's great when you start to make the connections between your memories and your fears. Now you have to make sure those fears stay far away; they will try, if you let them, to keep coming back. We have to retrain our minds away from thinking that we can't control money, that we don't deserve to do well, that not enough money is going to come in, that we don't have enough now, that we won't have enough tomorrow.

Believing, really *believing*, other realities makes other realities true: that we can control money, that we do deserve to do well, that there will be enough. How do we replace the old fears, the old reality? With new thoughts. With new truths.

I grew up with the belief that pervaded our household: "We don't have any money" was the message. "You'll always have to do without, so you had better learn how." I did learn how to do without—so you can imagine the shock I felt when I applied for a job as a stockbroker for Merrill Lynch in 1980 and was actually accepted. All I could think was, Wow! My dad is going to be so proud of me.

It didn't start well.

I wore my best outfit to the interview, my blue silk shirt over red-and-white-striped Sassoon pants tucked into my white cowboy boots—and you should have seen the looks on all the interviewers' faces. When they saw me, they actually asked if I had dressed that way to insult them. If there had been a rock in that conference room, I would have crawled under it.

Taking that job was breaking away from everything I had ever known. I was so out of my league. The most I had ever made before was $400 a month as a waitress, and even that was more than most of my friends were making back then. Every morning I would get up and feel sick to my stomach, but off I'd go to work with all these men in their pin-striped three-piece suits. When everyone else would go to lunch at their fancy restaurants, I'd get in my car and go to Taco Bell. It was the only part of the day when I felt comfortable in my surroundings.

The job itself was quite scary, telling people what to do with their money—and me having to make money just to keep my job. I had to go through a training program, but it didn't train me for the pressure, and it didn't give me the confidence. I was a commissioned salesperson, and either I generated commissions or I would soon be looking for another job. It was a never-ending battle: Would I meet my quota each month, or would I be out on the street? I needed something to override the fear that was eating me alive. I decided to change my perception of my situation and create a new truth for myself.

I created what I wanted for myself first on paper. Every morning before I went to work, I would write over and over again: "I am young, powerful, and successful, producing at least $10,000 a month." Why did I say "at least"? Because why limit it? What if the world wanted to give me more? Why did I use the present tense? Because this was the life I wanted to live in the present tense, not tomorrow, not someday. *Now.*

I wrote down that truth twenty-five times a day, said it to myself in the mirror, thought it each time I went up and down in the elevator. That's what I would say, and that's the truth I created. I still carry that truth around with me like a lucky charm in words, and it still works. I replaced the message of fear, and my belief I was inadequate, with a message of endless possibility.

You can, too, once you pull the fear out from wherever you've pushed it away to, face it, and use the power of your mind to put it behind you.

For twenty, thirty, forty years, or more, we've all been creating paradigms about ourselves, telling ourselves who we are, financially and in every other way. Part of this comes from what we were told about ourselves as children ("You'll be a secretary just like your mom"; "You'll be a gambler, just like your father"; "You'll never amount to much unless you do X, Y, or Z"). The rest is what we tell ourselves, fears and all, over and over until we believe it absolutely.

Your new future begins with your new truth.

YOUR EXERCISE

The power of positive thinking is not a new idea, but when it comes to money it is, because we're still so afraid. We're a culture of slogans—in ads, on bumper stickers, on T-shirts, needle-pointed onto pillows. Call it what you like—a financial mantra, a new truth, a new belief in yourself—but you must create a positive, empowering message for yourself and instill it into your powerful mind to replace the fear you're leaving behind, beginning now.

Install it, instill it, retrain your mind to believe it. Write it down twenty-five times a day, have it stamped on a T-shirt and sleep in it every night, say it to yourself on your way to work, when you pay your bills, when you begin to worry about money, when you feel afraid. Say it when you're shaving, when you're in the shower, first thing in the morning, last thing at night. A positive message to yourself, a message of possibilities. Do it when you resist it, do it when you don't believe in it, do it when you feel as if it's a useless drill, keep doing it until you believe it. Then it will be true. Three rules for your new truth:

⇥ Make it short enough so that you can remember it exactly, word for word, so that it's easy for you to say, "I have more money than I will ever need."

⇥ Put your message in the present tense; the future begins today: "I am in control of all of my affairs."

⇥ Make it an unlimited truth, to open the way to receive: "I am putting at least $200 a month into savings."

Sheila is starting to put the lobster platter incident to rest with her new truth: "I hold and benefit from everything that comes my way."

Mark is saying over and over again his new truth: "I have the power to put my money in good hands, and I trust the people I've chosen to keep it safe."

Liz is on the path to forgive herself the UNICEF mishap with her new truth: "I am not afraid."

Fears hate more than anything else to be defeated. They will try to invade your new truth like a virus, telling you what you can't do, not what you can do, telling you what you can't be, not what you are becoming, telling you what you aren't—not what you are and have every right to be. Don't listen. Just keep repeating your new truth the way I did in the elevator.

What is "income"? Something that *comes in*. Have your new truth with you as you now open the door to new wealth. Your new truth is bigger than your fears, bigger than your debt, bigger than your worries about the future, bigger than all the things you've meant to do with your money but haven't done. Now we will do them.

STEP 3

BEING HONEST

WITH YOURSELF

REALITY CHECK: THROW away a three-dollar magazine you never got around to reading—easy. Toss in the garbage five dollars' worth of food that's gone bad; you may reprimand yourself, but you probably do it all the time. Buy a sweater on sale for twenty dollars, then notice six months later that you wore it only once; it just didn't fit right; you give it away. Now try to rip up and throw away a dollar bill. I have found almost no one who could do this without great discomfort. Yet everything about the way the money establishment functions is calculated to distance us from our money, to anesthetize us to its power. The plastic card that slides through the machine so smoothly when we make our purchases; the automated voice of the bank's telephone answering system that robotically answers our money questions; the digital electronic readouts of the stock exchange language that flash on our TV screens for the privileged few who understand it. . . . All of these "conveniences" leave us many steps removed from the actual thing. Most of the money we use today is in the form of the plastic cards we use as currency or the checks we write, understudies to our money. Isn't that one reason it's so easy to spend—"it's only plastic"?

One way to get in touch with your money is to actually start *touching* it again, to handle cash, to feel and respect it, to delight in spending it the way you did as a child, to enjoy choosing not to spend it, to take pleasure in putting it away now for later.

This third step toward financial freedom, then, is about getting back in touch with your money and understanding that you have the power to decide how to use it. And it's about being honest with yourself. You have looked back to your childhood memories of money and connected them to your fears today and created new truths to keep the voice of those fears from paralyzing you against taking action. Now we are about to face your present reality. We will compare the money you have coming in with the money you have going out—real income, real expenses. With this step, by being willing to face up to what you are really doing with your money, your thoughts, actions, and words about money will begin to merge and become truthful. With this step, you begin to take control of your financial life in a concrete way.

WHERE DOES THE MONEY GO?

Have you ever taken a big wad of bills from an ATM machine, then found yourself, a day or two later, nearly out of cash and unable to reconstruct exactly where you spent it? And even when you retrace all your steps, you still come up $20, $40, or $60 short? It's upsetting, but most of us feel that way most of the time: a little short, a little panicky, wondering exactly where our money is going.

KAREN'S STORY

You could tell right away that Karen was an extremely efficient woman. She produced a radio show, ran her household, organized her children's lives, seemed to have everything under control—your basic superwoman. Except when it came to money.

> I guess it was when Richie's mother died that he decided we needed to do something special with that money. She left us $25,000, and that was the most we ever had in one lump sum. So Richie wanted us to figure out how to invest it right away, he wanted to keep it safe and sound but have it grow for our future. I think this money meant so much to him because it was the last thing he would get from his mom. I made an appointment with a financial planner a friend recommended, and we did go, right away. He was nice, but he wouldn't tell us where to invest the money until we filled out a questionnaire covering all our finances, not just about the money we wanted to invest, so we took the forms home. I told Richie I'd fill it out

because I handle most of the finances, but it's still there, sitting on my desk. I get queasy every time I look at it. I have a Visa card with a pretty big balance that Richie doesn't even know about. So I can't fill in the part about how much we owe—if I told him, he'd really be angry. And we have a few other unpaid bills, nothing serious, just sometimes we're a little short and I pay late. It just seems like a big tangled mess, so I keep procrastinating, and now Richie is the one who keeps asking about the forms. It's been about six months since we got those forms and God only knows how I wish I could just fill them out and send them back, but I can't. The money? Oh, it's still in our joint account, except now it's down, I think to about $22,000.

In time that $22,000 will inevitably go down to $20,000, then $15,000, and before you know it, it will be gone. Most likely the balance on Karen's secret credit card will be higher as well. What happened to Karen happens to most of us. We're afraid to really look at our finances head-on, to see where everything really goes.

We all work so hard for our money, yet don't let it work for us because we simply will not deal with it, will not check the amount we spend against the amount we bring in. And not dealing with money is just a different way of dealing with it—badly.

One of the first things I asked new clients to do was to write down on a piece of paper what they thought they spent each month. If the clients were married or living together, each, without consulting the other, was to write down what they thought their combined household expenses added up to each month. A simple enough question, right? We'll see.

WHERE DO YOU THINK YOU STAND TODAY?

Think carefully, then please write down your own answer: What does it cost you to live each month?

If you are married or living with someone with whom you share expenses, please ask him or her to write down the answer to the same question.

I am willing to bet you that after we complete this chapter, you will find that you're like most people. You'll find that you do not know.

How is that possible?

Most of us believe, or deceive ourselves into believing, that we need about $1,000 to $1,500 a month less than we actually do need to go on living the exact same way we live right now. Surprisingly, this figure seems to vary only a little bit regardless of income levels. If a client writes down that she needs, after taxes, $3,000 a month to live, invariably the truer figure is $4,000. If the client thinks he spends $10,000 a month, the actual figure is closer to $11,500. Where does this month-to-month self-deception lead us? Into financial chaos.

The reason we don't know how much it really costs us to live is this: Our planned spending doesn't cover expenses that don't occur every month or expenses that just crop up.

For example:

✦ Do you belong to a gym? If so, do you consider this cost per month even if you pay to renew just once a year?

✦ Do you wear disposable contact lenses? If so, do your monthly expenses include the $40 they actually cost you each month, or do you let yourself be surprised each time you have to buy a new year's batch for $500?

⇥ Do you pay your insurance premiums twice or four times a year? Do you calculate the cost of insurance in your monthly bills?

⇥ Where did you go on vacation last year? What did that onetime expense cost average over twelve months?

⇥ Do you pay someone to do your taxes every year? How much does that cost every month?

These big expenses hit once or twice a year, probably surprising you every time. And then there are seasonal expenses:

⇥ If you live in your own house, come summer do you forget about how much higher the oil bills run in the fall?

⇥ If you have a fireplace, do you buy two cords of wood a winter? How much do they cost a month?

⇥ How about the higher electric bills you get from using air conditioners in the summer? You're paying those bills, too, in February.

⇥ Do you have your windows washed once or twice a year?

⇥ If you have a lawn or garden that someone else helps tend, have you figured those weekly costs of the summer months into your monthly budget?

⇥ Did you send your children to summer camp last summer? Enroll them in ice-skating classes in the winter?

⇥ Do you have pets? Do you have them groomed at least once each season? Take them to the vet a couple of times a year?

⇥ Do you try to believe you spend little or nothing on clothes each year, when in fact you buy a few new things each season?

⇥ Do you get your hair cut and maybe colored every

couple of months? How much, then, does it cost every single month?

Here's another surprise. If you figure your expenses on a monthly basis, it's easy to forget that certain expenses occur each week. Some months have four Fridays (or Mondays, Tuesdays, and so on), for example, while others have five. If you make some sort of payment every week—child care, a cleaning woman, a mortgage payment withdrawn automatically every two weeks—the extra weekly payments will take place in four months of the year. These are exactly the sort of expenses that stay "hidden" and make you wonder why your figures aren't adding up right.

Plus, the smallest expenses add up fast—the ones too small, you might think, to be worth figuring into your budget at all.

For instance, do you go to the movies once a week? When you do, do you buy the tickets for yourself and your partner, have popcorn and sodas, go for a simple dinner afterward, as simple as pizza or a burger and fries? That's not so much, is it? No, it isn't, not on any given Friday night. Maybe $16 for the tickets, $4 for the popcorn and sodas, and $20 for a simple meal. But once a week over a year, that's $2,080. And too many of us forget to include expenses so "small."

Other "small" expenses might come up less often—but add up just as much. Magazine subscriptions, cosmetics, supplies for the yard, oil changes for the car, batteries for the flashlight, charcoal for the grill: Do you know what it really costs you to keep your life running smoothly over a year's time?

How about special occasions? Do you take your partner to an expensive anniversary dinner each year? How many birthday parties, housewarmings, and baby showers did you attend last year? Didn't you bring a present to each one? When you go to a friend's house for dinner, do you routinely bring a bouquet of flowers or a bottle of wine that costs, on average, $10 each time? Might you have done that twenty times or more last year? Do you know what the Christmas holiday season costs every month? Over time, and added to those other hidden expenses, these here-and-there expenses must also be considered truthfully each month.

Finally you need to allocate $50 to $100 each month for miscellaneous unpredictable expenses. You might need some dental work that's not covered in your insurance. You might have to travel to your brother's wedding. There's no way to avoid some surprise costs, so you need to figure them into your cash flow.

Most people were shocked to discover by how much they had underestimated—and that's when they had guessed as honestly as they could.

It's a scary realization, but there's a wonderful flip side to that fear. Once you take this step, you will feel better for knowing the truth. And you will begin to gain power over the money that's controlled you for so long.

YOUR EXERCISE: HOW MUCH IS GOING OUT?

I am asking you now to think about your money. Who cares more about your money than you? Shouldn't you know where it goes? It's one thing to say that you want to be financially powerful and responsible. To do that, you must face the truth honestly and know exactly where you stand today. This is essential.

Please get out your canceled checks, ATM statements, credit card bills, whatever will tell you how you spent your money over the past two years. These papers are more revealing than a diary; they contain the key to how you live your life.

Yes, it will take you some time to do this, but think how much time it will give back to you in the future. You work forty hours a week or more to earn your money. I am asking you to take a few hours to take your money out of the darkness, to see it in the light of reality, to see where you stand. Don't just read these pages—pick up a pen and take action.

⤖ Go through your checkbook, canceled checks, computerized statements, all your records for the past two years. Not one year, but two years. Maybe this year was an extraordinary time—you remodeled the house, bought a new car—but looking at a two-year period, you'll get a good idea of what it costs you to live the way you are living. All your checks, cash withdrawals, money spent every month, money spent once a year, money spent once a season, holiday expenses, everything.

⤖ Make categories for each month—such as telephone, gasoline, food, utilities, vet bills, golf fees, baby-sitting.

⤖ After all the categories are complete, total each category. Divide each category by 24. This will give you how much you spend per month on average for each category.

⤖ Now add together all the averages in each category. This will tell you what it costs you to live each month. Remember, these are *averages*. If your average is $3,000, most months you'll spend less—say, $1,800 or $2,000. But in some months you'll spend $5,000 or $6,000. To meet your expenses, you need to bring in that average number each month.

YOUR EXERCISE: HOW MUCH IS COMING IN?

Now we have to match exactly what we have coming in after taxes with the figure we have just learned is going out. Please write down now all the income from every source that you have coming in. Only calculate an amount you are fairly certain will continue coming in for at least one more year. If you loaned someone money, for example, and she has been paying you back regularly but owes only three more payments, don't include this figure. Or if you're working and about to retire or be laid off, don't count that paycheck, either. Be as realistic as possible as to how much you can really count on month in, month out. Possible sources of income:

- 🙼 Monthly paychecks after taxes
- 🙼 Predictable bonuses
- 🙼 Social Security income
- 🙼 Disability income
- 🙼 Bond income
- 🙼 Rental income, if you have any
- 🙼 Gifts from your parents or children, if you can really count on them year in, year out
- 🙼 Loan repayments, if they will continue for more than a year
- 🙼 Income you are taking or about to take from retirement accounts
- 🙼 Pension income
- 🙼 Miscellaneous

Take this total and divide it by 12, so you can see what you have coming in after taxes on a monthly basis.

Now compare your outgoing to your incoming. Now you know exactly where you stand.

WHERE DO I GO FROM HERE?

If you began this exercise knowing exactly where you stand financially, you'll have confirmed that you do spend each month what you thought you did, and that you also earn at least as much as, if not more than, you spend. Bravo!

The chances are better, though, that if you're like many of us, you've just confirmed that you spend more than you thought. Quite possibly you also spend more than you earn.

What can you do? You can do one or both of two things. Make more money and/or decide to spend less. Look at each of your categories again, and decide how much in each category you want to spend.

Notice my wording. I didn't say how much you are *allowed* to spend. I did not say to spend less. I said, decide how much you want to spend in each category. If you're spending more than you're earning, this solution is not about creating limitations. It's about making decisions—determining what you most want to spend your money on. If you can make more money realistically, without undue stress, in the immediate future (by changing jobs, say, or adding a second job), then you're in a position where you may be able to earn what you spend and go on living the way you do right now, if you choose to. If you take this route, make sure that the numbers balance out.

If you're like most of us, however, more likely you need to decide to spend your money differently. This does not mean that you have to take one drastic action that crimps your pleasures and quality of life, such as getting by with one car when your family needs two. Unrealistic budget cuts, like unrealistic diets, never work. Consider, instead, making the decision to spend $25 to $30 less per month from fifteen or twenty of your spending categories.

TRIMMING

There will be some categories where the amounts are fixed—rent, mortgage, taxes, and so on. There will be other categories—in fact, the majority of categories—where you can actually decide what the total spent per year will be. You can almost make a game out of it with yourself. If you cut and color your hair every eight weeks, see if you can schedule it for every nine weeks. You'll save the cost of one whole haircut each year and probably won't notice. Is there one magazine subscription you can do without? Can you have three Friday movie nights a month instead of four (or five, in the months with five Fridays)? Can you have your windows cleaned every eight months instead of every six months? Keep deciding to trim, a little here, a little there, until what comes in matches what goes out. Keep your new truth with you as you begin to consider how you want to spend your money. With each decision you make, you are gaining power over your money.

After you've done your mental trimming, put down in writing the yearly total you decided on for each category. Now keep track of what you spend in each category, month by month. The best way to keep track is to create a chart or system that will work for you. Each month when you pay your bills, check your spending by category. If you use up any allocation early, and want to spend more in that category, you'll have to make new decisions about what, if anything, you want to do by seeing where you stand with the other categories. Robbing Peter to pay Paul, so to speak, except that you're Peter—and you're also Paul.

For instance, say you decided you wanted to spend $2,000 this year on clothes but found a $200 coat you wanted in September, after the $2,000 was already spent. Check your other categories. Maybe you had to cut your vacation short and saved $200. Take the $200 and buy the coat. As long as the numbers always balance, you're in the driver's seat.

As a reminder, post the categories you're trimming on the fridge, or on your bulletin board, or on a yellow stickie in your checkbook. Mark your three Friday movie nights in your calendar, so you'll remember. Write down when you're due to make your hair appointments for every nine weeks in your calendar. Note in your calendar when you're due to have your windows washed again—in eight months instead of six. If the date is into next year, jot it down at the end of this year and transfer the dates.

You may find that you can come up with wonderfully creative ways to trim your spending so that you hardly notice. One family (both parents work and their teenage kids aren't home much) had the garbage picked up every two weeks instead of every week, trimming a painless $200 a year. A single mother went to the grocery store every eight days instead of every single Saturday, simply paying more attention to the food she already had in the house. By doing so, she trimmed nearly $400 from what she allocated for food. Another woman learned to do her own manicures and doesn't mind a bit. Savings: close to $500 a year. Another man, who described himself as a "compulsive spender on CDs," weeded out the CDs he didn't listen to much anymore and traded them with friends. Last year he had trimmed $600 and had just as many fresh CDs to listen to. That same client also did his taxes himself with a computer program, rather than going to his accountant. Savings: another $600. But only when you see in front of you how you spend your money now will you be able to decide how you would rather be spending your money. (If you look at everything and see no possible way you can decide to spend less anywhere, just keep reading. Later on we deal with ways of freeing up your money.)

How does this differ from being on a budget? With a budget you limit what you can spend each month, and that's that. Here, you are not limiting what you can spend each month but simply deciding how you want to spend the money you already know you have to spend. Rather than being dictated by a restriction, your actions are dictated by the choices you make.

As you read further into this book, and over the years as what you choose to spend your money on changes, your allocations will change.

You have just taken the hardest step toward financial freedom. With this step you have been honest with yourself. Now you know exactly where you stand.

The next steps will take you to where you want to be.

A NOTE ON STEPS 4, 5, AND 6

You have taken the first steps to financial freedom by facing the memories and fears that have kept you from dealing with your money. You have also started to recover the power and strength that enable you to be in control of your money—the money you have now and the money that will come to you.

But going back to the past is in itself not enough to create the future you want. Financial freedom requires not just insights but also actions, and to carry out these actions you must learn about money and how it needs to be treated. True financial freedom is not only having money, but having power over that money as well.

In these next chapters, you will learn how to manage your money and create more. In these chapters I will talk about the numbers that follow the dollar sign—facts, figures, how it all works. Don't let the numbers scare you. There is no financial computation you'll need to make that can't be done on a pocket calculator. You will soon be able to trust yourself with numbers more than you ever thought you could. You will soon see, too, that you have more than what it takes to manage your money on your own (a message, by the way, that the commissions-oriented financial industry would rather you never learn).

These three steps, as you'll see, are "must-do's" to ensure that the money you have now will grow, that the money you want to create will indeed come your way, and that your money will help take care of you and the people you love when you need it to.

Remember the goal you wrote down for yourself when you first picked up this book? Please pull it out now and look at it again. You are about to take the step-by-step actions to make that goal reality.

STEP 4

BEING RESPONSIBLE
TO THOSE
YOU LOVE

HAVE YOU EVER arrived at the scene of an accident on the highway and thought, Uh-oh, I've really got to get around to doing my will? Has a friend or colleague ever had a cancer scare that made you think, I have to make arrangements for my children in case anything happens to me? Does turbulence when you're flying remind you of all the affairs you don't have in order? But a few minutes later the traffic starts moving, your friend's scare turns out to be nothing, the turbulence dies down, your thoughts move on to something else, and everything is back to normal.

ALL THE WHAT-IF'S

The fourth step to financial freedom is being responsible, which starts with being responsible to those you love.

It is not okay when you get sick, or when you die, to leave financial chaos behind you for everyone else to clean up. It will be hard enough for those around you to bear the grief of your terrible illness or death; imagine, for a minute, their pain. Please don't also force them to deal with all the matters you could have taken care of while you were alive and healthy.

A big part of financial freedom is having your heart and mind free from worry about the what-if's of life. Each of us—from those who wish creditors would stop calling to those with millions—has to face the what-if's. It is not enough to say you'll "get to it" or to think vaguely that, because you have employee life insurance or a will you wrote years ago, you already "have" gotten to it. It is essential to know you have planned and prepared everything in the best way possible. In Step 3 you faced the reality of your present financial life. In Step 4 you face the reality of your death.

What I discovered with my clients was that their state of mind had a direct effect on their finances. Simply knowing that you have taken care of the people you love always, in my experience, frees up major blocks on this path to financial freedom. If you take this step, you will feel freer already—in mind, body, and soul.

If you really love your spouse, your children, your life partner, you must *say* you love them, *think* you love them, and *act* as if you love them—which means doing, really doing, the things listed in this chapter. I cannot tell you how many people

I have met through my work who have thought they had taken care of everything, only to have their loved ones discover that they had not. Please take these actions for yourself, for your peace of mind—and most of all for the ones you love.

THE FIRST LAW OF FINANCIAL FREEDOM: People First, Then Money

Can a good stock portfolio comfort you when your heart is broken? No. But a life rich in people you love can. The emotional foundation of your life is no less important than the financial structure you create. That is why, in building your financial future, you must begin with the people you care about. Each of the following topics is equally important to your future, and all are essential for you to know about in order to be responsible to yourself and those you love.

Wills and Trusts. What are they? How are they different? Do you need one? Do you need both? How old should you be when you get one? How much should they cost? What if you change your mind about what you want to happen to your estate? What happens if something happens to you and you don't have one? Can a trust benefit you while you're alive? Can you rely on your attorney for guidance in this matter?

Durable Power of Attorney for Health Care. What is it? Why should you have one? When should you have one? Is it complicated to create? Is it expensive?

Life Insurance. Do you really need it? If so, what kind? How much coverage should you have? What are the cheapest ways to buy it?

Long-Term-Care Insurance. Why is this the most important kind of insurance you can own? What does it insure? Who should and should not buy it? When should you buy it? How much will it cost? How can you tell if the policy is a good one? What if you don't qualify for it or can't afford it?

Estate Planning. Isn't a will or a trust enough? What more do I need?

WILLS

JEFF'S STORY

Jeff thought he had lost just about everything when his wife, Nancy, died of breast cancer at age forty-four, leaving him with their two young children to raise. As it turned out, his losses were just beginning.

Before I met Nancy, I had sort of thought I would never get married or have kids, but she was different. She had moved from New York to California six years before and found she just loved it here. About six months before we met, she bought a house for $225,000. It was kind of run-down, but she wanted to fix it up. That's how we met. I'm a contractor with my own firm, and I came over to give her some estimates. I ended up doing the job for free—because six months later we were living together. We worked on the house together and it was transformed. Supposedly it's worth about $300,000 now.

To our surprise, Nancy got pregnant—she had never thought she could—and soon we were married, with two daughters. After our daughter was born, Nancy's mother came to visit, and she didn't like me at all; I know she thought I wasn't good enough for Nancy. But it didn't really matter, because she lived in New York and we hardly ever saw her.

Last year, Nancy was diagnosed with breast cancer. She had surgery, radiation, chemo, the entire treatment. The process scared us because we never really knew if Nancy was going to be okay or not. We realized that we never had given much thought to these things and that we didn't even have a will. It was Nancy who insisted we have one drawn up. The house was still in her name, just as it was when we met, but in the will she left it to me. It was a given that I'd take care of the kids; I love my girls. She knew I'd find a way. In the end things happened so fast. Nancy wanted to die at home, but the health insurance didn't cover the hospice care. So when the time came, I paid for it with credit cards. It was hard. I wasn't working very much because I wanted to be with her all the way through this.

When Nancy died three months ago, I went back to the lawyer to see what came next. Maybe I should have just taken the kids and left town. The probate fees on the house are going to be enormous. No way do I have that; all our savings went to the hospice people, and now I have credit card bills, too, plus I gave up a lot of jobs to be with my wife. The lawyer says that unless I pay these probate fees, he will probably force the sale of the house. That's not all. Now Nancy's mother has flown out from New York, says she wants the kids, that she can give them private schools, and that I'm not a good father. That's not true, and the attorney says it will never happen, but now I have attorney's fees up to here. Even if I could get the money for the probate fees—which feels like making bail or something—I'll have to sell the house to pay the attorney's fees and the credit cards. So the kids and I will lose the house regardless. All that work we put into it. I thought nothing could get worse after I lost my wife. I thought wrong.

What is a will? A will is simply a piece of paper that states who you want to get what when you die. But it's also a legal document, which is where the trouble can begin. When you're dealing with a will, you're dealing with the courts.

When Nancy made up her will, she truly believed that everything—the house, their children—would pass smoothly to Jeff. She thought everything was in order. But a will often takes a circuitous route to get where it's meant to go, and in many cases it can be a very expensive route as well.

How do you obtain a will?

There are a few ways to get a will. You can have a lawyer draw one up. This should cost from a hundred to a few thousand dollars, depending on where you live and how complex your affairs are. You can buy a form will at a stationery store and fill in the blanks, which should cost about $10. Or you can get a computer program that will generate a will for you for about $35. If you use any of these methods, you'll also need to sign your will and, while you are signing it, to have two or three people witness your signature and sign the will as well. Some states require two signatures, some three, so to be on the safe side, ask three people to witness your signature. When you want to change anything in the will, you simply draw up what is called a *codicil*, which is an additional paper enumerating your changes. Follow the same procedure as when you signed the will in the first place.

If you want, you can draw up a will yourself on a piece of paper, which will cost you nothing. This is known as a *holographic will*. Just make sure that the paper you use has no other writing on it or the will will not be considered legal. Make sure, too, that the entire will is written in your handwriting and is dated and signed by you. If you make a mistake, don't cross it out. Start over. Anything crossed out is considered an interlineation, making the will null and void. Do not have anyone else witness a holographic will because, again, this will make it null and void. If you want to change a holographic will, it is better just to redo the entire thing.

Your will should specify an *executor*. This is the person who will make sure that all the legal, financial, and emotional matters are taken care of after you have died and that the wishes expressed in your will are carried out. Executors deal with the legal system and the accountant and all the beneficiaries. They contact the banks and insurance companies and inform them of your passing and send in the necessary documentation to change the names on all the accounts to the new owners. For tax purposes, all the property will have to be valued and the final tax returns compiled; and if any money is owed to the IRS, the executor must make sure that it has been paid or set aside before any assets are distributed to the beneficiaries of the will. In many states the executor gets a set fee for having done all these tasks, or, depending on where you live, you may just decide to specify a fee in the will.

So preparing a will is relatively simple. Where it can get complicated, as you saw with Nancy, is in its execution after you have died. All your will says is where you want your property to go. It does not necessarily get it there very easily.

After your death your will has to pass through the court system. Usually the executor has a lawyer handle this. Once the will gets to the court, two things happen. First, a judge has to authenticate the will, to make sure it is valid. After the judge probates the will, he or she will then sign a court order transferring title to the property covered in the will to the people who are intended to receive it, as reflected in the will. In Jeff's case, for example, title to Nancy's house would be transferred to his name once probate was completed.

This sounds easy enough, but can be a nightmare.

In the first place, the process can take anywhere from six months to two years or more, while ownership of the property remains in probate limbo.

Nor does this process come cheap. In the state of California, where Jeff lives, and in many other states, there are statutory probate fees—fees, that is, that are set by law. These are the first fees that have to be paid out any estate.

What this meant for Jeff was that the court would total the value of Nancy's estate and then charge a fixed-by-law percentage of that amount for these probate fees. The house was Nancy's major asset. Now, Nancy had put $50,000 down on the house, and in the few years they'd lived there, she and Jeff had paid off about $15,000 of the $175,000 mortgage she had originally taken out. This left a mortgage of about $160,000. So, since the house is now supposedly worth about $300,000, their equity in the house is $140,000. The bank is owed the rest. One would think that the probate fees would be based on their equity in the house—the $140,000 they actually have in it. But that's not how it happens. Probate fees are based on the fair market value of the house at the time of death, which means what the value of the house is on the open market. In this case the fair market value is now $300,000. California probate fees for Jeff would be $15,000, plus another $1,000 or so in court costs—just to claim title to the house that he and his wife already thought of as his.

Probate fees vary from state to state—but you get the idea. Probating a will takes time and money, no matter what state you're in. If your estate is very small, you might be able to avoid probate with a simple will. Assets valued at $10,000 to less than $100,000 (depending on the state) can be transferred to your heir by a simple process called *probate affidavit*. That costs very little, doesn't take much time, and makes it easy for your survivors to receive what you want them to. Probate affidavit forms are available in most banks at no cost. Be careful, though. Your estate could be worth more than you think. See pages 280–85 for assessing your net worth.

Keep in mind, too, that wills can be contested, which means

that anyone who thinks he or she should have something that the deceased willed to someone else has the right to come to the court and ask for it. Then the judge has to decide. Also, although people commonly use wills to specify guardians for their children, this is merely a recommendation and is not binding. It only express one's wishes. Even though Jeff is the legal father of his children, and even though the will expressed Nancy's desire that he be their sole guardian, the legal guardianship of children always rests in the hands of the court. Nancy's mother knew what she was doing when she flew to California to ask the court for the children. Will she get them? It's unlikely, but the court will make its decisions based on whatever it feels is in the best interest of the children. Meanwhile, Jeff has to hire—and pay—a lawyer.

Could Nancy have arranged her affairs differently, to save all this agony and expense? At least some trouble could have been avoided if Nancy had set up a revocable living trust.

TRUSTS

REVOCABLE LIVING TRUSTS

What Is a Revocable Living Trust?

A *revocable living trust* is a legal document that identifies any assets that will be held in the name of the trust and also designates the person who will manage those assets 1) while you are alive (typically, this is you), 2) in the event of your incapacity, and 3) after your death.

How Is a Revocable Living Trust Different from a Will?

A will simply tells your loved ones and the courts how you want to distribute your money and property after your death. It doesn't actually make the distribution happen. A court must do that. A trust is much more straightforward and flexible, for the simple reason that the court is taken out of the process. A trust lets you transfer legal title of your assets into the care of a trustee—usually yourself, but sometimes another person—and to name a *successor trustee* and beneficiaries. This way, assets quickly become the property of your beneficiaries upon your death. Most important, *they do not pass through probate*. The courts are not involved in the transfer of your estate.

Here's how a trust differs from a will. Let's say that my mother wants to leave me her home, just as Nancy wanted to leave her home to Jeff. The deed to the home is in my mother's name. If she has a will, she will have stated her desire that I inherit the house. But when she dies, I have a problem. How is the title of the house going to be changed from her name into my name? That's where the probate court comes in—a judge must read the will and approve the title transfer. If my mother leaves me the house in a living trust, however, and has signed the deed over to the name of the trust during her lifetime, probate on the house is avoided. The house comes directly to me.

A will states where you want your assets to go after your death; with a revocable living trust, you take the steps while you are alive to sign the title of your property over to the trust.

By the way, anytime you want to you can amend the trust, so you can always change your mind about who gets what. Think of a trust as a suitcase, into which you put the title to your house, your stocks, and your other investments. For each item, you can affix a label, saying who will get it after you die. You carry the suitcase with you while you are alive, and you're perfectly free to put new things in, take anything out, or change the labels. Then, upon your death, the suitcase gets handed by your successor trustee directly to your beneficiaries, at which time they can take out whatever you've labeled as theirs.

In many, many cases—especially in states with statutory probate fees—trusts are far superior to wills. Clients who came to me for financial advice, whether they were single, married, or living together, ended up with a thorough education on trusts.

As we just said in Nancy's case, if you die leaving a will, in all states the only way for property valued at more than $100,000 (or at as little as $10,000, in some states) to be transferred from the name of the deceased to the name of the beneficiary is to have a judge do it through the probate courts. With a trust you save time and you avoid probate fees and legal fees. If Nancy had a trust instead of a will, and had specified where she wanted the house to go, the house would have gone directly to Jeff. There would have been no probate fee of $15,000, no courts, and no attorneys. Nancy's wishes would have been carried out smoothly, and Jeff would at least have been allowed to grieve in his own home in peace.

If you own property or other assets, have children, or care about what happens to the people you love after you're gone, I urge you to look into a trust. When? As soon as possible. There is a fair bit of paperwork involved in switching assets into a trust, so the sooner you've set one up, the easier it will be to accumulate assets in the name of the trust.

SARAH AND ANNIE'S STORY

Where you want your money to go is one concern. Where you *don't* want it to go is just as important.

ANNIE: Ever since Daddy died, it's been a nightmare.

SARAH: My husband, Harry, fought with Peter, our son, for years, and always said he wouldn't get another dime. We had to give him money so many times; over the years, that was tens of thousands of dollars. The worst thing was when Harry died, Peter didn't even come to his funeral, couldn't be bothered. I will never forgive him for that. I decided then: that was that. I wouldn't let him have another dime, just like Harry said. Last year I moved here from Florida to live near Annie, my daughter, and my grandson, William. I trust Annie, she never wanted a thing. Peter is living in our house in Florida and wants it put in his name. No way. He can live there, but nothing more. Not one penny.

ANNIE: Mama kept all the money in a brokerage account in Florida. Daddy liked the person who handled it, so she thought, Why not just leave it there? What did we know? Daddy always took care of everything, so when we would get these statements from Florida, we just filed them away. Mama hardly goes out on her own anymore because she's afraid she'll trip and fall. But she loves to cook. Most nights William and I go over, and she makes us a great dinner. One night when we got there she was waving this power of attorney form around that Peter had sent her, and she was having a fit.

SARAH: I'm getting older, yes, but not senile, as you can see. Peter is trying everything to get his hands on my money. Can you imagine? He sends this note that says, "Mama, just sign here." Power of attorney. If anyone is going to take over for me, I want it to be Annie. I trust her with my life. I just want him to leave me alone. And when I die, I want the money, what's left of it, to go to Annie and William. Not a penny to that son of mine who wouldn't even come to his own father's funeral.

This story is dramatic—and it gets worse. But I've seen many cases like this. Money can tear apart families, even families that were closer to begin with than this one, faster than anything else.

I met Annie and Sarah because they were referred by a friend who thought they needed some financial help, and I was deeply relieved that they came when they did. Time was of the essence. I opened all the Florida statements that they had filed away, and they were stunned to find out that Sarah's assets added up to more than $3 million. They had no idea. I noticed something else: many, many trades of stocks and bonds had been going on in her account. How could Sarah have known this, when she didn't even open the statements or mail that came from the brokerage house? A few calls to the broker later and we found out that it was Peter who was trading the account. The broker figured it was okay because Peter was Sarah's son. This was no excuse and his actions could have cost that broker his job, but Sarah felt that Harry had liked him and that was good enough. Even so, we convinced her to transfer the entire account to a reputable broker here in California, where she lived. She also worked with an estate and trust lawyer, Janet, an associate of mine I have come to trust by watching how she has worked with other clients in the past, to make decisions about how to best protect her estate.

We put together her revocable living trust and began transferring her assets into it. The assets would remain in her name throughout the rest of her life, then would pass directly to Annie. Because of Sarah's age and frail health, we also gave Annie *durable power of attorney for health care,* which is covered later in this chapter. Because the estate was large, and because we all felt that Peter would do whatever he could to claim whatever he could, we took an additional precautionary step. We videotaped Sarah talking about the trust, expressing what she wanted to have happen to her estate when she was gone. As we went through the process, Sarah decided in the end that she wanted to leave Peter $10,000. Although frail, Sarah knew exactly what she wanted and what she was doing, and the video reflected that.

Everything went fine for about four years, but as Sarah's

health continued to weaken, she decided she wanted Annie to step in as the new trustee of the trust. This meant that Annie would be the one who could decide what was to happen with the money in the accounts, write checks against them, and generally oversee everything. They came back to my office, and it was an easy process to change the name of the trustee from Sarah to Annie. Janet then wrote all the institutions that held Sarah's money informing them that Annie was the new trustee.

About two weeks later Peter called to say that he was coming to visit Sarah; this was a first, and it made Annie very nervous. Still, she agreed to join her brother at her mother's condo for dinner the night he was due to arrive. When she got to Sarah's condo, however, the locks had been changed. After meeting with the super and calling a locksmith, Annie gained entry and found her mother gone, her suitcase gone, her checkbook gone—and the pills she needed to take every day still on the night table. Five days later the authorities found her in a hospital in Florida. She had collapsed from dehydration and starvation.

Annie and William, in a panic, flew to Florida to bring Sarah home, and her story emerged slowly. Peter had taken his mother to the bank and tried to close out her account—but wasn't able to, since Annie was now the trustee of her mother's trust. He was able, however, to clean out her safety-deposit box of quite a lot of cash that Sarah liked to keep there just in case. Then he flew her to Florida, made her sign another power of attorney form he'd drawn up. That was all Sarah would say about the last time she saw her son. As Annie and William were bringing her home, Sarah died.

After Sarah's death Peter was notified how much he was to get under the trust. He was furious. He claimed that his mother had promised to transfer the deed to the house over to him while she was in Florida. He claimed a lot of other things as well. He threatened to sue. But we sent his attorney a copy of the trust and a copy of the video, and that was that. Even though Peter was actually living in the house, the trust made Sarah's wishes crystal clear. Her trust overrode Peter's claims and threats. The trust protected what Sarah wanted to have happen to her money. Had Sarah had a will, not a trust, the probate fee on $3 million would have been $82,000.

One footnote to this story: Because there was a lot of money at stake here, and because Sarah and Annie were afraid that others might find out how much money they had, their privacy was a big concern to both of them. So there was yet another reason why they were better off with the money in a trust rather than in a will. Wills are public documents, and after someone has died and his or her will has been probated, anyone can go down to the courthouse and look up all the assets you owned and what they are worth. With trusts, only the people entitled to the assets will know what they are and what they are worth.

HOW DO I SET UP A REVOCABLE LIVING TRUST?

If you want to do it yourself, and if you're very good about taking care of paperwork, there are books in your bookstore that will show you how—$20, give or take. Computer programs for setting up trusts are available for about $50. If you decide to do it yourself, though, I urge you to have a qualified attorney look it over to make sure you did it correctly.

Most people decide—and I myself believe—that having an attorney draw up a trust is safest. Depending on the size of the estate and how expensive the attorney is, you should be able to get a simple revocable living trust drawn up for between $500 and $3,000. If you decide you want your attorney to fund the trust—that is, to transfer your assets into it—it may cost you more. Once the trust is set up, making simple changes to it should cost about $100. Obviously these fees will vary, depending on where you live and how complex your requirements are.

The language of trusts may seem daunting, but it isn't. Here's a rundown of the terms you need to know:

Revocable Living Trust

Trust: It's called a trust because you are entrusting this entity with your assets, for your benefit while you are alive and to carry out your wishes when you can no longer do so for yourself.

Living: It's called living because the trust will be set up while you are alive and will also live on after your death to carry out your wishes.

Revocable: Whoever is in charge of the trust—and it will usually be you—can change it at any time, so it is called revocable.

Components of a Trust: Trustor, Trustee, Beneficiary

Trustor, or settlor: The person who creates the trust and who owns the property that will be put into the trust. In the case history just presented, Sarah was her own trustor.

Trustee: The person who controls the assets in the trust. Most often the trustor is also the trustee. When you set up a trust, you do not have to give up your power over your assets. Most people continue taking care of everything just as they did before the trust existed. The only difference will be your title. If you and a spouse hold property as joint tenants or in community property, you do the same in the trust, and you can both be trustees. In fact, you can have as many trustees as you want, though having more than two is not usually recommended. Keep in mind that the trustee will have the say over most of what happens in the trust, so choose your trustees carefully, even if you are still going to be a trustee yourself.*

Co-trustee: Another person who has the authority to manage and invest the assets of the trust, although all trustees must agree to financial or investment changes. Parents often choose to make their children co-trustees, upon the deterioration or disability of the parents. Couples usually set up their trusts so that they're both co-trustees and therefore both must agree to any changes.

Successor trustee: This is the person who steps in to make decisions about the assets in the trust if and only if the trustee or co-trustees cannot or do not want to act in the decision-making process. Annie was Sarah's successor trustee and became her trustee once Sarah no longer wanted the burden of decision making.

Current beneficiaries: The person or persons for whom all of this is being held in trust. Sarah was the current beneficiary of her own trust.

Remainder beneficiaries: The person or persons who will inherit everything in the trust after the current beneficiary (who is usually the trustor as well) dies. In our case history Annie was a remainder beneficiary. Sarah had wanted William to inherit some assets outright, so he was a remainder beneficiary as well. Peter, to whom Sarah had left the $10,000, was another remainder beneficiary.

FUNDING YOUR TRUST

What good is an empty suitcase when you leave to go on vacation? Not much. Nor is an empty trust much good. By itself, the

---

*There are some states, New York for one, with restrictions about the same party serving as beneficiary, trustee, etc. In most states, however, this information holds true. Please check with an attorney in your state.

document establishing the trust means nothing until the trust assumes ownership of the things you intend to put into it.

In other words, once the trust has been set up your assets must be transferred into it. This means that if John and Jane Doe owned a house together in their own names, after they established their trust they would have a new deed issued that would list the owner as *John and Jane Doe, trustees for the John and Jane Doe Revocable Living Trust*. The Does would also change the titles on their stock portfolio, their insurance policies, bank accounts, and so on. Doing this is simply a matter of paperwork.

Computer programs and books about trusts provide sample letters to show you how to fund your trust. If you have a lawyer draw up your trust, he or she will have form letters available to show you. Or the lawyer can handle changing the titles for you; even if the fee is higher than that for simply drawing up the trust, it might be well worth it—different institutions have different requirements for making the change.

Failing to transfer assets into your trust can be costly. Let's say, for example, that you were lucky enough to have a certificate of deposit at the bank worth $100,000. Put that CD into your trust, and though there might be estate taxes for your beneficiaries to pay, there would be no probate. Forget to put it into the trust? That mistake would cost your beneficiaries up to $5,000. All assets that have a title on them—such as your bank account (both checking and savings), brokerage account, certificates of deposit, Treasury instruments, and all accounts that have your name on them—need to be transferred into the name of the trust. Every institution has a form that it uses to make this transfer easier for them. Make sure, if your lawyer is not doing this for you, that you contact each place, get the correct paperwork, and fill it out immediately to make the transfer.

PROVIDING FOR YOUR CHILDREN WITH A TRUST

Okay, you're thinking, this all makes great sense. But I'm only thirty-nine, and I did a will when we had children. The will says to whom the kids would go if something happened. My best friend, Joe, would be the guardian; we've already talked about it. Plus I don't really have that many assets yet, though I have a nice-size life insurance policy, just in case. That trust sounds like a good idea for when I'm older.

Not true. Particularly when you have children, the earlier you set up your revocable living trust the better, even if you don't have a lot of money. If your children are very young, and if anything were to happen to you, they could be at greater risk than you might imagine. Say you're killed in an automobile accident. It happens every day. Even if you have a will, your will does not have the power to assure that Joe, your best friend in this world, will be the legal guardian of your children. A will can only express your wishes. The court has the final decision when it comes to who is appointed legal guardian of your children. With a living trust, you can specify who handles the money position for assets in your trust.

This is true in a trust as well—there is no guarantee that the person you name to be your children's legal guardian will be the one appointed by the court. But with a trust, you can at least exercise control over their financial future. With only a simple will, the judge not only can appoint a guardian but can take charge of the funds you want your children to have (for private schools, camps, music lessons, prom dresses) until the children are eighteen years old. For instance, if your children are underage and all you leave them is a life-insurance policy, a guardianship for the insurance money is created upon your death, naming the executor or someone else as the guardian for this money. Each year the guardian has to go back to court to account for the money spent on behalf of the children during the past year. When each child reaches eighteen, regardless of his or her ability to handle the money, each one's share will be legally signed over, lock, stock, and barrel. And by the time he or she gets it, there will not be as much as there could have been, because every year there has been guardian fees and fees to a lawyer to do the guardianship reporting.

If you die with a trust, the courts still have the final say over guardianship. But you can at least make the important decision of how, when, and for what purposes your children will receive the money you are leaving them. You assign a successor trustee (your chosen guardian, for example)—or two or three, or however many you like—and specify when you want your children to receive their money, how you'd like that money to be used until that time, and, poof, it's done. The successor trustee(s) takes care of your children's financial lives on your behalf. No yearly reporting, no fees, nothing.

Think trusts are for old people who are likelier to die? Think again. Trusts are for people who are lucky enough to live among people they love. Trusts are for people who are responsible for those they love.

Think revocable living trusts are only for the rich? Not true, as we have seen. Bypass trusts (page 118) are for the rich, but that is a different kind of trust. In fact, revocable living trusts are even more important for people with fewer assets than for those with tons of money. Why? Because the less you have, the more probate hurts.

WHICH DOCUMENT DO I NEED?

If trusts are so great, why do so many people still think they should have a will drawn up and have their lawyers do it for them? Why don't the lawyers, especially in states where probate fees are statutory, recommend establishing trusts?

Guess who gets the probate fees? The attorneys do. If you were an attorney, would you rather make thousands in probate fees or just a few hundred to set up a trust?

More and more people are going the trust route and for all the reasons we've seen, I recommend a trust for most people. However, it is also very important to have a will as a backup, covering any assets you have not put into your trust—things such as furniture, personal items, and items of strictly sentimental value. And remember, if you have underage children, you should designate who is to serve as their guardian in your will, so that your wishes will be clear to the court.

If you have not created a will or a trust, or worry that you haven't done it properly, it might be time to see an attorney who specializes in drawing up these documents. Word of mouth is the age-old way of finding an attorney, so ask your friends, but please make certain you find one well versed in estate planning. If you do have friends, however, who think their attorney walks on water even if he or she doesn't specialize in trusts, you might want to call and ask that attorney to refer you to someone who does.

Another good place to find names of knowledgeable trust attorneys in your area is through your local university, especially if they have a law school. Call and ask one of the professors who specialize in estate planning whom they would recommend.

You can also refer to the *Martindale-Hubbell Directory,* available in any public library (and on the Web at lawyers.martindale .com). This is a comprehensive nationwide listing of lawyers, and it will have the names and addresses of all the lawyers in your state as well.

When you do get the names of some attorneys, please make sure that you interview at least three of them. An attorney plays a major role in making sure your estate is set up correctly, and your survivors will need his or her assistance after your death.

Here's what you should ask and what the answers should be:

⊰⊱ *How long have you been specializing in estate planning?* The answer should be at least ten years.

⊰⊱ *How many people have you drafted wills and trusts for in the past five years?* The answer should be at least two hundred people.

⊰⊱ *Will you be drafting the documents yourself or will someone else be doing the paperwork?* It is okay if someone else draws up the paperwork if they are supervised correctly. This may actually end up costing you less. You just want to know one way or the other.

⊰⊱ *How much do you charge?* You want a lawyer to charge you a flat fee to draw up a will and/or trust. The fee should include drawing up the document and explaining it to you (which could take a few hours, if the document is a trust) and funding the trust, which means doing the paperwork to transfer the titles on all your property and assets into the name of the trust.

⊰⊱ *If I have other questions, will you charge me if I call and ask?* There should be no charge for simple questions over the phone.

WHAT IF YOU DON'T HAVE A WILL OR A TRUST?

No problem, as long as you don't die.

If you do die—no, *when* you do die—your loved ones will soon find that by not taking action, you have left their inheritance up to the state.

Let's say you own your house, which was part of your divorce settlement, and hold it in your own name. Since divorcing, you've remarried and are hopelessly in love with your new hubby. Still, because of the terrible divorce you went through, you feel a little safer keeping the house in just your name. Your two children from your first marriage have never liked the idea that you remarried, and even though they're grown, they're extremely possessive of the house they grew up in. If anything were to happen to you, you would want your new husband to be able to stay in the house for as long as he likes, then have the title transferred to your kids. But you haven't got around to creating a will or a trust.

One day on your way home from work, you're killed in a car accident. Because you have no will or trust, the laws of the state go into effect—a process called *intestate succession*. Depending on the laws of your state, your husband may own half the house, and your kids (who do not approve of him at all) could end up owning the other half. If they wanted to, they could force him to sell the home. If nothing else, they could probably make him buy out their half, if they're willing to give up their attachment to the house. In any event, they'll all have to go through probate and come up with the money to pay the probate fees. Had the children been younger, the state would also have determined guardianship.

A trust specifying what you wanted would have been the best thing. A will would have been second best, even with probate fees. Without either, your loved ones still have the probate fees and your wishes will have gone unheeded.

DURABLE POWER OF ATTORNEY FOR HEALTH CARE

Talking about wills and trusts, I've heard people say, "I don't care about any of this, because I am spending every penny I have while

I am alive." In a way, I understand this. Once you die, it's not your problem anymore, is it?

But what if you don't die right away? What if you have a stroke or a skiing accident? What if you are incapacitated to the point where you are put on life support, with virtually no chance of survival? What would you want to have happen then? If you do not decide now, someone else may decide for you later.

My practice was riddled with people who came to see me when it was too late, when all the money in the world wouldn't have made a bit of difference. Too many times, failing to take action in time creates more misery in miserable situations.

For example, most health insurance policies today have limits stating the maximum that they will pay out for an illness. This maximum varies from policy to policy, but the average is about $1 million. After your insurance company has paid out $1 million in benefits, they're done. With the skyrocketing cost of hospitalization, I am sure you can imagine that it would not take long to reach the maximum of your health insurance policy if you happened to be on life-support systems in a hospital. Once those health insurance policy maximums have been reached, what happens? Your assets, as well as those of your spouse, will be used to pay the medical bills that keep piling up. Would you want that to happen, or would you rather be allowed to die? Having a durable power of attorney for health care is part of being responsible, not only to your loved ones, but also to yourself and the assets you've worked hard for.

For the sake of every one of you reading this book, I hope that you won't ever be incapacitated or hospitalized, and that a long healthy life awaits you. But in case it doesn't, I urge you to make the simple arrangements for durable power of attorney for health care, for yourself and for the people you love. Do it now, while you're strong and healthy. It might be the most important document you ever sign. Most of the other subjects covered in this chapter concern your death. This one concerns your life.

DENNIS AND SALLY'S STORY

"I promise you that if anything ever happens, I'll make sure that you do not have to spend your life on those machines," Sally told her husband.

That was my promise. I don't even know why the subject came up. We had just come home from Dennis's forty-fifth birthday dinner, and I guess he was thinking about getting older, but there was nothing wrong. Nothing. Three months later I came home to find a message on our answering machine, to get down to the hospital as soon as possible. Dennis had been in an accident at work. I was sick when I saw him, tubes in and out of every opening in his body. I loved him so much. I asked the nurses if he was in pain, and they said, "I doubt very much if he can feel anything." They were acting as if he were already dead. The doctor came in right away and said there was little hope—in fact, in his opinion there was no hope—that Dennis would ever come off those machines. I kind of lost it then, and I kept screaming over and over, "But I promised! No machines." They had to give me something to calm me down.

Dennis's family started to arrive one by one. As the days and weeks passed, it became very obvious that even though the wounds were healing, Dennis would never be my Dennis again. He would never come off those machines. The doctor said that in order for us to disconnect them, I needed to have a something or other for health care. I didn't know what it was then, but I sure know now. I didn't have it in writing, I just knew about my promise, I kept telling them that. The doctor was starting to see if there was any way around it when Dennis's sister stepped in. She said it would be over her dead body that they would disconnect these machines. She said she and her brother were like one and there was no way he'd want to disconnect the machines.

That was eight years ago now and nothing much has changed. Dennis is still on the machines. This is still so freaky to me. It was as if Dennis somehow knew something like this would happen, and that is why he made me promise. My promise meant nothing, but I hope he knows somewhere inside him that I'm still trying to keep it.

She's still trying today. When I asked Sally if it's sad to see her husband this way after so many years, she said, "Not as sad as the fact that I didn't keep my word to him." This disagreement between the sister and Sally went to the court system after seven years and Sally lost—which makes it all the more important to have a written document regarding health care. The sad thing about this is that it did not have to be this way. If Dennis and Sally had that "something or other" for health care—durable power of attorney for health care—in force, none of what has taken place after the accident would have happened.

The first part of putting a durable power of attorney for health care in place is deciding what you would want to have happen to you if you were in a situation like Dennis's. It requires talking to your loved ones and making your feelings known. You can choose from three basic options.

1. You want to prolong your life as long as possible, without regard to your condition, chance of recovery, or the cost of treatment.

2. You want life-sustaining treatment to be provided, unless you are in a coma or ongoing vegetative state, which two

doctors, one your attending physician, will determine in their best judgment.

3. You do not want your life to be unnaturally prolonged, unless there is some hope that both your physical and mental health might be restored.

You must also decide in whose hands you want to put your life—that is, who will make the final decision to take you off life support, if the decision ever has to be made. This person is known as the *agent*. Choose someone who loves you, yet who is strong enough to do what you would want him or her to do— not an easy position to be in.

IS THIS THE SAME AS HAVING A LIVING WILL?

A living will is not the same thing and, in my opinion, not as complete. A living will does make your wishes about life support known to the doctors, who then take them into consideration. It doesn't appoint someone you trust to make the final decision. A durable power of attorney for health care not only enables you to put your feelings and wishes into effect, but also specifies who will make the decision if you cannot. Living trust, living will, durable power of attorney for health care: remember, these are very different documents.

HOW DO I SET UP A DURABLE POWER OF ATTORNEY FOR HEALTH CARE?

The forms to establish durable power of attorney for health care vary from state to state but are available, free of charge, at every hospital. Just make sure you get the form that is valid in your state. You can also write to Partnership for Caring's National Office, 1620 Eye Street NW, Washington, D.C. 20006 or call 800-989-WILL (9455) (download forms from the website www.partnershipforcaring.org). If you are arranging for your trust or will, your attorney can take care of this at the same time. Be sure to distribute copies to your doctor, agents.

Don't put this step off. The moment you need to do this document, it's too late to create it.

LIFE INSURANCE

Life insurance was never meant to be a permanent need. Its original purpose was to protect people while they were younger, before they had a chance to build up a nest egg, in case the family breadwinner died early and unexpectedly. If the breadwinner lived his or her life according to plan, however, the family would accumulate enough assets to make itself safe and then let the insurance go.

Today, however, a huge industry exists to sell you as much insurance as it can, whether you really need it or not.

I know how the industry works, because I'm a licensed insurance agent, and I know the workings of most policies inside out. I also know how the commissions work. If you knew how large those commissions on whole-life policies really are—often 80 to 90 percent of the first year's premium—you would know why people say, "Life insurance isn't something you buy. Life insurance is something that's sold to you."

If you're single and have no dependents whatever, you can skip this section, because there's no need for you to have life insurance at all. However, if you have people who depend on the money you bring in with every paycheck, there is information here that is essential for you to understand. The four questions to ask yourself about life insurance are these:

⇢ Do I need it?

⇢ If so, how much do I need?

⇢ If so, how long will I need it?

⇢ If so, what kind of life insurance policy do I need?

YOUR EXERCISE

Question 1: Do I Really Need Life Insurance?

You're a single parent with two kids, and you die unexpectedly. Or you're married in a two-income household, and your spouse is killed in an accident. Whatever your own family circumstances, would those you left behind be able to carry on financially?

Back in Step 3 you compiled a list of all your expenses. Now is the time to review that list and see how much it would change if your children were suddenly parentless or if you or your partner were to die. Fixed expenses would remain the same. Some expenses would decrease. Some would increase—long-distance phone calls to friends for comfort, eating out so you wouldn't be so lonely, entertainment. Would your childcare situation change? What about the future financial goals you had—paying for the children's education, for example? Could you still cover that? What if you or your partner had to stop working as well? How would you cope? How much would it really take? How much do you really have?

Now compare the hypothetical money coming in against the hypothetical money going out in this scenario and any other scenarios you can imagine. What impact would a possible death have on the money coming in? If your survivors would have enough, then you do not need insurance. You may still want some for peace of mind, but you don't need any—and there is a big difference between needing insurance and wanting it.

If your loved ones would not have enough, then you know you need insurance to protect yourself and them.

Question 2: How Much Life Insurance Do I Need?

Most people think, "Oh, all I'd need is enough to get my family by for just a little while. As a result, they usually have the $50,000 or so worth of insurance that's part of their benefits package at work, and feel that is enough. But since an unexpected tragedy affects people in different ways, you never know for sure what might happen after you are gone. That's why this is a decision, which must take into account every tragic possibility, and must be discussed with the people who would be affected by it. All the questions must be asked. Do they feel comfortable knowing that they have enough money to get by for a year, or two, or eight? Many experts will tell you to purchase six to eight times your annual salary, but experts are not the ones who have to live your loved ones' lives. Maybe in your situation you would rather know that everyone will be okay no matter what, even if no one is able ever to work again. Maybe you want your children to be provided for more than ten years, rather than just eight. There is no magic formula. Each of us has our own financial what-if comfort level. The final decision is a balance of what makes everyone concerned feel secure and how much you can realistically afford to pay for that security.

As a rule of thumb, figure you need about $100,000 in insurance for every $500 of monthly income required. Let's say your household needs $3,000 a month to cover all your expenses. Your worst-case scenario is that the people who survive you have no employment or other income, so they'll need the full $3,000. You'd divide this by $500 and get 6, so your insurance policy should be in the amount of 6 × $100,000, or $600,000. The following table shows you the simple calculation. You can plug in your own numbers in the blanks at the right.

	EXAMPLE	YOUR NUMBERS
Your projected monthly income need is A	A $3,000	A _____
Divide A by $500 to get B	B 6	B _____
Multiply B by $100,000 to get C	C $600,000	C _____
The death benefit in your policy should be C.		

How does this work? You want your insurance settlement to be a sum of money that your beneficiaries can invest to generate enough income to cover your expenses without dipping into the principal. If your monthly expenses are $3,000, that's $36,000 a year. Assuming a conservative interest rate of 6 percent, you would need $600,000 to produce that $36,000 a year. That principal would go on throwing off income forever because your survivors are using only the interest.

Okay, that's the worst case—but now let's say that if something happened to you, you know you or your spouse would keep working. All you need from the insurance proceeds, before taxes, is $1,500 a month. You have three choices. You can purchase the minimum amount of insurance needed to cover that shortage of $1,500 a month, which is $300,000 worth of insurance: $1,500 divided by 500 is 3; 3 times $100,000 is $300,000. Or you can purchase $600,000 worth of insurance to cover yourself completely, in case at some later date you won't be able to work after all. Or you can purchase any amount in between that would make you feel comfortable.

Let's say you and your spouse decided to be completely

secure and bought the $600,000. Your spouse dies, but you still want to work; for now, all you need is $1,500 a month from the death benefit to cover all your expenses. What do you do with the $600,000? You will want to invest enough safely for the principal to generate that $1,500 a month in interest every year, without touching the principal, and invest the rest for growth in case the day comes when you can't work any more or you lose your job. Let's figure again. How much needs to be invested for income, to cover the $1,500 a month you need, and how much for growth?

To find out how much you need to invest in order to generate $1,500 a month before taxes, multiply $1,500 by 12 to find out how much you need a year—$18,000. Let's assume that the going interest rate is 6 percent (a conservative figure, but we are trying to make you safe, and to be safe, it's always essential to think conservatively). So we need to figure out how much you need to invest at 6 percent to generate $18,000 a year. We divide 100 (percent of any whole) by 6 (the interest rate we're after), which gives us almost exactly 17. Now we multiply $18,000 by 17 to see how much needs to be invested at 6 percent to generate $18,000 a year: $306,000 ($306,000 × 6% = $18,360). You received a total of $600,000 in insurance proceeds, and now you know that you have to invest $306,000 for income generation for as long as you continue to bring home the $1,500 paycheck. The remaining $294,000 is what you can invest for growth—and also serves as backup if something happens to you. You have covered all your bases.

If you had decided simply to purchase the minimum amount of insurance needed in this situation, which was $300,000, you would invest all of that to generate the $1,500 a month income you need and would hope that you are able to keep working while you build up more of a nest egg.

When money is an issue, though, as it is for most of us, we don't always have the luxury of buying enough life insurance to assume the worst. With most people there's almost always a discrepancy between the maximum of insurance wanted and the minimum of insurance needed. Your needs, comfort level, and what you can afford all have to be taken into account. If you're using a professional to help you figure this out, make sure he or she has your needs and pocketbook in mind and isn't just thinking of all that the commissions will buy. I would suggest that you're better off trying to figure out how much insurance you really need and can afford, then calling the following numbers to get quotes to compare the best-priced policies. Here are the numbers and Internet addresses of the insurance quoting services (make sure that you check with at least three of the following services; you would be surprised how much they can differ):

AccuQuote
800-442-9899
http://www.zaccuquote.com

Insurance Quote Services
800-972-1104
http://www.iquote.com

Matrix Direct Insurance Services
877-844-8371
http://www.matrixdirect.com

InsWeb
916-853-3300
http://www.insweb.com

Liferates of America
800-457-2837

Quote Smith
800-556-9393
http://www.quotesmith.com

Master Quote
800-337-5433
http://www.masterquote.com

Select Quote
800-343-1985
http://www.selectquote.com

Termquote
800-444-8376
http://www.term~quote.com

Question 3: How Long Will I Need Life Insurance?

Remember, life insurance was never intended to fill a permanent need. As the years go on, the money that you are putting away in your retirement plan (see Step 5), that you may be accumulating on your own, and that you are accruing in your home as you pay off the mortgage will continue to change how much insurance you really need, or whether you need it at all. One of the goals of this book is to make sure that by the time you are retired, you'll have enough coming in from your retirement plans to support you—and support your loved ones after you're gone. Once you have enough to live on in this way, most likely there will be no need for life insurance. (However, never, never cancel or attempt to change a policy without checking with your doctor and having a thorough physical. If there's a medical reason, you may want to keep insurance you otherwise would not have needed.) Bottom-line goal: By the time you are sixty-five at the latest, your need for life insurance, and your need to pay the premiums on your life insurance, should be gone.

Question 4: What Kind of Life Insurance Do I Need?

In my opinion there is only one kind of life insurance that makes sense for the vast majority of us, and that is term life insurance. When you sign up for term insurance, you're buying a just-in-case policy for a finite length of time that you need protection. Term policies are not very expensive because the insurance company knows you have relatively little chance of dying while the policy is in force. Most likely they won't have to pay a death benefit, and the premium is accordingly relatively small.

With a whole life or universal policy, on the other hand, the insurance company knows it will almost certainly have to pay the face amount or the death benefit. You're expected to die with it. So they price it accordingly. It's true that whole life and universal policies have cash values, so if you decide not to keep it, or if you suddenly need money while you're alive, one source would be the cash value of these policies. But commissions on life insurance policies are some of the most lucrative commissions in any business—and *you're* paying them. If your goal in buying life insurance is to put money aside, there are far, far better ways to do so without having to pay these kinds of commissions, as we'll see in the next chapters. With low-cost term insurance, even though you do not accumulate a cash value, you're paying low commissions on the protection you need, for as long as you signed up for.

LINDA'S STORY

The agent was so nice, Linda thought, and he was selling something she thought she needed.

> I've always had it in my head that I want my kids to have insurance when I die, and $1.5 million is the figure I always thought sounded right. I have a comfortable income from my work—in fact, I was the one who paid the settlement in my divorce—but I have no savings, really, and the income will stop when I die. The kids don't really see their father, and he has children from his second marriage, so this is all they'd get, ever. My father always said life insurance was a great way to save. I always remembered that. I finally got around to it three years ago—I was fifty-three.
>
> The agent was so nice. He came all the way to my house, which is way out of town. On a Saturday! I was so impressed.

When he came, I told him what I wanted and he had his computer with him, so he did the figures right there. He said it would be $22,500 a year for twenty years and that was that; the kids would have their money. In my head I added it up. It meant that I'd be putting in $450,000, and they'd get $1.5 million—a good deal, no? So I said fine, and every June 1 since, I've sent in my $22,500.

This last year, though, I got a notice that said since interest rates have been so low, I would have to pay the $22,500 for an extra three years to keep the $1.5 million death benefit, and if the rates stayed this low or went lower, I might have to pay longer. I called up the agent, and he said that it is possible, even though it isn't probable, that if interest rates didn't pick up, I might have to pay that money for quite a while longer than I was told. The best that could happen is that I'd have to pay it for twenty-three years in total. But I think he was saying that I might just have to go on paying it forever.

Had I known that, I would have thought twice about this. It just doesn't seem right. I asked him what if I stopped now and cashed in the policy, how much would I get? He said $36,000. But I've already paid $67,500! I got so confused. He had told me the same thing my father always said, that this was a great place for saving money, regardless of the insurance, because they were giving a guaranteed seven percent interest rate. So how do I end up with only $36,000? And what do I do now?

This is when I met Linda, now fifty-six, who still had it fixed in her head that she wanted $1.5 million in life insurance for her kids. But think about it: For the insurance company to pay that $1.5 million, plus all the commissions and expenses buried in the policy, don't they have to earn more than $1.5 million from Linda's money? Of course they do.

This is why they are having Linda pay that extra $22,500 a

year for three years right now. If their performance on how they invest Linda's money, and the money of everyone else covered by their plans, falls short of what they want, no problem. They'll just tell Linda she'll have to keep paying that $22,500 a year for as long as they like. And why does Linda, after putting in $67,500, have only $36,000 in cash value in her policy? Simple. Especially in the first few years of the policy, the bulk of her money goes to pay the agent's commissions; the insurance company also has to take its share. It is totally possible that the agent received that very first year a commission of $18,000, well worth his time that Saturday when he came out to her house. So, $18,000, give or take, of her first payment of $22,500 went out the window as soon as she paid it. In all likelihood the agent also "earns" around $2,000 every year she pays her premium from then on. Not bad.

What is also important to remember when buying universal/ whole life or, for that matter, any insurance is to study the chart or illustration your agent will show you of what your premium is going to buy you.

All illustrations have a *projected earnings* side and a *guaranteed earnings* side. The projected side shows how this policy is projected to perform if everything goes according to plan. I can still remember seeing projections on certain life insurance policies of what they would be worth if interest rates stayed at 14 percent, which is what they were when these policies were being sold. Policyholders were in for a rude awakening when interest rates came tumbling down and the policies stopped paying the 14 percent. Projected earnings are "in a perfect world" earnings.

If you look at the guaranteed side of the illustration, it will show you the absolute minimum death benefit, given the highest mortality charges (the maximum the company can charge you for the insurance) and the lowest possible interest rate they can pay you. If you look at the guaranteed side and decide that yes, it still feels like a great deal, buy it by all means, but I doubt you will feel this is the case. If Linda had looked at the guaranteed side of her illustration, she would have seen that the $22,500 would go on for the rest of her life in the worst-case scenario. She hadn't understood that and wouldn't have taken the policy if she had. Her agent had emphasized only the projected values. A responsible agent will always, even without your asking, point out the worst-case possibilities as well.

This is not how it works with term insurance. With lower-cost term insurance, the insurance company is taking an actuarial gamble that Linda will still be living when her policy reaches the end of its term and that they won't have to pay the $1.5 million. Both her children, who were doing just fine, and I tried to talk Linda out of having insurance at all, even term. By taking her money and investing it carefully, Linda could have built up $1.5 million for her children without paying any insurance premiums. Even so, Linda had her heart set on having a $1.5 million insurance policy for her kids. Therefore term insurance was the only sensible answer.

I suggested that we first apply for a $1.5 million twenty-year level term policy, which would guarantee that her premiums would stay level and not go up for twenty years. At the end of the term, that's it: no cash value, no insurance. At that time, the only way to get more insurance would be to reapply, but Linda would be seventy-six then, and the cost would be prohibitive. However, if she died within the next twenty years, her children would still get the $1.5 million she had dreamed of leaving them.

Our plan was that if she were accepted for this twenty-year level policy, we would cancel the first policy, withdraw the cash value, and invest that plus the difference in good no-load mutual funds (page 252) for growth. Then we ran the numbers.

When we priced the twenty-year level term policy with a death benefit of $1.5 million, based on Linda's age and health, the cost was $5,600 a year for the next twenty years—$16,900 less than she was paying on the whole life policy. Had she been younger, the cost would have been less; it would also be less if the death benefit were lower. This meant that Linda could take the $36,000 cash value from her first policy and add to that the yearly savings of $16,900 for the next twenty years, investing it all for growth.

Her main question was how much her kids would have if she died in the twenty-first year after the term policy ran out. The answer depended on how much those funds returned.

AT	8 PERCENT	$941,000
AT	9 PERCENT	$1 MILLION
AT	10 PERCENT	$1.2 MILLION
AT	11 PERCENT	$1,375,000
AT	12 PERCENT	$1,564,000
AT	13 PERCENT	$1,782,000
AT	14 PERCENT	$2,033,000
AT	15 PERCENT	$2.3 MILLION

With an insurance policy, the death proceeds are income tax-free, (though not estate tax free) and she would have to take that into consideration as well.

Linda then asked me to do another calculation. What if she lived her normal life expectancy and never again put in another penny after twenty years? Assuming a 9 percent interest rate from the start, how much would she have then? Her life expectancy is eighty-seven, according to the charts, which would be eleven years after the twenty-year policy ran out.

At 9 percent the money she invested outside of the insurance policy would have grown to $1 million by the time she was seventy-six. Then, even if she never put in another penny, that money would grow, to $2,580,000 by the time she was eighty-seven. (There are also a number of ways to invest the money and not have to pay taxes on it while it is accumulating; see Step 6.)

In the end Linda agreed. She figured that since the average rate of return, for stocks, even in a simple mutual fund, was around 10.1 percent, and that 9 percent was being conservative, she'd rather have control over her own money than be at the mercy of an insurance company telling her that she needed to pay $22,500 forever. Her insurance agent tried to talk her out of canceling her policy. Until she ran the numbers again, for him.

Happy ending—although if Linda had taken this course from the beginning, she would be in even better shape. At fifty-three her premiums for the exact same $1.5 million term policy would have been only $4,425 rather than $5,620. That alone is a big difference, never mind the fact that she would not have wasted $31,500, the difference between the $67,500 she paid in those three years and the $36,000 she got back. If she had gone the term route from the beginning, she would have had more than $3 million when she was eighty-seven and projected to die, rather than $2.5 million, if the money earns the conservative 9 percent. That was a costly three years.

SHORT-TERM? LONG-TERM?

A twenty-year policy felt right for Linda, but you'll have to decide the term that's right for you. Term insurance is available in all different term lengths, from yearly renewable term, where every year your premium will go up, to level term for longer terms—five, seven, ten, fifteen, and so on—where the premium is fixed for the term. The longest level term I know of is a thirty-year level, which is not available in all states. (See "Long-Term-Care Insurance," below, for information about how to choose an insurance company and agencies to call for the best rates.) Insurance companies are always coming up with new concepts, so scan the papers for offers that sound promising.

Linda thought we had finished discussing insurance, but I asked her one more thing. What if she ever had to go into a nursing home? She was so concerned about leaving money to her children. Did she know how fast nursing home costs would eat away at her assets?

LONG-TERM-CARE INSURANCE

ANNA AND ART'S STORY

"I'm only fifty-three," said Art. "I'm not going into any nursing home, and I'm not spending my money on *any* nursing home insurance."

Art can't tell his story now; his speech is still too slurred from the stroke. I will tell it for him.

When Anna and Art came into my office, I hardly noticed Anna, she was so tiny. Art, on the other hand, was huge, built like Smokey the Bear, with a great booming voice. Though soft-spoken, Anna, a schoolteacher, was not the least bit intimidated by her husband of twenty-seven years. Art had been offered early retirement, and they had come to see me about whether he should take it. After going through all their finances, we decided that although it was going to be close, they should take the offer, which was an excellent package. Only one thing worried me.

Anna had a heart condition, which had already necessitated two operations. She was also scheduled for a third operation in four months. The good news was that as a teacher, her health insurance coverage was excellent. But knowing of her condition, and considering Art's age, I suggested that we look into long-term-care (LTC) insurance for Art.

LTC insurance covers some of to all of the expenses the policyholder will incur if he or she were to enter a nursing home; it's that simple. As you will soon be able to tell, I love long-term-care insurance. I believe that it's one of the most important policies you can have. Long-term-care insurance is called into service more than any other kind. Yes, yes, I know, a nursing home would be decades off if you ever even had to enter one, right? Your parents aren't even in a nursing home. If you're twenty, thirty, or forty, I agree, this is not a policy to think about right now—for yourself, at least. But as you read this chapter, think about your parents. If you are hitting that magical fifty mark—well, you should read this chapter for you as well. It is when people reach fifty that I start suggesting LTC insurance. At fifty-three Art was about to hear me suggest it.

Like most health or life insurance policies, LTC policies require that you qualify for them, and I knew that with her weak heart, Anna would never be eligible. But Art would, and such a policy, if he ever needed it, would provide protection for Anna that could make all the difference in the world to her.

You see, what happens all too often with couples is that one of them ends up in a nursing home, and it takes every penny of income they both have coming in just to pay for those nursing home bills. The person who is healthy and at home is left with no money to live on and so has to start using the savings, retirement plans, and the principal that they had spent a lifetime saving. Before you know it, all the savings are used up, and then, when the partner in the nursing home dies, the one who is alive and well is left penniless and perhaps with many years remaining to live. I see this happen all the time, and it's devastating, which is why I brought up the subject of LTC insurance with Art and Anna. The subject went over like a lead balloon. "Do I look like a man who is ever going to end up in a nursing home?" Art boomed, and I had to admit he had a point. I said okay for now but one day soon we would talk about it again.

That day came just five months later. I received a call from Anna, who sounded very weak. She was slowly recovering from the heart surgery she'd had the month before, but her news this time was about Art. While she was still in the hospital, he had had a massive stroke, leaving his right side paralyzed and slurring his speech. If either of them got worse, how would they manage? They both remembered that I had said good nursing home care in the area in which they lived today cost $3,500 a month—a huge amount, given their financial situation. Did I think there was any way Art could still qualify for LTC insurance? No, I didn't, not now.

But Anna and Art got a very lucky break. The company that handled Anna's retirement plan was starting to offer group LTC insurance, and as part of their enrollment campaign they were accepting all employees and spouses, regardless of their current health. I don't generally like group plans as much as individual insurance, but the plan offered Anna and Art protection that most people in their situation couldn't get at all.

What if you never use long-term-care insurance? It will be wonderful if that's the case. The purpose of insurance is to cover catastrophes. You should always hope you'll never have to use it.

This is the question people ask me all the time about LTC insurance. Now, let me ask you a few questions.

Do you have fire insurance? If you own a home, you have to

have it. If you do, have you ever used it? Only 1 out of every 1,200 people ever uses fire insurance. But that doesn't mean it isn't a good idea.

Do you have automobile insurance? If you have a car, you do. If so, have you ever used it? Many of us are afraid to file a claim even when there's a reason to, for what it might do to the cost of our premiums. Only 1 out of every 240 people ever uses car insurance. But most of us still have it.

How many people do you think use long-term-care insurance? One out of every two, among those who have it. It is used more than any other kind of insurance, yet it's the kind of policy that way too few of us have.

Why do you think you'd need LTC insurance if you already have medical insurance? Because *there is not one medical insurance policy in existence that covers long-term care.*

If this situation were this dire, are you thinking it would be better all around just to dump the bills on Medicare? You couldn't, because Medicare won't pay them. Medicare will only pay 100 percent for the first twenty days of an LTC stay and will pay only if the facility is a Medicare-approved skilled nursing home. This means that the home must be approved by Medicare and have registered nurses on hand twenty-four hours a day, seven days a week. In the year 2000, only 8 percent of all the people in nursing homes were in skilled nursing homes. The other 92 percent need or needed custodial care, not skilled nursing care.

Even if you needed skilled nursing care, you would have had to spend three days in the hospital before being admitted to a skilled nursing facility, and both stays would have had to be for the same illness. Also, after those first twenty days, if Medicare miraculously paid in the first place, for the next eighty days in the year 2000 you would be responsible for paying the first $97 a day out of your own pocket before Medicare kicked in. This daily amount changes, so please check out the current amount by going to http://www.medicare.gov. In essence, then, Medicare pays for the first twenty days in just a few cases, and then it's your turn. In fact, as of the year 2000 Medicare paid for less than 8 to 10 percent of all the people in nursing homes. If you want to count on being one of those 8 to 10 percent, good luck. Anyway, do you believe that Medicare is going to be thriving by the time you're in your eighties?

Well, what about Medicaid, then? Doesn't Medicaid pay for nursing homes? An agency of last resort, Medicaid currently takes over, at any age, when you're financially destitute. It's welfare. Medicaid is a federal agency but run in each state by the state. Currently it's true that 40 percent of the people in nursing homes are paid for by Uncle Sam—but Medicaid is not the answer.

For one thing, "financially destitute" is a tricky concept. If you are reading this book, you're reading it so that you won't be financially destitute, and I'll tell you what I tell everyone I advise: If your plan is to divest yourself of your assets should a nursing home become inevitable, please turn to another financial adviser. Historically, many people have made themselves poor on paper to qualify for Medicaid by transferring assets and trying to make it look as if their money has disappeared. This is a demeaning process and can be devastating to the spouse, if there is one, who remains at home. The spouse who needs long-term care is then sent to a Medicaid-approved nursing home, which is not necessarily a place where you want to spend your last days. These are often overburdened facilities, and quite simply, our government can no longer afford to fund them. The government is also urging us all to consider LTC insurance—for peace of mind, to assure quality care, for the freedom to choose, and for asset protection.

If the government is trying to get out of the long-term nursing home business right now, you can be sure they will be out of it entirely by the time the baby boomers reach nursing home age. The good news in all this is that the government is also making it cheaper and more advantageous for us all to sign up for the care we might one day need.

Anna and Art haven't had to use their long-term-care insurance yet, but their story ended up more happily than most such stories. They at least are protected, if the day comes when they need protection.

There is nothing we can do when unexpected illness hits, but we can take the steps today to make sure that our loved ones' "tomorrows" are financially protected. This is not a topic that anyone, including me, likes talking about, but as we get older, and our parents or children get older, we're going to have to deal with it whether we want to or not. In the baby boom generation most of us have more parents than we have children—and those parents are getting older. It is important to really think about what would happen if something did happen to you or someone you love. Do your parents or other family members assume without your talking about it that you would take care of them? If so, would you still be able to take care of yourself and your family? What are the costs of a home in your area or in your parents' area? If you're single, married, living with someone, a parent: Who would take care of you? And would taking care of you make it hard for them to take care of himself or herself?

Long-term-care insurance is becoming a subject of much interest today, and you'll be reading more about it as more and more people are beginning to see why it's such an important quality-of-life issue not only for the person who needs the care, but also for the loved ones left to try to pay for it. Beginning in 1997, corporations have been able to pay for LTC insurance coverage for their employees and take the cost of the premiums as a business expense for the company. This employer-paid LTC is not taxable to the employee. Individuals can now consider it as a medical expense. For the self-employed, LTC insurance is now a business expense. There has also been talk lately that LTC premiums will one day become completely tax-deductible or that we'll be able to buy it with the money already put away in our retirement accounts. Keep an eye out for more news about this topic—if this is the first time you've heard about it, it won't be the last.

LTC INSURANCE: WHY IT'S A BARGAIN FOR MANY OF US

In my opinion the best age to purchase an LTC policy is around fifty-nine, although it can still be a bargain at any price if you're older. Regardless of your age, if you carry an LTC policy and do have to go into a nursing home one day, you will almost certainly pay less for all your payments combined than you would for one year in that nursing home. And many people live in nursing homes much longer than in the past. The average length of stay is 2.9 years, 8 years if you have Alzheimer's. And one out of three people who reach age sixty-five will spend some time in a nursing home over the course of his or her lifetime.

Long-term-care premiums are based on how old you are when you purchase the policy and are projected to stay stable at that amount for the lifetime of the policy. Let's say you are fifty-nine, in great health, and purchase a policy. I know of a wonderful policy here in California, and other states are pretty comparable, that would give you a $130 daily benefit, no elimination period, and 5 percent compounded inflation protection in a six-year plan, and for which you'd pay $2,561 a year for the premium. If you had waited until you were sixty-five to buy that policy, and again are in good health, the premium would cost $3,758. Big difference. And the premiums are projected to stay stable for the whole time you carry the policy.

(These policies are not like car insurance policies, where they can raise my neighbor's rates if he happens to use his policy too much but not raise mine because I've never filed a claim. These LTC policies can raise the rates, only if there is an across-the-board increase for all those in the same state, region, or county who have this particular plan.)

It's also true that the younger you are, the likelier you are to be in good health. LTC policies are either not available at all to those with serious health problems, or are prohibitively expensive.

Let's do the math. The average age of entry into a nursing home is eighty-four. Let's say in the year 2003, you are fifty-nine years old and you bought a tax qualified policy offering you six years' coverage at a $130-a-day benefit, 5 percent compound inflation benefit, and home health care, and a zero-day elimination period. This is a top-of-the-line policy. For this policy at the time, if you were able to get a preferred rate, health-wise, you would have to pay $2,561 a year.* Assuming no rate increases, you pay this for the next twenty-five years, until you are eighty-four, and then you in fact do have to go into a nursing home. You would have paid $60,025 in premiums. The average cost of a nursing home thirty years from now is projected to be $13,000 a month. So you will have paid less for all those years of insurance than what five months in a nursing home will cost you if you happen to need it.

If you're that sixty-five-year-old who waited to buy it, it would cost you $3,758 a year for the exact same policy, or a total cost of $71,402, if you went into the nursing home nineteen years later at the age of eighty-four ($3,758 × 19 = $71,402). This is still a great deal, but as you can see, the sixty-five-year-old will have spent $71,402 for just nineteen

---

* Costs are always subject to change.

years of premiums, or $7,377 more than the fifty-nine-year-old, who spent $60,025 for twenty-five years of premiums. This is assuming that the sixty-five-year-old is still in good health and can qualify for the preferred rate. By the way, once you need to use the policy all premium payments will be waived; from that point on it is free while you are receiving benefits. This is not one of those policies where you will out-smart the insurance company by waiting to buy it. It doesn't work like that. Rule of thumb: The longer you wait, the more it will cost.

Good nursing home care in the year 2000 costs about $4,500 per month in some areas, and in major cities some of the most pleasant homes are already $100,000 a year. Who knows what it will cost where you live in ten, twenty, thirty, forty years? You cannot afford to wait to find out.

HOW CAN I TELL IF I CAN AFFORD IT?

In the past, some people walked into my office wanting to buy an LTC policy, but we found, when we looked at their financial big picture, that it wasn't right for them because they couldn't really afford it over the long haul. This insurance is meant to keep you from going into the poorhouse in case of a long-term stay, not to put you into the poorhouse just to pay for it. If you sign up at fifty-nine, you have to be able to afford it—both now and in the years after you retire. It will do you no good to buy a policy at fifty-nine, retire at sixty-four, and find, at seventy-four, that you can no longer afford the premiums. You would have been better off not purchasing the insurance in the first place but investing the money instead.

There are policies available that have what is known as a *return of premium option*. This option means that if you'd paid your premiums for a number of years and either don't use the policy or can no longer afford it, you can get your premiums back. This sounds good, but this option will raise the cost of the premium some 35 percent. In most cases you're better off getting an LTC policy without this option and investing that 35 percent extra on your own.

How do you know if you can afford it? By taking a good hard look at your future financial picture. Make some calculations to see what would happen to your ability to pay for this insurance when you retire and no longer have a paycheck coming in. Ask yourself what would happen after retirement if your partner died: Would you lose a Social Security check? Would his or her pension stop or be reduced? Could you afford it if the rates went up? The insurance agents you're talking to should be concerned about these same questions, and run as fast as you can from anyone who begins to pressure you. If you can afford it, LTC insurance is great. If you can't afford it *well into your retirement,* it won't do you a bit of good.

If you can't afford it, you can still be responsible to those you love. If you are worried about your aging parents, or when the time comes that you begin worrying about yourself, you can seek out the advice of an attorney who specializes in elder care. If your parents live far away, see an elder care attorney near where they live, not where you live, because the assistance available varies widely from state to state and even can vary from region to region within the same state. In any case, an elder care attorney will go over all the options available to you—and these keep changing—given your particular situation.

HOW DO I CHOOSE A LONG-TERM-CARE INSURANCE COMPANY?

When I first started researching long-term-care insurance in 1986, there were only about four companies selling it. Today, there are about 130, and that number fluctuates at any given time by 30 or 40, depending on which companies have decided to give it a try and which have decided to check out of the LTC business.

This is a little bit of good news and could be a lot of bad news.

As long-term-care insurance becomes more and more popular, people will be shopping more competitively to buy it, which will keep insurance companies on their toes. That's good news. The bad news is that this industry is in such flux that companies are trying it, and some are deciding it's not for them. Not profitable enough after a few years? They just close up LTC shop. This has already happened—with a few huge companies that tried LTC and decided against it after a while. Another case in point: One of the first times *Consumer Reports* rated LTC insurance carriers, their number one–rated company was out of the business by the time the magazine hit the stands.

When you buy your LTC insurance, you don't plan on using it for many years from then, if ever. It is imperative that the company you buy it from will still be there if ever you need it. Let's say you bought your policy at age fifty-nine, when you were perfectly healthy. Fine. Then let's say the company you bought it from decides it doesn't want to be in the LTC business anymore when you turn sixty and have been diagnosed with some terrible disease.

What does this mean for you? Do you get your money back? No, of course not, they'll tell you. Why should you get your money back? We were covering you for all those years, and if you had had to go into a nursing home, well, we would have been there for you. Your insurance may be picked up by another company but that's not a chance any of us wants to take. So you must buy your policy from a company with a firm commitment to the LTC arena.

ESSENTIAL QUESTIONS

Thus the essential question is: Is the company going to be in the LTC business for the long haul? Here are the questions you must ask each company you are considering in order to find out. These are good questions to ask when considering buying any policy, but essential in the case of long-term care.

Questions About the Company:

↦ *How long have you been selling LTC insurance?* The only acceptable answer is: Ten years, minimum. If the answer is one year, two years, or three, they are still experimenting.

↦ *How much LTC insurance do you currently have in force?* The only acceptable answer is hundreds of millions of dollars or more. With that much money in LTC care, they are already making a handsome profit—and not thinking of getting out of the business.

↦ *How many times have you had a rate increase for those who already own a policy?* The only acceptable answer is two times or fewer.

Note that the "already own a policy" clause is important. You are not looking for rate increases for people who have not yet purchased a policy. You are looking at rate increases for people who have already taken the plunge, bought the insurance, and are therefore vulnerable to the whims of the insurance company. You want a company that treats its current policyholders as respectfully as it treats all the prospective buyers it is trying to attract.

↦ *In how many states are you currently selling LTC insurance?* The only acceptable answer is: Every state. Because each state regulates its own insurance policies, and because it's tedious and expensive for insurance companies to be licensed to sell every kind of insurance in every state, if the company is selling LTC insurance in only one state—yours—you can be sure they are still experimenting.

❧ *Is your company on the block to be sold?* The answer you want to hear is: No. Even if the company has a great LTC track record now, what would happen if the company that bought it wasn't a company you felt safe with? A few years ago, for example, American Express, which had a good policy, decided to sell its LTC business. They sold it to GE Capital in the end. So prospective American Express LTC buyers should have been more interested in GE Capital than in American Express. (Happy ending: GE Capital is still committed to LTC.) So one has to watch it carefully.

❧ *What are your ratings from the following independent companies, all of which rate the safety and soundness of insurance carriers?*

AM BEST	A-PLUS OR BETTER
WWW.AMBEST.COM	
(908-439-2200)	
MOODY'S	AA OR BETTER
WWW.MOODYS.COM	
(212-553-0377)	
STANDARD & POOR'S	AA OR BETTER
WWW.STANDARDANDPOORS.COM	
(212-438-2000)	
FITCH RATINGS	AA OR BETTER
WWW.FITCHRATINGS.COM	
(212-908-0500)	

The only acceptable answer is: At least two of the insurance rating companies listed must have awarded these ratings or better. Insist that the insurance company send you the ratings in writing, or call the ratings companies yourself.

Acceptable answers to every single one of these questions will tell you if the company is safe. Here are the questions you want to ask about the policy itself.

Questions About the Policy

⇥ *What does it take to qualify for benefits?* In order to qualify for your benefits, and have your insurance company start paying your LTC bills, you are going to have to prove to this company that you really need long-term care. This is called "making it through the gatekeepers." You won't see a penny until you qualify.

In a tax-qualified plan—which is quickly becoming the most common type of plan—the first gatekeeper is not to be able to carry out certain *activities of daily living (ADLs)*. In order to function normally, most of us need to be able to 1) bathe ourselves; 2) feed ourselves; 3) clothe ourselves; 4) transfer ourselves (get in and out of bed, chairs, and the like unattended); 5) be continent; and 6) use the toilet. With a good policy, if you got to a point in your life where you could not do two out of these six ADLs, then you would qualify for benefits.

The second gatekeeper is *cognitive impairment,* which simply means that you qualify if you come down with, say, Alzheimer's disease or cannot think or act clearly on your own and therefore cannot care for yourself.

By the way, don't be surprised if you run into two types of plans: tax-qualified (like the above) and non-tax qualified. An important note here is that with a tax-qualified plan (TQ) your LTC insurance premiums may be tax-deductible as a medical expense, if your premiums, along with other deductible out-of-pocket medical expenses, come to 7.5 percent of your adjusted gross income. A non-tax qualified plan (NTQ), which has become less common in recent years, doesn't offer the possible tax deduction but *does* let you claim your benefits with one other gatekeeper, which is known as *medical necessity*. This is where a doctor states that it is medically necessary for you to have long-term care; for example, if you are unstable and in danger of falling.

In the past, I have always liked NTQ policies more than TQ policies. That said, today many insurance companies are no longer even offering NTQ plans. The government has stated the possibility that the benefits you might one day receive in your NTQ plan could be taxed; so if you ever use the benefits, you might have to pay taxes on them (although most likely you would have at least a partial offset for deductible medical expenses). Therefore, your choices are becoming more limited, with the result that a tax-qualified plan is probably the way to go.

To find out more about the differences, you can call the Health Insurance Counseling and Advocacy Program (800-434-0222) to find an office near you that can provide more information.

⇥ *How much is it going to cost?* Not as much as you would think—if you find the right company. Below is an estimate of what it would currently cost you based on your age and assuming you are in great health for the following benefits with an LTC policy with General Electric Capital Assurance Company LTC Choice Six-Year plan . . . 5 percent compound . . . 0-day elimination . . . $130/day facility and 100 percent of that amount for home care . . . Automatic survivorship benefit . . . Preferred rate for a tax qualified program. The definitions of these terms are provided below.

Please note: there is a huge difference in pricing among

companies offering LTC insurance (or any insurance, for that matter). I have seen policies from different carriers offering essentially the same benefits but with a difference of up to $1,500 a year—a big difference, especially for retirees, and especially when premiums can be raised. When you are comparing these prices, make sure that you are comparing apples with apples—comparing policies that have the exact same benefits across the board. Otherwise your price comparisons won't give you the information you're really looking for. The benefit period, the elimination period, the benefit amount, the inflation rider, and home health care will all need to be identical when comparing prices among different companies. Here are explanations of what those terms refer to.

The *benefit period* means the length of time the policy will pay for your long-term care. I recommend choosing at least a six-year plan.

The *elimination period* means the amount of time you have to pay out of your own pocket before the policy will kick in. I recommend a zero-day elimination if money for premiums is not an issue. If it is, then go for no more than a fifty-day elimination. Can you imagine where your loved ones would get the money to pay for the first hundred-and-twenty days of your stay, for instance, if the cost of a home was $10,000 a month? I would rather see you pay a little more now than possibly a lot more later.

The *daily benefit amount* means how much the policy will pay per day if you use the benefits. Policies are now being sold in two ways: the original way, where there is a specific fixed amount of money that the policy will pay per day for your covered LTC stay, or for home health care. If the policy that you are considering is sold under these guidelines as of 2002, I would recommend purchasing about a $100- to $150-a-day benefit (depending on your location without considering inflation benefits) amount for LTC care. The actual amount you purchase ultimately depends on where you plan to use the policy and how much of your needs you expect it to cover. You would figure the exact daily benefit amount you should purchase by calculating how much other income you will have at that time that could go to pay for an LTC stay.

A policy that offers just a daily benefit amount works like this: If you bought a six-year policy that offers a $130-a-day benefit amount, you would have a policy that would pay up to $130 a day for six years in a facility.

The other way a growing number of policies are being offered is based on a *pool-of-money* approach. The pool-of-money design is one where you start off the old policies purchasing a specific benefit amount for a specific period of time. But in the new policies, the insurer takes the dollar amount you have purchased and conceptually puts it in a benefit account. That account can be accessed at claim time for any kind of covered service. Using the example of a six-year plan at $130 per day, this means the insured has $284,700 (without considering inflation benefits) available to fund his or her care needs. This results in a policy that will pay for home health care (see below) or a nursing home in any order, in any combination, for any length of time. Even though the original policy that was purchased this way had a six-year benefit period, in reality there is no six-year limit on benefits, just the $284,700 limit that was established when the policy was purchased. If the cost is more than $130 a day, that money is taken from the pool (subject to certain limits), if it is less than $130 a day, that money is not taken from the pool. When the pool of funds is used up, the policy or your coverage is over. But this way you can use the pool of money to best meet your needs.

The *inflation rider* means how much the daily benefit amount paid will increase year after year. I recommend 5 percent

ANNUAL PREMIUMS, ASSUMING GOOD HEALTH, AS OF 2002:
PLEASE CHECK FOR RATE CHANGES, WITH 100 PERCENT
HOME CARE.

AGE	COST
40–45:	1596
46:	1634
47:	1660
48:	1686
49:	1699
50:	1725
51:	1763
52:	1828
53:	1879
54:	1956
55:	2033
56:	2136
57:	2265
58:	2394
59:	2561
60:	2728
61:	2921
62:	3102
63:	3320
64:	3539
65:	3758
66:	4015
67:	4311
68:	4710
69:	5135
70:	5611

compounded inflation. Unless you are over seventy, in which case a 5 percent simple inflation or a higher daily benefit to start is the way to go. If inflation benefits were added to the benefit amounts example above, then both daily benefit limits and the amount of money in the pool will go up by 5 percent per year until benefits are exhausted.

The *home health care (HHC) clause* means that you can receive certain kinds of long-term care at home if this care is administered by professionals, friends, or individuals deemed qualified by the insurance company to provide HHC. Some plans state that if you belong in a nursing home but prefer to be at home, the policy will pay your LTC benefits at home. I tend to view HHC as coverage you would need at home for the short term—for a broken hip, for example. With HHC, you are expected to get well. With LTC, you are not expected to get better.

As of the writing of this book, many carriers include far more than just home care in that portion of their policy. There are policies that offer benefits for assisted living centers, adult day care centers, adult congregate living facilities, and other community-based care providers. So it is important that you find a policy that has a good emphasis on home care benefits. Make sure you ask what is covered.

Why is it important that an HHC policy offer so many different kinds of care alternatives?

It is important that you have a choice in what kind of care you may want versus having to take the kind of care that your carrier is willing to pay for. So given that most of us would prefer to avoid being put in a home or institutionalized at all, it is important that you know there are policies out there today that have options that include being able to move into a private residence that has been converted to allow barrier-free access and has some monitoring staff available around the clock, but where you have a private room, furnished with your personal furniture and decorated with your personal items. It's less of an institution; it's more palatable. Most important, in my opinion, it's the growth market for the future. Nursing homes are now getting more and more skilled care for patients who used to be in hospitals. More and more custodial patients are finding better care options outside the nursing home.

Given that the trend is moving toward care outside of a nursing home, is it better to purchase an exact daily benefit amount policy or a pool-of-funds policy?

Given the situation today, I am leaning now toward the pool-of-money design because the insured are covered, in the best contracts, without much regard to site of care. They have an increasing freedom to choose, which allows for a degree of independence.

What you need to keep in mind when looking for a good policy that deals with HHC is this: The best policies today recognize that true home care is typically not delivered every day. It's intermittent and relies on an informal caregiver being in place. In the old design, the HHC side of the contract had a daily limit. Emphasis on the word daily. What often happens is the insured receives visits from an aide three times per week. The insured also receives a visit from an RN once per week. If these visits occur on the same day, in most cases you would have out-of-pocket costs because the *daily* limit applies. Today's better plans recognize this and treat HHC benefits with a *monthly* maximum. So if we once again use the example of the policy with a $130-a-day benefit amount but use the pool of funds approach, that $130-per-day benefit will automatically have about a $4,000 per month limit ($130 × 31 days) for HHC, allowing for complete coverage even on days when multiple services are received.

How much coverage is needed for the HHC portion of the policy?

In years past I used to recommend 50 percent of the LTC benefit amount for HHC. So if your LTC daily benefit amount was $100, the HHC daily benefit amount would be $50. I now recommend that your HHC benefit be 100 percent of what the LTC benefit amount is for three reasons:

1. In major metropolitan areas, HHC services cost every bit as much as nursing homes today.

2. So much more is covered under HHC provisions that while typically costing less than nursing homes today, I expect supply and demand will drive the costs of these services up.

3. If you purchase the pool-of-funds policy, there is no penalty if costs of your HHC are much lower, because the money stays in the pool available for you to spend on other types of care or extending the time the current care plan will be paid for. (Back to the $284,700 example—it will take twelve years to exhaust this benefit if expenses are only $65 per day, even if you bought a six-year plan.)

If you or a loved one you're responsible for ends up in a nursing home, all the great things you wanted to do with your money, all the sums you eventually accumulate, all can be lost. Don't let this happen. There is nothing worse than seeing someone in his or her seventies or eighties devastated emotionally by losing a spouse to a nursing home, then also having to endure the financial devastation that can follow. Although our bodies age, we all still feel deep inside that we're twenty or thirty years old, and we don't want to deal with things like this. But we must. We may even feel that our parents are still invulnerable. But they're not. If you have two sets of parents alive today, between you and your partner, the chances that at least one will end up in a nursing home are 90 percent. Love and loyalty aside, if you are to pay for this, it may leave you very little money with which to create more money and not very many ways to hold on to what you already have.

With long-term-care insurance in place, this most likely will not happen. You will have gone a long, long way toward being responsible not only to those you love, but also to yourself and the money you've worked so hard to earn.

LONG-TERM DISABILITY INSURANCE

Long-term disability (LTD) insurance is another kind of insurance that can protect you if a catastrophe happens that prevents you from being able to earn a living. Depending on the kind of work you do, an injury, an illness, or certain chronic conditions could cut off your income for a long time or even permanently. These policies will usually pay 60 to 70 percent of your current salary in the event of such a disability.

Suppose you do heavy labor and are laid up with a back injury, or you are a psychotherapist and lose your speech because of a stroke. When this kind of disaster strikes, an LTD policy can really save the day. You may think that you do not need one because you are protected by workers' compensation. Remember that workers' compensation covers you only if you are injured while performing your job. LTD insurance will pay for you whether you hurt yourself on the job or at home or on vacation.

In many ways this insurance is every bit as complicated in terms of finding a good policy as long-term-care insurance is. To find a good carrier, you might want to ask many of the same questions I listed under LTC insurance.

In looking for a good policy, here are some elements that you need to understand and some further questions to ask:

⇥ *What percentage of income will the policy pay?* Most policies pay a percentage of what you are earning; typically the range is from 60 to 90 percent of your current salary. The higher the percentage, the more expensive it usually is. Many companies have a cap on how much they will pay monthly, if bought through your employer. For large employers, it is usually $5,000 a month.

⇥ *How long is my elimination or waiting period?* Just as with LTC policies, this is how long you will have to wait till the company starts to pay. A normal waiting period is three to six months.

⇥ *Till what age will they pay?* Most policies pay only until you are sixty-five years of age.

⇥ *Do you cover me if I am disabled because of illness as well as in an accident?* The answer should be: "Yes."

⇥ *What if I can only work part-time because of my disability?* You want a policy that will pay according to how much you can and cannot work. If you can work part-time, the company should pay you a portion of your disability payments. The term for this is *residual benefits.*

⇥ *Is the policy guaranteed renewable?* Here you want to hear absolutely "Yes"—you do not want to have to qualify each and every year for benefits.

⇥ *Is it "owner's occ" or "any occ"?* Do you feel as though I just started talking a different language? This question is very important. What it asks is under what circumstances the company will pay you. Will it pay you only if you cannot perform any job whatsoever, or will it pay if you cannot perform *your* job? Suppose you're a musician and you lose some of your hearing. You might be able to function and sell pencils on the street corner, so you are not necessarily "disabled," but you can't do your job. If you have an "any occ" disability policy, it will pay you only if you cannot perform any occupation, so you would not be able to collect benefits for your loss of hearing. If your policy were "owner's occ," it would pay as long as you, the policy owner, cannot perform your own occupation.

PRICING

LTD insurance is even more expensive than LTC insurance, so it pays to shop around. The most cost-effective way to buy it (usually) is through your employer if they offer it. In many states it is mandatory that your employer offer it to you in your benefits package, so depending on where you live, you may already be covered. Make sure you ask your benefits person to find out if you are covered and, if so, how much coverage you have and how it works. If you do not feel that it is enough, or you do not have any, you might consider looking into purchasing some on your own.

The main companies that specialize in disability insurance are:

UNUM PROVIDENT LIFE INSURANCE
WWW.UNUMPROVIDENT.COM   800-227-8138

CNA-CONTINENTAL CASUALTY
WWW.CNA.COM   312-822-5000

USAA
WWW.USAA.COM   800-531-8000

NORTHWESTERN MUTUAL LIFE
WWW.NORTHWESTERNMUTUAL.COM   800-748-9493

To save some time, you might want to ask the insurance quoting services that are listed on pages 84–85 for quotes as well.

A/B TAX-PLANNING TRUSTS/NON—U.S. CITIZENS TRUST/SPECIAL NEEDS TRUST

SHERRY'S STORY

Sherry was worried. Her husband's father was dying, and she feared that when he died it would be the financial death of the whole family as well.

> Tim, my husband, and his brother, Daniel, work for their dad at this machine shop he owns. They've worked there forever. I keep the books and see all the papers, so I know pretty much what's going on. The shop makes pretty good money, but it's just all these machines mainly, and a lot of the money goes back into the business to keep the machines going. Some of them are getting pretty old, but the business is still worth about a million bucks.
>
> The way it's set up is that Tim's dad owns the whole business. He says one day it's all going to be Tim's and Daniel's, so not to worry. He's pretty old and not well at all, and Tim's mother is probably not going to live that much longer, either. I don't mean they're both going to die tomorrow, nor do we want them to, but they are both in their mid-eighties, and death, I keep telling Tim, is a fact of life. Pop owns the business, and when he dies, if Mom is still living, she inherits it. He has a will saying so. Then *her* will leaves everything to Tim and Daniel. The shop is a family business, so what happens next is that Tim's and Daniel's wills both leave the business to each other. We're all really close, but it still doesn't feel right to me, or to Daniel's wife, Christine, either. What will happen to me when Tim dies? What happens to Christine when Daniel dies?

When Christine and I ask them, they're just like Pop—they both just say, "Don't worry, I am taking care of it. End of discussion." But I *am* worried.

Sherry was right to be concerned. How many times have we said or heard the words: "Don't worry, I'll take care of it"? These words don't handle the problem; at times, in fact, as was the case here, they create the problem. Sure, we all intend to get around to taking care of things, but there's a big difference between thinking we will and actually doing it. Being responsible to those you love is *knowing* that you have taken care of everything, rather than just *thinking* you have. Being responsible also means being open to talking about issues such as death, sitting down with everyone involved to discuss their concerns, fears, misguided assumptions, and questions. Seldom do the words "I'll take care of it" take care of anything.

When Sherry came to see me, I told her her family could be in big trouble. Even though Pop and Mom had a will, in truth they had not taken care of the very problems they sought to avoid.

To begin with, their total assets were worth more than $1 million, which, in 2002 or 2003, is the maximum amount you can leave to anyone other than your spouse without having to pay estate taxes to Uncle Sam. For deaths occurring after 2003, the unified credit will be adjusted to permit a higher amount of property to be exempt from estate tax. The new limits will be:

FOR DEATHS OCCURRING IN	AMOUNT OF EXEMPTION
2001	$675,000
2002–2003	$1,000,000
2004–2005	$1,500,000
2006–2008	$2,000,000

2009	$3,500,000
2010	UNLIMITED—NO ESTATE TAX
2011 OR LATER	$1,000,000

(Please refer to this chart if using this book after the year 2003. Please substitute the correct yearly figure from the chart whenever you see the amount $1 million used in the following pages. Please further note that under the current law, the amount of property exempt from estate tax will increase through 2009 and the estate tax will disappear completely in 2010, only to return with a vengeance in 2011. But it is almost a guarantee that the law will change in the next few years, so it's important to stay current with these changes and make sure that your professional advisors stay current with changes, too.)

In the year 2002, if Pop and Mom die, and Tim and Daniel inherit a business worth $2 million, they are going to owe estate taxes. And because the ownership of the business and house and bank accounts will have passed to them under a will rather than a trust, they could be hit with huge probate fees as well.

Is there a way for Sherry's family to reduce the federal estate tax that would be owed on an estate worth $2 million? Yes. Tim and Daniel's father could really take care of it by setting up a *tax-planning trust.* This is a trust for those with estates, as of the year 2002 or 2003—worth more than $1 million. (See chart above for later years.)

Depending on whom you talk to, these trusts can be known as *credit shelter trusts, bypass trusts,* or *A/B trusts:* they're all the same thing. I like to call them bypass trusts, because I just love the thought of bypassing taxes.

BYPASS TRUSTS

As of 2002, the bypass trust can eliminate federal estate taxes on estates of married couples valued at $2 million. In the next few years, a bypass trust can eliminate estate taxes on estate values up to:

YEAR	ESTATE VALUES
2001	$1,350,000
2002–2003	$2,000,000
2004–2005	$3,000,000
2006–2008	$4,000,000
2009	$7,000,000
2010	NO ESTATE TAX
2011	$2,000,000

Federal estate taxes fall into the realm of the IRS and don't vary from state to state the way probate fees do, so don't confuse estate taxes with probate. Probate fees are determined in each state and cover the cost of processing a will through the court system. (Please note, however, that some states also impose their own estate tax.) Federal estate taxes are the share of the estate owed to the IRS if you leave more than the amount of exemption, which is featured on page 116, to anyone other than your spouse. Unless, that is, you eliminate or minimize the sting by setting up a bypass trust.

In Sherry's family's case, here's how the inevitable deaths of Mom and Pop would play themselves out with and without a bypass trust.

SHERRY'S FAMILY: SCENARIO ONE

There are two main ways to reduce or eliminate federal estate tax on the first spouse's death. One is the unlimited marital deduction, and the other is the exemption or credit shelter amount that can be left estate tax free to any beneficiaries including your spouse. Husbands and wives can leave an unlimited amount of wealth to each other without owing any estate tax whatsoever, as long as you're married to a U.S. citizen. (If you're married to a non–U.S. citizen, you need to consult an estate lawyer now! Page 129.) Each individual can pass on to his or her beneficiaries other than a spouse, the exemption amounts listed on page 116. (But please be aware that these amounts could change with any future legislation, so be sure to stay abreast of any new legislation as it develops.)

When Pop, Sherry's father-in-law, dies, assuming he dies first, and all the assets are passed to Mom, she would owe nothing in estate taxes. She receives the million-dollar estate and owes nothing. But let's say Mom dies in 2002. Now she has the whole $2 million dollars on her side of the balance sheet but can only leave the credit shelter amount for that year of $1 million to her kids without their having to pay estate tax. No one ever got the benefit of Pop's credit shelter amount because he just passed everything to Mom.

So when Mom dies the kids will have to pay a total estate tax bill of $435,000.

If, however, before either Mom or Pop dies, $2 million is separated out of Pop's individual name and into two shares, each for $1 million, and Pop's share is held in trust for the benefit of Mom when he dies, and the family follows certain rules, then the IRS will see the money as if it never left Pop's side of the balance sheet. The $1 million that's Pop's "half" can be passed down free and clear when Mom dies, because it's less than or equal to the credit shelter amount for 2002 of $1 million. As for Mom, the $1 million on her side of the balance sheet can be passed down in the same way when she dies. Remember, in the year 2002, you each get this $1 million credit shelter amount. But most of us who are married don't take full advantage of it. We just simply leave everything to a spouse who was able to get everything anyway, so in effect the first spouse to die wastes the credit shelter amount exemption. To take full advantage of it, use a bypass trust. The deceased's half of the money goes into the trust, preserving this exemption.

WHAT ARE THE RESTRICTIONS ON THE HALF HELD IN TRUST FOR MOM?

She can be her own trustee over Pop's half so she has full management and control over it. Depending upon how the trust was drafted, she can have an absolute right to all the income generated by his half, and she can spend any part or all of the $1 million if she needs it. The key word is "needs." She has to spend her entire $1 million before she starts spending his. Finally, mom can't change who gets Pop's share of the estate after he dies. The beneficiaries named by Pop are the ones who will get the money. And Mom will have to file separate tax returns each year, one for her half and one for Pop's. That's it. These are minor restrictions to endure for a savings of $435,000.

PROBATE

The way things are set up now, Sherry's family will encounter another problem when either Pop or Mom dies: probate. Remember, as it stands now, the business is in Pop's name alone, and he is passing it on with a will to Mom, who will then (with her will) pass it to her sons.

To transfer the title to the assets when Pop dies, or to have Mom's name put on the papers, there are procedures in most states that allow you to sign an affidavit with a certified death certificate so you don't need to go to probate court to transfer assets from spouse to spouse. But look out if your state doesn't allow this and you haven't checked the form of ownership on the deeds to real property like your home. If there are names on the titles other than Mom's or Pop's, you may be in for a rude surprise. If this is the case, or you don't know how you hold title to real estate, or what the words by your name on the deed mean, seek legal counsel. Ask your attorney to put what you want to know in writing so you understand the consequences of the many types of ownership forms out there. The words "joint tenant" and "tenants in common" (or the absence of any such words) have different meanings and can make the difference between a $150 fee to transfer ownership and thousands of dollars in fees or even more, depending on the value of the real estate.

But the simple procedures available to most surviving spouses to change title to a home, business, bank, or brokerage account cannot help Daniel or Tim when Mom dies. If everything is left to them via her will, they'll have to go through the probate procedure and be hit with unnecessary probate fees. The probate fees that Daniel and Tim will have to pay in California are $52,300 plus about $1,700 in court costs for a total of $54,000.

If you add together the probate fees and the estate taxes, Tim and Daniel will owe about $489,000 when Mom dies—and no, they can't send the IRS or pay the lawyers' fees with some rusty old machines. Where would they get that kind of money? They don't have it, and it would be owed within nine months of

Mom's death unless they qualified for certain limited extensions.

PAYMENT OF ESTATE TAX

Estate taxes are due nine months from the date of death. Under very special circumstances, you can get an extension for twelve months, but it's not as easy as you might hope, and you also have to pay interest on the sums due. When you have acquired enough money to have to pay estate tax, the government thinks you will be smart enough to have planned for the day you'll owe the money and just assumes, often wrongly, that you'll have it on hand. This can be a real problem if you didn't plan at all, because you and your parents (or whoever you'll be inheriting money or property from) have never discussed it.

If you're left an inheritance of assets such as real estate that might not be so easy to cash in fast, or assets that you didn't want to cash in, and you have no liquid cash of your own, you could be in a very precarious situation. Advance knowledge of what will happen when the time comes gives you time to prepare, either by getting a life insurance policy that would help pay the death benefits or by liquidating assets sooner rather than later.

Sherry's family's situation is different from most. In their situation the main asset they will be inheriting is a family business. Under the Internal Revenue Code Section 6166, they might be allowed to pay off their estate tax over a nine-year period of time, with interest. Even so, they'll have to come up with almost $50,000 a year, which will no doubt put a crimp in the balance sheet.

For most people, it would be worse. Most people owe estate taxes nine months from the date of death, and that's that. If you can't pay your estate tax, interest will be charged. Currently that rate is three percentage points higher than the current rates on certain short-term Treasury obligations. If you inherit a closely held business, the rate is a flat 4 percent. It's great to get an inheritance—unless you're not prepared for it.

ADDITIONAL INHERITANCE PROBLEMS

Let's take Sherry's story one step further. Assume that after Tim and Daniel inherit the business, one or the other of the brothers dies. They have left the business to each other via a will, so the surviving brother will have to come up with money to pay estate taxes, even before he inherits anything, since estate taxes have to be paid before the deceased's property can be distributed.

What is more, and family business notwithstanding, Sherry or Christine will be at the mercy of the surviving brother and not protected in any way.

Sherry had very good reason indeed to be worried.

SHERRY'S FAMILY: SCENARIO TWO

AVOIDING PROBATE

Is there a way for Sherry's family to avoid paying probate fees? Yes. As we've seen, these assets should have been put in a revocable living trust (page 59) instead of being left to one or the other brother via these various wills, so that they would pass smoothly and without probate fees from family member to family member. In this case a revocable living trust would ultimately save them $54,000. That alone is surely worth the $2,500, give or take, it would cost to set one up.

AVOIDING ESTATE TAXES

If Sherry's family were to set up a bypass trust now, before Mom or Pop died, the scene that would inevitably play itself out would be a much, much brighter one.

In the first place, Mom would retain control over everything she and Pop worked for without any court intervention. When she died, Tim and Daniel would inherit the shares in the company—and would not owe one penny of estate taxes in the year 2002 for the first million they inherited. (After that, they'd have to pay somewhere between forty-one and fifty cents for every additional dollar they inherited.) In this scenario, rather than owing $435,000 in estate taxes, they would owe nothing. Zero. And you can add in another $54,000 of savings, because neither probate fees nor court costs would be owed, either. For estates valued at more than $1 million for the year 2002 or 2003 or in later years, the applicable credit shelter amount (see page 116), this is an urgent matter.

This plan will not work unless it's put into place before one of the spouses dies. How? Simple. You amend your revocable living trust (or will, but I hope you'll have a trust) to specify that after one or the other of you dies, the assets from his or her half of the estate will be put into a new trust, this bypass trust. In effect, you're putting the money from a revocable trust into an irrevocable trust, because the ultimate beneficiaries have been specified by the spouse who has died, and they cannot be changed.

In the majority of states the revocable living trust is the original trust created jointly by the two spouses. It is the instrument that enables the surviving spouse, after the first one has died, to divide the estate into two shares, the survivor's trust and the bypass trust. In the revocable living trust, set up while you're both alive, you specify what happens when one spouse dies and the other is still living and then what happens when both spouses have died.

In some states, however—and check with your estate planning attorney on this—it may be better to use two individual trusts from the beginning, one for the husband and one for the wife. It works the same way, though. The trust set up by the first person to die becomes irrevocable on death but provides that the assets are held for the benefit of the surviving spouse for his or her lifetime. The surviving spouse's trust continues on the way it always has. After the death of the surviving spouse, it pays out, from both parts of the bypass trust, what's promised to the beneficiaries. In community property states, Arizona, California, Idaho, Louisiana, Nevada, New Mexico, Texas, Washington, and Wisconsin, we start with a revocable living trust, which provides for what happens when one spouse dies and when both die, and the trust specifies that the revocable living trust can be split into two trust shares upon the death of the first spouse. The trust continues on as it always has, but you must create the bypass trust at the first death.

After the first spouse dies, the surviving spouse will have to carefully value everything, all the marital assets, and divide them up, at least on paper. (In order to get the maximum benefit in capital gains treatment if you ever want to sell appreciated assets in the future, you'll need to get a valuation on your assets sooner or later anyway.) This will require the assistance of a good attorney. If the attorney can't explain the plan to you in a way that you can understand completely, then go to someone else. Don't pay the attorney the full amount (you may be required to pay a retainer) until all your questions have been answered. If someone tells you it's too technical to explain, most likely they don't understand it, either. There are some technical points, but there is no reason you can't understand the main terms of the trust and why it says what it does.

In the case of Sherry's family, if Pop or Mom dies before they can be persuaded of the value of a bypass trust, it will be too late and the error will be costly.

DO I NEED A BYPASS TRUST?

It's easy to tell whether you need a bypass trust. With your spouse, do a quick addition of everything you own—any expected life insurance proceeds due on policies owned by you or your spouse, the equity in your house, your retirement accounts, additional investments, your cars, everything. Now subtract any money you owe. If, to your amazement, you are married and your assets are worth more than the current credit shelter amount (see page 116), which for the years 2002 and 2003 is $1 million, then, yes, you need a bypass trust.

Think you're a long way from needing a bypass trust? Repeat the calculations from time to time, perhaps when you do your taxes every year. Your mortgage is closer to being paid off. Your retirement funds are growing. Maybe you inherited a little money here or there. No matter how much you have— even $10 million—your spouse will be okay if you die first; spouses, remember, can inherit billions without paying estate tax if they are U.S. citizens. But once your spouse dies, or if the two of you happen to die together and those surviving you have more than the current credit shelter amount, it's estate tax time—unless you have this trust in place. With this kind of trust, you can double your credit shelter amount in this situation. The minute you're lucky enough to hit that credit shelter mark, which is $1 million for the year 2002 and 2003, unless you plan to leave all your money above the exempt amount to a charity, you need a bypass trust.

I am very serious about this. If you and your spouse fall short of the current credit shelter amount, but are getting up there, I urge you to set up a bypass trust. You never know when a two can become a one, so don't chance it. A bypass trust will cost about $2,500 in attorney's fees to set up, unless you own a lot of real estate and have lots and lots of cash, in which case it will cost more, or unless you're just amending a revocable living trust you already have, in which case it will cost less. But wouldn't you rather leave your hard-earned money to your loved ones than to the IRS?

In the case of Sherry's family, because Tim and Daniel will eventually die, Tim and Daniel should also set up a revocable living trust, setting up in turn a bypass trust; what's good for the goose is good for the gander. Tim's and Daniel's children should not have to go through what their fathers are going to go through if Mom and Pop don't take action. At the very least, the brothers should each have a revocable living trust that leaves the business to each other in trust with their share of the income it generates to Sherry and Christine.

They should also think hard about what they want. Let's say that one of the wives predeceases her husband. Maybe that brother will want his share of the business to go directly to his kids, not to his brother. If there isn't some provision for this, the first brother to die might leave his children with nothing. I am sure that Tim and Daniel don't intend to deny their children an inheritance, but the way their estates are set up right now, that might well be what happens.

UNINTENTIONALLY DISINHERITING YOUR CHILDREN

If you have a child from two or more marriages and want to protect them all, please, please go see a lawyer *now*. And if you have more than the current credit shelter amount in assets, want to protect all your children, and don't go to see a lawyer, you are being tremendously irresponsible to yourself, your money, and your children.

In the case of Sherry's family, let's imagine that Pop and Mom do manage to get their act together and, with the aid of a bypass trust, leave the business to Tim and Daniel in the most respectful way possible. But Tim and Daniel don't follow suit; they keep their wills. Let's say Tim dies first, the business goes to Daniel, and Daniel's will says everything goes to Christine, who in turn has a will leaving everything to her children. What about Sherry? What about Tim's own children? Did he mean to disinherit them? Did he intend for Daniel's kids to get the whole business and his to get nothing? That's not what he meant, but that's what could happen. Or if Daniel dies first, did he mean for the same scenario to happen to his children? No, of course not. Both brothers need to set up revocable living trusts themselves to protect their families, as well as each other.

FOR SPOUSES WHO ARE NOT U.S. CITIZENS

This doesn't happen often, but it affects more people than you would think—and it's important. It's true that there is an unlimited marital deduction when it comes to estate taxes between spouses. But that holds true only if your spouse is a U.S. citizen. If not, the most you can leave him or her is the credit shelter amount allowed for that year (see page 117), which in 2002 and 2003 is $1 million.

In other words, if Mom in Sherry's family was not a U.S. citizen, and if Pop left her the business through his will, she would owe $435,000 in estate taxes. And if she were to pass the business down to her sons in the year 2002, they would owe additional estate taxes.

There's a way around this. If you or the spouse who isn't a U.S. citizen has a child who is a U.S. citizen and who is reliable, that child, when he is of age, can act as one of the trustees for or with the non-citizen spouse, thereby passing on the assets without being taxed. However, if the estate is worth more than $2 million, the laws are unbelievably complex, so you must see an attorney at once.

A FINAL NOTE ABOUT SPECIAL NEEDS TRUSTS

Whenever I set up an estate plan, I made it a point to ask about any special needs of the children. Over the years I have been surprised at how many of my clients have children who, in one way or another, will need long-term management of the assets that they will eventually inherit. Children who suffer a disability of any kind or the effects of substance abuse, or simply are unable to hold on to money—whatever the case, many of them really end up needing help.

In severe cases of disability, your special loved one might be on SSI, or Supplemental Security Income, and possibly even on Medicaid. Even if you're helping the child, too, Medicaid can sometimes step in in dire cases and help with, for example, life-long medication. Parents have to be very careful about how they leave money to children on SSI or Medicaid who will need financial watching over later on, when they are not here. Leave such a child, say, $50,000, and that child might lose his or her federal subsidies and no longer be able to go on once the inheritance is gone.

The answer to this may be a *special needs trust.*

Under the law, if certain limitations are built into a trust, they will make it impossible for creditors to reach the funds in the trust. For example, if I am the beneficiary of a trust that holds the $50,000, but I'm not the trustee, then I have no control or management over this money. Only the trustee has the power to give me money. Because I have no legal right to demand it, my creditors can't take the money I owe them from the trust. Therefore I'm not really considered the owner of the $50,000, and it can't be considered my asset in determining my eligibility for government assistance. In some states laws have been passed that take this basic trust principle and use it specifically to allow money to be held in trust for the benefit of a developmentally disabled person while still allowing that person to retain all public benefits.

The greatest protection is provided for someone who suffers a developmental disability, one that impairs his or her ability to provide self-care and custody, which constitutes a substantial handicap. The primary purpose of these special needs trusts is to provide that person with a lifelong supplemental and emergency fund of assistance. Currently there exist basic living needs, such as dental care, which public benefit programs do not provide. While the parents are alive, they often provide for these needs when necessary. In the interests of love, human dignity, and humane care, they want to keep providing for these needs after they're gone.

Because the cost of care for developmentally disabled people is very high, the assets in trusts set up to provide for their care don't count against the beneficiary in qualifying for government assistance. The way they work is that the trustee is directed to pay for the beneficiary's special needs, which is to say, the requisites for maintaining the beneficiary's good health, safety, and welfare when, under the discretion of the trustee, such requisites are not being provided by any public agency, office, or department of the state or of the United States. "Special needs" include, but need not be limited to, dental care, special equipment, programs of training, education and habitation, travel needs, and recreation.

If you are trying to protect someone who is not developmentally disabled but receives SSI, the same type of planning is advised but may not be protected to the same extent and may require more careful work on the part of the trustee. But when you love a special person, you already know there are more considerations needed at all times, and you probably don't mind the technicalities, if you know they offer the greatest hope of protection for your special one.

ON BECOMING RESPONSIBLE

What was the goal you wanted to accomplish by reading this book? Did you want to find a viable way to reduce your debt, put more money into retirement plans, figure out how to invest your money? Perhaps you're thinking, Well, now I know all about wills and trusts, but that won't help me with my Visa bill, will it?

Oh, but it will. What you need to know and believe is that when you have taken care of others, you have responded to the higher values of your existence—people first, then money. It's as if, on a material level, you're giving thanks by taking care of those who helped you enter the world, those to whom you gave life, those who have guided your passage through your life. By taking these actions, you remind yourself of who you really are and what is important to you, what is important in this life. This knowledge is a powerful force. I think it is almighty. The force starts to push forward like a bulldozer, clearing out all the obstacles that prevent you from living the life you deserve to live. As you complete the rest of the steps in this book, these obstacles will continue to be cleared away. Unlikely as it may sound to you now, you will be closer and closer to paying off your Visa bill, taking that trip to Italy, or whatever your goal happens to be.

Please take the actions outlined in this chapter. Do one this week—make a call, get quotes for insurance, ask your parents about what would happen if they had to go into a nursing home. One action this week will clear you to take one action next week, and so on, until you have become responsible to those you love.

STEP 5

BEING RESPECTFUL
OF YOURSELF
AND YOUR MONEY

MONEY IS A living entity, and it responds to energy exactly the same way you do. It is drawn to those who welcome it, those who respect it. Wouldn't you rather be with people who respect you and who don't want you to be something you're not? Your money feels the same way.

> ### THE SECOND LAW OF FINANCIAL FREEDOM:
> ### Respect Attracts Money—Disrespect Repels Money

This is one of the reasons why the rich get richer. If you're respectful of your money, and do what needs to be done with it, you will become like a magnet, attracting more and more money to yourself.

For some of us, this goes against the grain. We've all heard that "money is the root of all evil," and it's easy to have the notion that caring for our money is a task that should be beneath us. We know there are more important things in life—like people, as we saw in the last chapter. But that doesn't mean you should neglect your money. Remember, your financial life is like a garden. If you tend a garden carefully, nourishing the flowers, pruning, and weeding, it's going to be a lot more beautiful than if you simply water it halfheartedly now and then.

Wouldn't you like your financial garden to be beautiful and bountiful? Don't you deserve it? If you treat your money with disrespect, you are actually not giving yourself the respect that you deserve. And when you fail to respect yourself and your money, you actually repel wealth from yourself, and you block more wealth from coming your way.

The consequences of not respecting money may show up in your life in any number of ways. You might lose some of what you have just by neglecting to pay attention to it. As soon as you pay off one credit card, your car breaks down and now you owe even more. Maybe you didn't get that job you felt certain was yours. A wonderful relationship, or so you thought, just goes out the window over money. However this repulsion takes place in your life, the root cause of it is disrespect of yourself and your money.

When I say this to some people, many of them get very defensive and say, "But Suze, I am the most respectful person I know when it comes to money." When we look closely at all their actions relating to their money, however, we eventually see that they are not as respectful as they would like to think.

When you start really respecting yourself, those you love, and your money, the result is that you start having control over your money. What follows from that is control over your life.

YOUR EXERCISE

Please write down all the ways in which you are both respectful and disrespectful of yourself and your money. Contemplate this for a while, and you'll begin to see how the actions you take in your life, and with your money, can erode your relationship with yourself and your money. Some questions:

⇥ Do you spend more money on your friends than you can afford to? Why?

⇥ Do you find yourself buying more presents for your children for the holidays or their birthdays than feels right to you? Why?

⇥ Will you spend money on others but never a penny on yourself? Why?

⇥ Do you send things Federal Express or next-day air because they'll come pick it up, rather than going to the post office to mail it far more cheaply? Why?

⇥ Have you ever bought a dress and decided, when you got it home, that it really didn't suit you, then neglected to return it to the store in time to get your money back? Why?

⇥ Do you give to charities because you really believe in the cause or to impress people? Why?

⇥ Do you put away as much money as you possibly can for retirement each year? Why not?

⇥ Do you borrow things from friends and fail to return them? Why?

⇥ Do you sometimes "forget" to pay off personal loans from friends with the same regularity that you'd pay off a credit card? Why?

❧ Do you constantly return videos a day late and have to pay the late fee, even though you've already watched them? Why?

❧ Do you send your clothes out for dry cleaning when all they need is a quick once-over with an iron? Why?

❧ Do you often go out to dinner simply because you don't feel like cooking? At what cost over time? Why?

❧ Do you sometimes pay your bills late when you didn't have to? Why?

After you have written your answers, go back and think of occasions when your respect led to something great happening or when your disrespect brought with it some unhappy consequences. It's very subtle, but the way we treat ourselves and our money touches upon every aspect of our lives.

Those people who are respectful of themselves, respectful of others who have money as well as those who do not, respectful of what money can and cannot do, are said to be people with a golden touch. I'm sure you've said it yourself about someone: Whatever she touches turns to gold. But a golden touch with money isn't something you're born with, like perfect pitch. It is something you can learn, something you *must* learn if you want to be blessed with financial freedom.

YOUR EXERCISE

Please take out your wallet or whatever you keep your money in right now. How are your bills organized? Are the ones mixed in with the tens? Are they all facing different ways? Are they stuffed in there in such a way that you have to unravel them to see what they are? How you actually keep your money is where respect for it starts. Keeping your bills neat and in order, caring for them the way you care for other important things in your life, will serve as a constant reminder of the respect that you and your money deserve.

This is what Step 5 of the nine steps to financial freedom is about—being respectful of yourself and of your money and taking actions to give that respect meaning.

PAYING YOUR BILLS TO YOURSELF

A few years ago I was asked to counsel the employees of a company that was offering early retirement to those employees fifty years old or over. I've given seminars to such employees before and also personally counseled more than one thousand people who have been offered early retirement, and I've seen how terrifying such an offer by an employer can be. If the employee is emotionally ready to retire, and financially ready to retire, it can be great. Seldom, though, do we have all our emotional and financial ducks in a row at such an early age. Many people are afraid to take offers of early retirement. Yet however afraid they are to say yes to the offer, they're more afraid to say no. Why? Because if they say no, they're at the mercy of their company, with no guarantees of employment for as long as they'll need it. And once they turn down the offer the first time, they may not have a second chance.

This time I discovered something very interesting. Even though most of these people had worked for this company for twenty-five years, and most of them were earning the same salaries the whole time, there was an even split of the people who came for counseling, with only a few exceptions. The vast majority of people who came either had around $400,000 in their 401(k) retirement plans or else they had around $150,000—big difference.

What accounted for the difference? Were some simply better investors than the others? No. Nearly all these people had all their money in the company's stock, even though they had other investment options. Had some been in the company plan longer than others? It wasn't that, either. Most of them had been in the plan for about the same time, give or take. Had some withdrawn large amounts of money from their retirement plans, even at a penalty? There were a few of these, but they were the people who only had anywhere from $10,000 to $50,000 left in their plans, and they were a small minority.

One single factor accounted for the difference. Those who had $400,000 or more had from the beginning put in the maximum amount they were allowed to put into their 401(k) account. Those who had $150,000 had simply put in 6 percent of their salaries because that was all the company matched. Their attitude was: Why put in more than the company will match? (Sound familiar?) One good reason for these people would have been $250,000.

To look at it a different way, that extra $250,000 would give them an extra $1,500 a month without their ever having to touch the principal, or a hefty amount to invest for growth to cover inflation concerns, or to leave to their family when the time came. For most of the people I counseled, that $250,000 meant the difference between knowing that they would never have to find work again unless they wanted to and being afraid that one day there would be no choice.

THE IMPORTANCE OF INVESTING

There are only three honest ways in this life to get money. The first is to work for it. The amount of time most of us are able to work will be limited—by age, health, elimination of our jobs, whatever—and there will be many years, for most of us, when we're spending money but not earning it. Do you know that most of us will spend more time in retirement than we ever did working?

The second way to make money is to inherit it. Are you among those who are hoping that an inheritance will be your saving grace? If you're waiting around for the heavens to rain money down on you, I hope you paid close attention to Step 4. With the life expectancy inching up to the eighties and beyond, you might well hit your own retirement years before you ever see a penny. What is more, for the majority of us, inheritance is rarely a sure bet. One nursing home stay, a few investments gone bad, a large probate or estate tax bill—anything can happen.

The third way to make money is the most powerful and respectful way there is. This is to invest the money you save during your working years wisely, so that when you no longer want to or are able to work, your money will work for you. The earning years of your retirement money can go on forever— money is a living entity, remember? If invested with respect, if invested in time to let it grow, these earnings will take care of you well and go on to take care of those you leave behind.

ADDING YOURSELF TO YOUR PAYROLL

It is not respectful to yourself, to others, or to your money not to plan for your future. It is not respectful to yourself, to others, or to your money not to take full advantage of the 401(k)s or IRAs or the other retirement plans that are available to you. It is not respectful to yourself, to others, or to your money not to face your debt, to learn the basics of investing, and to stand guard over your money, making sure that every penny you're spending is a penny that must be spent. What day you pay your bills, when you send in your taxes, and what hidden costs you pay for your checking account all can make a difference in how much money you have and how much money gets attracted your way. We all think that a bigger paycheck would be the answer to our financial woes, but that is rarely the case. Respect starts with the money you are earning right now and what you do with it.

THE THIRD LAW OF FINANCIAL FREEDOM (PART 1):
The More You Make, the More You Spend

Remember your first paycheck from your first job, how it seemed like so much money and how everything seemed possible? Remember your first raise, how your expenses expanded to spend it, and you wondered how you ever managed to get by on that first paycheck? With every subsequent raise, you've probably increased your spending to use up every penny of it—even though you got by perfectly well before your most recent raise, the one before that, and the one before that.

THE THIRD LAW OF FINANCIAL FREEDOM (PART 2):
The Less You Think You Make, the Less You Will Spend

No, no, no—this does not mean you should make less money; I hope you make as much money as you can! But there is a simple and remarkably effective way to make yourself spend less. You invest more. By putting more money into your retirement accounts, your take-home check will be less and you will quickly train yourself to spend at a lower level, just as you used to do when you were making less money. (If you still don't see how you can spend less, reread Step 3, which will show you how to do so.)

If you do this now, if and when that day comes when you're asked to attend an early retirement seminar, or when those rumors in your office about downsizing become reality, you'll be ready. You'll be the one with the $400,000 or more with which to face the future.

You may say, "But Suze, I can barely afford to pay my bills as it is. How do you expect me to live today and still put money away for my retirement?"

If you think you cannot make it today, while you're working and have a paycheck coming in, how in the world do you think you're going to make it in the future, when you will have essentially the same bills to pay but no paycheck coming in? The answer is that you won't. But if you set it up now, even on a modest salary, you can put aside an impressive amount of money.

Some years ago a couple came to my office—early forties, nicely dressed, two children, annual salary of $35,000. The wife didn't work outside her home, because the children were too small, although she planned to go back to work in a few years. They owned their own house and had fourteen years left on their mortgage. They paid their credit card bills in full every month. They already had a sizable nest egg, because the husband had been aggressively investing the maximum in his 401(k) plan at work. They had a few other investments that were doing nicely, earmarked to fund their children's education. I remember asking them, "How is it possible that you can do all this on just $35,000 a year?"

He answered: "We only spend what we see. The company takes out the maximum for my 401(k), and I also have them send money directly to our credit union. The credit union sends money directly to a mutual fund to invest it. Our take-home money isn't much, but at least we know we can spend it all and not have to worry. So it works." I asked them why they had come to see me, and they said they wanted to make sure they were covering all their financial bases. With immense respect for the job they were doing, I sent them home and told them not to change a thing.

MAKING YOUR MIND YOUR FRIEND

Your mind is the most powerful tool you have, and in the same way my clients just mentioned did, you must make it believe that you make less than you do so that you will naturally spend less.

Your mind believes that if you bring home a monthly paycheck of $3,000, then you have $3,000 to spend. And you'll spend it, all of it. If you get a raise and start bringing home $4,000 a month, you'll spend all of that, too, and wonder how on earth you managed on less. But if you start bringing home $3,500 a month, your mind will adjust to it, and you'll naturally spend less. The way to do it is exactly the way my clients do: just put it away before you ever see it.

You won't be depriving yourself. You'll be paying yourself. You'll be on your own payroll and soon be able to enjoy two of life's great pleasures: counting your money as it grows and dreaming of how you'll spend it when the time comes.

TIME AND YOUR 401(K)

JUDY'S STORY

"I would happily up my 401(k) to the maximum," Judy said, "but I can't afford it."

It was actually quite a few years ago when my mom died and left me what I thought was a nice inheritance. At the time, I had just a few credit card bills—not more than, say, $2,000. But I sure loved having more money in the bank. My partner and I had been living together then for about eighteen years, and we had always had a nice sharing relationship financially. But things seemed to change after I got that money. Before I knew it, I had spent more than half of it, on things I had never really given much thought to before. And Deb, well, she started to spend more, too. Before I knew it, our credit card bills were up to around $7,000. And that was before we bought our new apartment. But now I'm getting nervous about the future. I have a 401(k) plan at work, and I put in 6 percent, which is what the company matches. Deb doesn't even have a retirement plan at work. I probably should put more money away for retirement, I know it makes sense, but I really can't afford to, not with the mortgage and everything.

Judy had it backward. In fact, she couldn't afford not to put more money away for retirement. Having worked at the same corporation for twenty-seven years, she had missed out on thousands upon thousands of dollars she could have saved painlessly, effortlessly, and tax-deferred. By receiving a little less in each paycheck, she would have earned herself far, far more in the long term for her retirement, which would be upon her not too many years down the road.

THE FOURTH LAW OF FINANCIAL FREEDOM:
It's Not What You Make—It's What You Get to Keep

With Judy, as with the rest of us, it is not the amount of money earned that is important. It is how much of that she does not have to give to the IRS, how much she really does get to keep.

Money that goes into a retirement fund is money you do not have to pay taxes on until you take it out. Depending on your income tax bracket, you might be able to keep up to 38.6 percent more of your money (the highest federal tax bracket as of 2002 and 2003; rates are scheduled to change in subsequent years.) right off the top. Because of the tax savings, contributing the maximum to your retirement account right now will not deprive you of as much current income as you might fear. And where it will make a vast difference is in what you'll have to spend later.

Let's say that I convinced Judy to raise her 401(k) contribution to $500 a month or $6,000 a year, and let's say, too, that she is in the up to 38.6 percent tax bracket for federal taxes in 2002 and the 11 percent bracket for state taxes. She will have saved $135 a month on her 2002 and 2003 federal taxes and $55 a month on her state taxes. If she didn't put this money away, she would really get to spend only $310 a month after paying her taxes.

Your situation might be a little different, depending on what tax bracket you are in or whether the state you live in imposes an income tax, but the concept always holds true.

Finally I convinced her, and she promised to up her contribution to the maximum that very week, which she did. She called me a few days later: the very day she raised her contribution, her boss had called her into her office to give her a midyear raise. This was the first time in all these years she had been given a raise before the end of the year. She was stunned.

I wasn't. This sort of occurrence, however you want to explain it, is not uncommon; I've seen it happen many times. I attribute it to the second law of financial freedom: *Respect attracts money.*

Judy had decided to respect herself, chosen to put the creed into action and take the steps to nurture her money. And by doing the right things with her money, she attracts more money.

EXERCISE

If you are covered at work by a 401(k), 403(b), or SIMPLE plan, I want you to go into your human resources office and up your contribution to the maximum, if it isn't there already. If you have not signed up for your retirement plan, please do so now. If you are self-employed or your place of employment doesn't offer a 401(k) or similar plan, please read on and take the actions that are right for you. Once you've done this, write down the date you took the action and begin to keep track, see what happens in your financial life that never would have happened before. For Judy, it was a midyear raise. Soon you will see that there is a direct correlation between taking a step toward financial freedom yourself and watching your money take a step right back toward you.

IF YOU'RE AFRAID TODAY, YOU'LL BE MORE AFRAID IN THE FUTURE

You need not feel afraid about increasing your contributions to the maximum. None of these changes is cast in stone, and you could always change back if you felt you had to. Among all the people I've had do this, by the way, not one single person has ever regretted it—or changed his or her contribution back to where it was. You cannot afford not to try this out. There will be a day, you know, when you won't be able to bring in a paycheck, and you must prepare for that day now.

Companies are offering 401(k) plans because most of them do not offer pensions anymore. When many of our parents retired, things were different. Back then, almost everyone received a monthly paycheck from their longtime employers after retirement—that's why retired people were called pensioners. Also, even a generation ago people were not living to ripe old ages, the way we are now, and retirement was a shorter-term eventuality. For most of us, the pension check is a relic of the past.

If you're counting on Social Security to see you through retirement, count again. That is not the most secure bet you could make. When Social Security was first created, the average life expectancy was sixty-two. The architects of Social Security expected that very few Americans would live long enough to collect it. Surprise! Now that the average life expectancy extends well into the eighties, most of us will spend more years in retirement than we ever did working. This is placing a tremendous strain on the Social Security system, so much so that recently the government has changed the ages as to when you can collect your full Social Security benefit. Starting with people born in 1938, the normal Social Security eligibility age will rise by two months for each year, until it reaches sixty-six if you were born in 1943. It then stays at sixty-six for everyone born through the end of 1954. If you were born after the year 1954, then the age to receive full benefits starts to climb again by two months a year until it is finally capped at sixty-seven for those born in 1960 or later.

Not only does the change affect when you start collecting your full benefit amount, but it also affects you if you decide to take your Social Security payment before your full benefit eligibility age. For instance, if your full benefit eligibility age is now sixty-six but you wanted to take your Social Security benefits at age sixty-two, your benefits will be 25 percent lower. People whose normal retirement age is now sixty-seven will see a 30 percent benefit reduction if they choose to take their Social Security at age sixty-two.

The way it used to work was you could get your full benefits at age sixty-five, but if you did take them at sixty-two you only had a 20 percent reduction. But now, not only do you have to wait longer to get your full benefit if you were born after 1938, but if you take your Social Security at sixty-two, you get less as well.

On the bright side, the yearly rate of increase in benefits for those who wait past their full eligibility age to start collecting Social Security will gradually rise, up to 8 percent for those born in 1943 or later. It is 6 percent for someone turning sixty-five in 2000. This incentive is not offered beyond age seventy, however.

The eligibility age for Medicare, the nation's health insurance program for the elderly, is not affected by the Social Security changes and will remain at sixty-five.

If all this is confusing, take a look at the chart below. The figures on the left refer to the year you were born and the figures in the second column refer to your actual full benefit age calculated by the SSA. The last three columns show you what will happen if you decide to start taking Social Security before reaching your full retirement age.

Year of Birth *Note: Persons born on January 1 of any year should refer to the previous year.	Full Retirement Age	Age 62 Reduction Months	Monthly % Reduction	Total % Reduction
1937 or earlier	65	36	.555	20.00
1938	65 and 2 months	38	.548	20.83
1940	65 and 4 months	40	.541	21.67
1941	65 and 6 months	42	.535	22.50
1942	65 and 8 months	44	.530	23.33
1943–1954	66	48	.520	25.00
1955	66 and 2 months	50	.516	25.84
1956	66 and 4 months	52	.512	26.66
1957	66 and 6 months	54	.509	27.50
1958	66 and 8 months	56	.505	28.33
1959	65 and 10 months	58	.502	29.17
1960 and later	67	60	.500	30.00

If you want to know what your Social Security benefit will be, please note that as of October 1, 1999, you will get an estimate of your Social Security benefits mailed directly to you automatically three months before your birthday at your home address. So, if you were born in June, you should get your statement in March. If your birthday has come and gone and you have not yet received your statement of earnings in the mail, call up the SSA at their toll-free number (800-772-1213), and request that your statement be sent to you. Or you can access the SSA website at http://www.ssa.gov. and request your statement on-line; you can even fill out the form on-line. But, again, this should be a yearly automatic process.

So, as you can see, the government has the ability to make changes whenever they want; in my opinion, if you are counting solely on Social Security, you could be in danger. You, your money, and what you do with it today will be the only thing you can count on for your future. Since no one is doing it for you, you have got to do it for yourself. For most of the people I have come in contact with, their saving grace is their 401(k) or other retirement plan. Almost certainly it will be for you, too.

RETIREMENT PLAN BASICS—HOW THEY WORK

The employer-sponsored plans known as 401(k) and 403(b), allow you to contribute a portion of your salary, usually around 15 percent, into the plan. A 401(k), which takes its exciting name from a section in the tax code, is an all-around plan that almost any employee of any company can enter into. A 403(b) plan is what you have if you work for a nonprofit organization, such as a hospital, university, or research organization. The 401(k) and 403(b) plans work in much the same way; if I refer to a 401(k) plan here, it will also apply to you if you have a 403(b) plan.

How Much Can I Put into My Plan?

The percentage and the amount you can contribute may vary from employer to employer; some employers limit the percentage of your salary you can contribute. Regardless of the percentage your company allows, the maximum dollar amount the government generally allows as of the year 2002 is $11,000 per year for 401(k) plans and 403(b) plans. This limit is scheduled to increase over the next few years, as follows:

YEAR	401(k)/403(b)
2003	$12,000
2004	$13,000
2005	$14,000
2006	$15,000

In addition to the above limitations, individuals who are at least 50 years old by the end of the year can make an additional contribution to their plan. For 2002, the additional 401(k)/403(b) contribution limit was $1,000. This limit will increase by $1,000 each year until it reaches $5,000 in 2006, and will be indexed for inflation in later years.

In addition, with a 401(k) the government has interesting regulations that affect how much you can contribute if you are making a lot, $75,000 or more. (This figure also changes for inflation.) When you earn this kind of money, the government considers you to be a "highly compensated employee," and out of fairness to all employees it does not want the average percentage for those earning $85,000 or more and putting the maximum into the plan to be far greater than the average percentage of all other employees who are not as highly compensated. The term "highly compensated employee" means any employee who, during the current year or preceding year (1) was at any time a 5 percent or more owner; (2) received compensation from the employer in excess of $85,000; (3) received compensation from the employer in excess of $50,000 and was in the top-paid group of employees for such year, or; (4) was at any time an officer and received compensation greater than 50 percent of the amount in effect under section 415(b)(1)(A) for the year. A plan where the more-highly paid individuals contribute much more than the less well-paid is called "top-heavy."

This means that if you are highly compensated in the government's eyes, you might not even be able to contribute the full

$10,500 to your 401(k). In fact, if employees at your company who are less well paid are not putting in anything at all, you may not be eligible to contribute anything whatsoever. Make sure your plan administrator has addressed this potential problem. Otherwise, if you are highly compensated and have put too much in your plan, they'll have to give the money back to you, and it will be taxed as ordinary income.

How Do I Put Money into My Plan? What Happens to the Money?

The percentage that you decide to contribute, once okayed by the company, will be taken from your paycheck before taxes and deposited into the plan.

The company administering the plan then invests your money for you. You will usually have a choice of several investment vehicles, which might include mutual funds, bond funds, or individual equities such as the stock of your own company. Typically, the choices will offer a range of risks and returns. Some investments are highly predictable, such as bonds, which produce steady income at minimum risk. The stock market is more variable, and the most aggressive growth funds may swing up and down considerably in value, while they offer a higher return over time.

Usually you will be given extensive information about your investment options, and you can divide your contributions as you see fit among the different investments.

Most plans today allow you to transfer money within the plan from one investment to another or to change how you want future contributions to be allocated among the investments. All it usually takes is a phone call. So if you have invested all your money in a stock fund, for instance, and the stock skyrockets and you sell your shares within the plan because you made 30 percent on your money, you will not owe a penny at that time in taxes. While the money sits in the plan you do not have to pay taxes on it.

Should I Invest All My 401(k) Money in My Company's Stock?

It's never wise to put all your eggs in one basket, particularly in stocks. The stock market has ups and downs, and individual companies may fall on hard times very quickly, due to management mistakes, changes in the economy, or sheer bad luck.

This doesn't mean your company is a bad investment or that you shouldn't express your loyalty by being a shareholder. But even great companies—think of Microsoft or Procter & Gamble in the year 2000—can see frightening declines in their stock. By all means, invest in your own firm, but spread your money around so that you're protected if the unexpected happens. *Diversification* should be your watchword.

When Do I Owe Taxes on a Retirement Plan?

The taxes on a retirement plan will be deferred until you take your money out, at which time it will be taxed as ordinary income. But if you withdraw funds from a retirement account before the age of fifty-nine and a half, you will pay ordinary income tax on the money. You will also pay a 10 percent federal penalty on any amount withdrawn, as well as a state income tax penalty. With a SIMPLE, it works the same way after the first two years. But if you take out the money within the first two years you participate in the plan, an early withdrawal tax of 25 percent will apply.

However, there are exceptions.

Getting Around the 10 Percent Early Withdrawal Penalty

Very few people know about this, but it's true.

If you're fifty-five or older in the year of retirement from your company, you can withdraw whatever you like from what's known as a *qualified employer retirement account* without any tax penalty whatsoever.

You will pay tax on this money as if it were ordinary income. The tax will be withheld from your withdrawal off the top in the form of a 20 percent withholding tax. You'll get a refund of this withholding tax if when you file your return you owe less than was withheld. If you owe more, you'll have to pay the balance.

This holds true only for employer-sponsored retirement plans such as the 401(k)and 403(b). If you take your money out of your 401(k) and put it for you (without you touching it) into, for example, an IRA rollover, this 20 percent withholding rule won't apply to you.

What If I Leave My Present Employer?

When you leave your place of employment, many times you can leave your 401(k) right there and not have to take it out until much later. Other times you might want to withdraw your money, and some companies may encourage you highly to take it out when you leave, although if you have more than $5,000 in the plan, they can't force you to do so. In any case, there might come a time when you need a place to which you can transfer the money.

You usually have two choices. If you're merely changing jobs, you can move it to the 401(k) plan at the new company if the company has no time restrictions as to when you can enter its plan. If it does, until you qualify to join the plan (after you've been there a year at the latest, by law), you can take advantage of the other option. The other option is to arrange for a trustee-to-trustee transfer of the money from your current plan into an *IRA rollover account.* If you do this, you can continue to shelter all the money from taxes and invest it for your retirement. You can open an IRA rollover at a bank, mutual funds company, insurance company, or brokerage firm. IRA rollovers are governed by the same regulations as an IRA account (described later in this chapter). As of 2002, you no longer have to keep rollover money in a separate IRA in order to roll it into a new employer's plan. A 401(k) cannot be rolled directly into a Roth IRA.

Substantially Equal Periodic Payments to Avoid the 10 Percent Withdrawal Penalty

There is one other way to get money out of your retirement accounts and avoid that 10 percent penalty if you are not the permissible age or if your money is in an IRA or IRA rollover. You can do this by using a technique called *substantially equal periodic payments (SEPP)*. Simply put, you have to take out a specific amount of money every single year until you are 59½ or for five years, whichever period is longer.

So if you are fifty-seven and you start to take money out of your IRA account under SEPP, you will have to do so until you are sixty-two. If you're fifty-two when you start, you'll have to continue withdrawing the money until you're fifty-nine and a half—again the rule is whichever time period is longer.

The amount you can withdraw is calculated by one of three methods; the method you choose will determine the actual dollar amount you must take out yearly. This exact predetermined amount must be withdrawn every year for five years or when you reach fifty-nine and a half, whichever is longer. Very few people know about this loophole, IRS code 72(t)(2)(A)(IV), but it's there if you need it. Make sure you deal with a financial adviser, accountant, or brokerage house who is familiar with this law.

When Do I Have to Start Making Withdrawals from My Retirement Plan?

The longer you can let it sit there, in most cases the better off you'll be. But the government won't let it sit there (tax-free!)

forever. They want their taxes on your retirement money. According to a formula specified by the IRS, you have got to start taking money out of your retirement plans (except for Roth IRAs) by April 1 in the year after you turn seventy and a half. There is one big exception: If you are still working, your retirement money is in an employer-sponsored plan such as a 401(k), and you are seventy and a half or older, and you do not own more than 5 percent of the employer, you do *not* have to make withdrawals until April 1 following the calendar year in which you do retire.

What If I Don't Have a Retirement Plan at Work?

Ask your boss to get you one. Take a poll and you will see that almost everyone you work with probably wants one, too. Choose the best person to approach your boss to ask about establishing a 401(k) company plan or a SIMPLE for all of you. Offer to do the research yourself or with a colleague. Many excellent plans are offered by different mutual funds companies, all of whom will set up a plan for your company's needs; Fidelity Investments (800-343-3548 or visit www.fidelity.com) and Vanguard Group (800-662-7447 or visit www.vanguard.com), for example, are two of the largest 401(k) money managers and wonderful places to start looking.

INDIVIDUAL RETIREMENT ACCOUNTS

If you are working for a company that still won't offer you a retirement plan, your only other option is an *IRA,* or *individual retirement account.* You can make an IRA contribution of up to $3,000 for yourself, and if you're married, you can also contribute $3,000 for your nonworking spouse. The IRA contribution is scheduled to increase in future years, in accordance with the following schedule:

YEAR	CONTRIBUTION LIMIT
2002–2004	$3,000
2005–2007	$4,000
2008 AND LATER	$5,000

Individuals who are 50 or older as of the end of the year can contribute an additional amount. For years 2002 through 2004 the additional amount is $500. For 2005 or later, the amount is $1,000. In order to make a contribution, the combined income of both spouses has to be at least equal to the amount contributed to the IRA. You can also have a traditional IRA in addition to an employer's retirement plan, but your contributions may not be tax-deductible.

As of January 2000, there are three different kinds of IRAs that you can choose from: a traditional IRA, the spousal IRA, and the Roth IRA. Here are the new specifics.

The Traditional IRA

If your earning allows it, the traditional IRA gives you a current-year tax deduction. If you are eligible, you can contribute $2,000 to your IRA, and if you are in the 27 percent tax bracket as of 2002 and 2003 (rates will change in subsequent years), you will save $810 that year in income taxes ($3,000 × 27%). What is more, while the money is in the IRA, both your contributions and the IRA's earnings grow tax-deferred, which means that the income taxes on any growth of the funds are deferred until you actually withdraw any of the money, at which time you will pay ordinary income tax on the amount withdrawn each year. With a traditional IRA, in most cases you cannot withdraw the money prior to age fifty-nine and a half without paying a 10 percent penalty on the amount withdrawn. (Exceptions to this are if you use SEPP, page 154, or for the reasons listed below.) On the other end, if you do not need the money, it can sit there until you have to start making withdrawals by April 1 of the year after you turn seventy and a half. But remember, if after that date you have not taken out the required amount there is a 50 percent penalty on the amount that should have been withdrawn. The spousal IRA follows the same guidelines.

Who Can Withdraw Money Penalty-Free from a Traditional IRA?

As of January 1, 1998, the penalty for premature withdrawals from IRAs was eliminated in two additional instances:

1. If the money is used by a "first-time home buyer" to purchase a principal residence. The distribution may come from the buyer's IRA or from an account belonging to the buyer's spouse, or the child, grandchild, or ancestor of either the taxpayer or the taxpayer's spouse. There is a lifetime limitation of $10,000 that can be treated as penalty-free "first-time home-buyer" distributions.

2. Distributions for higher education expenses at an eligible education institution to the extent that such distributions do not exceed the qualified higher education expenses of the taxpayer, taxpayer's spouse, or any child or grandchild of either the taxpayer or the taxpayer's spouse for the taxable year.

Who Can Take Advantage of the Traditional IRA Deduction?

The traditional IRAs, including spousal IRAs, have rules regarding deductibility that are determined by whether the taxpayer is covered by a qualifying pension plan at work and, if so by what the taxpayer's filing status and income are for the year. Under the new law, the "phase out" income ranges will be increased over several years, until in 2007 the range will be $50,000–$60,000 for single taxpayers and $80,000–$100,000 for married filing jointly (MFJ). However, a spouse will not be considered covered by a pension plan simply by virtue of the other spouse's being covered. The spouse without a qualifying pension plan will be able to make a fully deductible contribution to an IRA if the modified joint AGI does not exceed $150,000. Between $150,000 and $160,000, deductibility is phased out.

The Roth IRA

The Roth IRA differs, in that you do not get to take a current-year tax deduction in the year that you put the money in, or, for that matter, ever, but—here's the lure—from the moment of deposit, no matter where you deposit it or what your return, your contribution grows tax-free. When you take your original contributions out, you will not pay any taxes or penalties whatsoever. That's right, you can take your initial contributions out anytime, regardless of your age, without taxes or penalties (subject to a special rule on withdrawals of converted IRAs within five years of the conversion). And to get your hands on the earnings tax-free, the only rules are these: The money your contributions earn has to stay in the account for at least five years before you can withdraw it without taxes or penalties, and you have to be at least fifty-nine and a half years of age. The other ways to get your hands on the earnings penalty-free are if the owner has died or is disabled, or if the distribution is made for a qualified "first-home" purchase ($10,000 lifetime limitation is applicable) as long as the five year rule is met.

Who Can Take Advantage of the Roth IRA?

Not all taxpayers are eligible for the Roth IRA. As of 2002, up to $3,000 (subject to the same earned-income rules as the traditional IRA) can be contributed by single taxpayers having less than $95,000 in adjusted gross income (AGI). (See chart on page 156 for later years' contribution limits.) Married taxpayers filing jointly have full eligibility if they have an AGI of $150,000 or more. Eligibility is lost at $110,000 AGI for single taxpayers and $160,000 AGI for MFJ. Taxpayers can have a combination of Roth IRA and traditional IRA accounts as long as the combined contributions don't exceed the yearly maximum allowable for either type (which can be as much as $3,000, as of 2002, but may be less).

So what do these income qualification levels tell us? In my opinion, the government does not want people in really high tax brackets to be able to take advantage of the tax-free accumulation phase offered by the Roth IRA. With those who can take advantage of the Roth IRA, I recommend you do so. But always make sure to check with a financial advisor or professional.

IRA Conversions and Qualifications

If your yearly adjusted gross income is $100,000 or less, the government also allows you to convert any or all of your traditional IRAs into a Roth IRA. If you do this, what you need to know is that even though you may be under the age of fifty-nine and a half when you take the money out of your traditional IRA to convert to a Roth, the 10 percent penalty tax will not apply—but you *will* owe ordinary income tax on any money that you converted.

To Convert or Not to Convert, That Is the Question

Because the Roth IRA and the conversion feature continue to cause tremendous confusion, many websites and help departments at brokerage firms have been set up just to answer this question for you, given your particular circumstances—most of them in the hope that they will end up with your IRA money one way or the other. Try them out and do the calculations for yourself, using the sources available to you, and see if it makes sense for you in your particular situation to convert or not and then check your answers with a professional. If you have access to a computer check out the website www.rothira.com, which has links to many on-line calculators that will give you the answers to your conversion-related questions. Also, on my own website www.suzeorman.com, in the resource section I have links for you as well that will answer this question for you.

If you do decide to do a conversion, make sure that you can pay for the taxes out of your savings or your income, but not from the money in the IRA. Also, remember that no one ever said you have to convert all the money that is in your traditional IRA into a Roth; you may just want to convert a small amount so the tax bite is not so bad. Before you do anything, however, I would suggest getting a professional opinion—from someone who does not want to get your IRA money to invest, such as a CPA or an enrolled agent who does not take money under management.

Roth IRA and Roth Conversions

Q. If I open up a new Roth IRA and contribute $2,000 a year or convert my traditional IRA to a Roth IRA do I still have to wait till I am fifty-nine and a half to take the money out without penalty?

A. No. The rules that govern Roth IRAs and converted Roths are different than the rules that govern traditional IRAs.

In a contributory Roth IRA you can at any time you want, regardless of your age or time the money has been in the account, withdraw your original contributions without any taxes or penalties. So let's say you are now thirty-nine years old and for the past three years you have put $3,000 a year into your Roth IRA. You have put in a total $9,000 of original contributions. At any time you want, you can withdraw up to $9,000 without penalties or taxes. Remember, you are only thirty-nine, not fifty-nine and a half, but that does not matter. The money has only been in there three years, but that, too, does not matter. Your yearly contributions can be withdrawn at any time, with no restrictions whatsoever and without taxes or penalties.

However, the *earnings* that your contributions have made have to stay in the account until you have attained fifty-nine and a half years of age and the account is more than five years old. So let's say that the $9,000 over those three years grew to $9,800. Yes, you could withdraw the $9,000 at any time, but the growth on that money or the $800 has got to stay in the Roth IRA till you are fifty-nine and a half and for at least five years before you can withdraw it without taxes or penalties.

Roth Conversions

When you convert money from a traditional IRA to a Roth IRA, the withdrawal privileges work like this. The money that you originally converted has got to stay in the Roth account for more than five tax years or until you are fifty-nine and a half, whichever comes first, before you can withdraw it without taxes or penalties. You do not, however, have to be fifty-nine and a half to withdraw the converted amount to avoid the 10 percent penalty, you just have to have met the five-year holding requirement. So let's say that you are thirty-nine and you convert $50,000 from a traditional IRA to a Roth. That $50,000 has got to stay in the Roth IRA for at least five years. After that time, even though you are just forty-four, you can withdraw all $50,000 without any taxes or penalties. The earnings on that $50,000, however, cannot be withdrawn without penalties or taxes until you have attained the age of fifty-nine and a half.

Q. When does the five-year period begin for contributory Roth IRAs? This confuses me, since I am putting money in every year.

A. The timeclock starts for all your contributions from the year of your first contribution. So let's say in the year 2002 you deposit $3,000 into a Roth. The five-year timeclock began—on

January 1, 2002. Every contribution made from this point on will be timed from the year 2002.

Q. When I die, will my beneficiaries have to pay income taxes on the money that I leave them in a Roth IRA?

A. No. That is one of the beauties of this account. The money that you leave your beneficiaries via a Roth will be income tax free when they take it out.

Q. Do I have to start taking money out of a Roth IRA when I turn seventy and a half, like I do with my traditional IRA?

A. No. You can leave the money in there for as long as you want.

Q. Can I convert my 401(k) to a Roth IRA?

A. Not directly. You first would have to roll over your 401(k) to a traditional IRA and then from the traditional IRA, you could do a Roth conversion if your income allows, but taxes will be owed on the amount converted.

Q. Can I have a 401(k) and a Roth IRA?

A. Yes, in most cases. In fact, you can have almost any retirement plan and also have a Roth IRA if you meet the AGI income levels listed below.

Q. Does this mean I can have a traditional IRA and a Roth IRA?

A. Yes, as long as between the two IRAs you have not in one year contributed more than the $2,000 annual cap for IRAs.

Q. Are there income limitations to who can have a Roth IRA?

A. Yes, the maximum adjusted gross income limitations are as follows: for those filing an individual return, $110,000; for joint returns, $160,000.

Q. Is there an income limit to be able to convert a traditional IRA to a Roth IRA?

A. Yes, you cannot have more than $100,000 of AGI.

Q. If my spouse and I file separate tax returns and we each make under $100,000, can we qualify for a Roth conversion?

A. The answer is no.

Q. What if I convert my traditional IRA to a Roth and then find out I have over $100,000 AGI for that year. *Now what?*

A. No problem. The government now allows you to transfer back to a traditional IRA without any penalties.

Q. When do I owe the taxes on the money that I have converted into my Roth IRA from a traditional IRA?

A. Starting in 1999, you owe them in entirety for the year of conversion.

Q. What if I converted my traditional IRA to a Roth at the time the market was really high? Since then, the market has taken a tumble. I now owe a lot of taxes on an IRA that in reality is worth a lot less. Is there anything that I can do?

A. Yes. You have until October 15 of the year after the conversion to "recharacterize" the account back into a traditional IRA. You can then convert it back again to a Roth IRA as long as you wait until the later of 1) the year after the year of the original conversion, or 2) more than thirty days after the date of the recharacterization. (Please note that I said the *later* of the two.) Just be sure that your income allows you to be sure that your income allows you to be eligible still to do a conversion at this later time. For instance, let's say that you have a traditional IRA worth $100,000 and you converted it to a Roth. Six months later in the same year, the market has gone down and now that $100,000 is only worth $78,000. Since you converted your traditional IRA when the value was worth $100,000, if you do not do anything, you will owe income taxes on $100,000. What you could do is recharacterize back to a traditional IRA, then reconvert back (30 days later or the next calendar year, whichever one is longer) to the Roth with hopefully a lower conversion value. This is something that you should always keep in mind. It could save you lots of money, but make sure you check with a tax professional before doing anything, since these laws can change.

IRA Guidelines

A few thoughts to keep in mind. Are you eligible for a company retirement plan like a 401(k) and do you also qualify to fund a Roth IRA? If so, it can be confusing as to whether you should fund your 401(k) plan or the Roth IRA first. It would be best to fund both to the maximum if you can. But if money is tight and it is an either/or situation, then this is what I would do. If you have a 401(k) plan where your employer matches your contribution, meaning that for every dollar you put into your retirement plan at work, they put money in for you as well to match in full or in part, I would first fund my retirement plan at work up to the point of the match. Once I reached the limit of the match where the employer was no longer matching my contribution or if my 401(k) plan or 403(b) plan did not have a matching program to begin with, I would figure out what tax bracket I was in. If I were in a high tax bracket *and* I also liked the investment choices that my retirement plan at work was offering me, I would continue to fund my 401(k)/403(b) plan to the max. Then I would fund my Roth IRA if I could. If, however, I was not currently in a very high tax bracket or I did not like the investment choices within my retirement plan at work, I would first fund my Roth IRA, and then if I had the money available, I would fund the retirement plan at work. If you have been investing in a nondeductible IRA, you, too, should definitely consider switching to a Roth IRA; for most people it makes the nontax-deductible IRA obsolete. If you are not covered by a company pension plan, and can really use the tax write-off right now from a traditional IRA deposit, but you are a spender and not a saver and—realistically—will fritter away the tax savings from a traditional IRA instead of investing them each year, then you might want to lean more toward the Roth IRA as a savings against future taxes that you would have owed with a traditional IRA. In other words, pass up the current tax savings for the future big picture. If you are very young, just starting out in your career, and in a low tax bracket, by all means look into a Roth IRA, which can jump-start your retirement savings by a lot, even if you switch tactics later. Let's say that from ages twenty-one to thirty you invested $2,000 a year into a Roth IRA averaging an annual return of 10 percent every year and then you never deposited another cent into that account and just let it grow; at age fifty-nine and a half, you'd have $474,000 that you could access totally tax-free. Big difference, if you think that all it would have saved you in taxes in a traditional IRA (if you are in a 15 percent tax bracket) would be around $300 a year, or $3,000 over ten years. As you can see, it makes no sense to have to pay taxes on $474,000 later on in life (when you might be in a very high tax bracket) just to have saved $3,000 over ten years early in your career. By the way, if your tax bracket changes and you want the deduction of a regular IRA, you can make that change anytime you want. Rather than making a deposit into your Roth IRA that year, switch to a traditional IRA.

Benefits of Withdrawal of a Roth IRA vs. a Traditional IRA

With a traditional IRA, upon your death your spouse is the only one allowed to take over your account as if it were his or hers. Thus surviving spouses (if withdrawals had not already started) can continue to use the tax deferral strategies until they really need to live off the money, or until age seventy and a half when withdrawals have to start. However, if you are currently not married, then your named beneficiary for these funds will have to start taking withdrawals that year and continue them over his or her entire life expectancy. But what usually happens is that the beneficiaries wipe the account clean over a short period of time. This often results in a significant tax bill for your beneficiaries. This can be avoided with a Roth IRA. In this case, your beneficiaries would also get the money tax-free. No doubt this will make you the most loved relative in the family.

Comparison of the Traditional IRA and the Roth IRA

Another possible advantage of the Roth IRA is that you do not have to start withdrawing money at age seventy and a half. With a traditional IRA, you have to start making withdrawals by April 1 of the year after you turn seventy and a half. Because of this, a Roth IRA could also help you tax-wise down the road. When you have to start taking money out of your traditional IRA—even if you don't need it—these add to your tax bracket, which affects the bottom line all the way around. One last factor is that if you really need help saving money, if you tend to sneak into your future piggy bank when you want money available to spend on today's eventually useless treasures, gear yourself toward a traditional IRA where it is harder to get at the money without sustaining penalties before age fifty-nine and a half.

COMPARISON CHART

	TRADITIONAL IRA	ROTH IRA
TAX DEDUCTIBLE	YES	NO
TAXABLE AT WITHDRAWAL	YES	NO (IF A QUALIFIED WITHDRAWAL)
PENALTY FOR PREMATURE WITHDRAWAL	YES, PRIOR TO AGE 59½	YES FOR EARNINGS WITHDRAWN PRIOR TO FIVE YEARS AND AGE 59½. ORIGINAL DEPOSITS CAN BE WITHDRAWN PENALTY-FREE AT ANY TIME
MANDATORY WITHDRAWAL AGE	70½	NO

What's the Difference between a 401(k) and an IRA?

Well, it's about as much as $8,000 or $8,500, depending on your age, in the year 2002, of possible contributions you can put away. In 2002, the most you could put into an IRA for yourself was $3,000 a year, or $3,500, if you are over 50. This is a big reason to push for a 401(k), where the max in 2002 is $11,000. Even with a SIMPLE (see page 170) you can possibly put away $4,000 more a year than you can with an IRA.

Maximizing the Impact of a Roth or Traditional IRA

Most people wait to contribute to their IRA until they file their taxes in April of the year after—a mistake that adds up. For the tax year 2002, if you qualify, you have the right to put up to $3,000 in your IRA in January 2002. But most people will wait until April 2003 to do so. This is an incredible waste of money. If you possibly can, I urge you to put that money away at the beginning of the year rather than at the tax deadline.

If you invested your $3,000 in January 2002 and that money sits there averaging an 8 percent return, by the time April 15, 2003, comes along you will have $310 more in the account. If you simply keep this up, you would have thousands of dollars more over the years you maintained this account.

Look at the larger picture. If in fact you put $2,000 away each year for the next twenty-five years and this money averaged an 8 percent return, after twenty-five years you would have $157,098 in your IRA. If instead you waited to make this contribution until the end of every December, you'd have $146,211, which is $10,887 less.

If you don't have $2,000 at the beginning of the year, and so can't make the investment all at once, start putting $166 (or whatever you can) each month into your IRA for the next twenty-five years; you will still come out better than if you had waited to do it in one lump sum at year's end. How much better? About $4,700 better. You would have $150,967 rather than $146,211.

RETIREMENT PLANS FOR THE SELF-EMPLOYED

If you're self-employed and are not incorporated, you also have excellent options for funding your retirement. You can open up what is known as a SEP, a Keogh, or a SIMPLE. All three of these are great ways to plan ahead. In order to qualify for these three retirement accounts, your earnings must be reported on Form 1099-misc. or be earned as fees for services you've provided. (Company employees, on the other hand, are usually provided with W2s to report the money they've earned.)

If you have people working for you, after a certain period of time you'll have to fund the SEP, Keogh, or SIMPLE plan for them as well.

Simplified Employee Pension Plan (SEP)

You can open a *SEP,* or *simplified employee pension plan,* and put away up to 25 percent of your income or $40,000—whichever is less—per year in payments for yourself. SEP-IRAs can be set up at banks, mutual funds companies, brokerage firms, discount brokerage firms—almost anywhere you'd like to invest (read Step 6 and decide). If you have employees who have worked for you for three out of the past five years, you will have to put money in their SEPs as well, to the tune of the lesser of 25 percent or $40,000. Please keep in mind that these figures change yearly, so check with a tax professional to find out the current limits. The above figures are for the year 2002.

Keogh

A *Keogh plan* (named after Senator Eugene Keogh, who came up with the idea) can also be used to fund a retirement for the self-employed. Keoghs are more complicated than SEPs but used to allow you to set aside more money than you could with a SEP. That is no longer true. The amounts are the same as with a SEP. You must also find a Keogh for anyone who has worked for you for at least one year. And you must contribute the same percentage for those who work for you as you do for yourself.

Keoghs are divided into two types of plans. The first is known as a *money purchase plan*, and the second is known as a *profit-sharing plan*. With both, you can invest the money just about wherever you like. However, due to the new, more generous limitations for SEPs, there is currently no reason to set up either type of Keogh, since a SEP plan is easier to administer.

SIMPLE

SIMPLE, or *Saving Incentive Plan for Employees*, lets you put up to $7,000 a year (for 2002) into a plan for yourself. There is no percentage limitation for a SIMPLE, as there is for a SEP or Keogh. If you have any employees who have worked for you and have made at least $5,000 in compensation over the past two years and are projected to do so again, they, too, are eligible for a SIMPLE. The SIMPLE contribution limits are scheduled to increase in future years, as follows:

Year	SIMPLE Contribution Limit
2002	$7,000
2003	$8,000
2004	$9,000
2005 (AND LATER)	$10,000

Individuals over the age of 50 can contribute an additional amount on top of the limit, as follows

Year	Over 50 additional SIMPLE limit
2002	$500
2003	$1,000
2004	$1,500
2005	$2,000
2006 (and later)	$2,500

As a self-employed person with employees who are eligible, you are required to follow one of two contribution formulas for your employees: either the matching contribution formula or the 2 percent formula. Under the matching contribution formula, you must match dollar for dollar what the employee elects to put into it, from 1 percent up to 3 percent of their compensation. You get to decide. However, if you choose the lower match, you cannot do that for more than two out of any five years. With the other formula—the 2 percent contribution formula—you simply decide that you are going to contribute 2 percent of the employees' compensation, up to a maximum of $4,000 a year for each employee.

Note that all contributions are considered vested the second they are made. This means that they belong to your employee even if he or she leaves your employ the very week after you made the match.

WHICH DO I WANT—SEP, KEOGH, OR SIMPLE?

One thing to know, particularly if paperwork makes you crazy, is that there's more paperwork involved with a Keogh than with a SEP or a SIMPLE (for which the paperwork requirements are almost nil). With a Keogh, from the moment you have more than $100,000 in the account you have to file what's called a 5500ez form at tax time. Not all that bad, but it's still paperwork, and paperwork that's not required with a SEP or a SIM-

PLE. If you don't have employees, or if you do and you don't mind contributing the same percentage of their income for them as you contribute of yours for yourself, the SEP is the way to go. If you have employees whom you do not want to contribute a lot of money for, or if your income is so low that you can put more away with a SIMPLE plan, then go with it. If you're self-employed, you must take advantage of one of these options. Whichever way you go, you cannot lose.

TIME CREATES MONEY

Employed, self-employed—it doesn't matter. When it comes to money, time is probably the most important factor in the growth process. The more time you give to your money and the more time it has to grow are the two key ingredients to attracting and creating large sums. The amount you will have accumulated when retirement comes will determine what kind of lifestyle you will then be able to afford.

✦ If you're forty-five, and start putting $100 a month into an account that averages a 10 percent return, you'll have $71,880 by age sixty-five.

✦ If you start ten years earlier, at thirty-five, your $100 a month will have grown to $206,440 by age sixty-five.

✦ If you can start saving $100 a month at age twenty-five, you will have $555,454 by age sixty-five.

Time accounts for the difference. For every year that you wait to take the step of establishing respect for your life, it costs you about $25,000 a year of future growth. That is a lot of money. By waiting twenty years, from age twenty-five to age forty-five, to start saving just $100 a month, you pass up almost $480,000.

MULTIPLYING YOUR MONEY

Time plays an essential role in building your future wealth, not only because the longer you contribute, the more you'll have, but also because with time, the contributions you have already made will do more work for you. This second feature that makes time so powerful is called *compounding*.

When you leave your money invested over time, the amounts of money that your contributions are generating on their own are the worker bees of your money hive.

For instance, let's say you are investing $6,000 a year, and that $6,000 is earning 8 percent. Let's assume that your investment will be able to average that 8 percent over the next twenty years, and that you continue to add $6,000 at the beginning of every year as well. There will come a point in time when the earnings on your account will add up, by themselves, to more than the $6,000 you are putting in every year. This is when those worker bees really start to make that money honey.

Take a look at the following chart and see how many years it takes before you are earning as much in interest as you are putting in. Look a little farther down the road, and you'll see that in just a few more years you could be earning three times more a year in interest than what you are contributing!

Why? Because of the magic of compounding. It is for this reason and this reason alone that you cannot afford to let one year pass without making a contribution into your retirement plan. When it comes to the wonderful effects of compounding, you can never make up for lost time. This is why in the example just given, twenty years makes such a tremendous difference in what you will have in the end: $480,000 worth of difference.

YEAR	401(K) YEARLY CONTRIBUTION	INTEREST EARNED AT 8% PER ANNUM	
1	$6,000	$480	
2	$6,000	$998	
3	$6,000	$1,558	
4	$6,000	$2,163	
5	$6,000	$2,816	
6	$6,000	$3,521	
7	$6,000	$4,283	
8	$6,000	$5,106	
9	$6,000	$5,994	YEAR 9: INTEREST NOW EQUALS YOUR CONTRIBUTION
10	$6,000	$6,954	
11	$6,000	$7,990	
12	$6,000	$9,109	
13	$6,000	$10,318	
14	$6,000	$11,623	
15	$6,000	$13,033	YEAR 15: INTEREST IS MORE THAN TWICE YOUR CONTRIBUTION
16	$6,000	$14,556	
17	$6,000	$16,200	
18	$6,000	$17,976	YEAR 18: INTEREST EQUALS MORE THAN THREE TIMES YOUR CONTRIBUTION
19	$6,000	$19,894	
20	$6,000	$21,966	

This table illustrates the power of compounding at an 8 percent return; the higher the return, the better the results. In this case you have invested $120,000 over these twenty years. At 8 percent throughout, you have earned in interest $176,536: you have earned, in other words, 147 percent of what you put in! The interest you have earned is far greater than what you put in in the first place, and think how much greater the rewards would be for every bit more than the $6,000 a year you could put in. Compounding is extraordinary, and the main ingredient of compounding is time. Give yourself that time.

Whatever your return, however, you can't afford to miss out on the golden opportunity that time allows. You work so hard for your money. Now let your money in return work hard for you.

CONSIDER THE FUTURE VALUE OF YOUR MONEY

Start training yourself to understand not just what your money is worth today, but what that same money will be worth in the future. Like a slide projected on a screen, your money becomes much larger over time. Consider the "big picture"—that compounded future value—when you are looking at the money you could save or spend today. Whenever I had a client come to my office who wanted to do something that day that would cost a lot of money, I always calculated what it would really cost by looking into the future. That's the true cost of today's desire.

I once had a client come in and say, "Suze, I want to take a year off work, and $20,000 out of my savings, to go live in Europe for a year." No problem, I said, as long as she could understand what that meant for her future. That $20,000, if left invested at a 10 percent annual return, would, in twenty years' time, when she turned sixty-five, be worth $135,000. Did she feel comfortable spending $135,000 to take a year off, not to mention the money she'd lose by giving up a year's salary? "But Suze," she said, "in twenty years $135,000 won't even be $135,000, because of inflation." But using a 3 percent inflation adjuster, in twenty years that $135,000 would still be worth $75,000. The trip would cost her $75,000.

It is so important to see what things are really costing you, and the way to see this is to see money over time. It is when you start looking at money like this—finding out how what you do today affects your future before making your decisions, which must be based on reality and not just on hope—that you will really begin to understand money. Desire the trip, understand what it will really cost, decide whether you can afford it, and if you can, then take it by all means. Or scale it back, if that makes more sense. Or wait a year. If not this year, then the right actions with your money will still get you to Italy next year or when the time comes.

And when you're doing the right things with your money, when you're being respectful, the right time will always come.

DOLLAR COST AVERAGING

One thing that your mind will try to tell you is that when you invest money, whether in your retirement account or on your own, you have to keep it safe and sound, that you can't afford to take risks with it. Wrong. The truth is that you really can't afford not to take risks. You *have* to invest this money for growth, especially if you are under the age of fifty. The younger you are, the more aggressive you can be.

As long as you have at least ten years during which you won't have to touch this money, invest the majority of it for growth.

Put your money in whatever stock or equity mutual funds your 401(k) offers. If you are in a SIMPLE, IRA, SEP, or Keogh, and just want to keep your life as easy as possible, look into good no-load index and managed growth mutual funds (page 247). Your investment mix can also include a very small percentage in international growth funds if your company offers it. Over the years, stocks or equities have outperformed every other investment out there—so again, the younger you are, the more aggressive you can be.

When you start approaching retirement, and know that you will soon be living off this money, it's time to consider easing up on your more aggressive investing. Even so, it's always best—and perfectly safe and sound—to have a nice mix of funds and keep your money diversified.

BUT I DON'T WANT TO LOSE MY MONEY

Of course you don't, nor does anyone want you to. When you begin paying yourself every month, as you do with a retirement plan, not only do you get more long-term bang for your buck, you also take some of the risk out of investing this money. So you don't have to be afraid. When you put the exact same amount of money month in, month out, into the same investment vehicle, you are taking advantage of the investment strategy known as *dollar cost averaging*. It puts time, your money, and the market all on your side at once. (We'll talk about this more later.)

I believe this with all my heart, but regardless of what I say or what anyone says, you should invest only if you want to. The reason I say only if you want to is that even though investing for growth may be the right thing for you to do economically, it's not the right thing to do if it keeps you up at night worrying or makes you afraid all the time. As you'll see in the next chapter, you must always trust your own gut feelings about money. If you can't live with risk, you must invest where you feel safe investing. Perhaps your new truth will make you feel stronger about taking risks. Maybe reading throughout the rest of this book will make you feel differently about risks and your fears about money. But respect yourself first, and however you choose to invest, take care to understand how things work—or you might end up doing what Michael did.

MICHAEL'S STORY

With time on your side, you win when the market is up—but you also win when it goes down.

> My company has a 401(k), but I never joined it. I knew that it would be a good way to build up retirement money, but I never knew which investments to put my money in, plus I was afraid to make the wrong choices. I'm more a cash kind of guy. But now I'm starting to make more, and I'm thinking of getting married to my girlfriend. I've been feeling more like a grown-up, I guess, and I was really thinking it was time to invest.
>
> Since it was the beginning of the year, I thought why not start the year off right, and I signed up, and started to contribute the maximum I could, which they told me was $750 a month based on what I made. I put all the money into this one aggressive growth mutual fund that seemed as though it had done really well over the years. The first month, fine, and the second. But then the market dropped, and the fund tumbled way down. I couldn't believe it. By the time I had added my third payment, my $2,250 was only worth about $1,950—I had already lost money. I was somehow seeing my fear come to life. But I decided to stick with it. Two months later, after I put in another $750 for each of those months, I should have had $3,750, more if it was actually earning money, but when I looked at my statement I only had $3,343. I was still losing money. This was when I couldn't take it anymore, so I went back to the human resources department to withdraw from making any more contributions to the 401(k). I mean, there's no point in losing money. I thought at least I

could wait till the market started to go up and maybe then I would rejoin.

Michael's trouble was that he understood only the concept that when you buy something you want it to go up, better known as "buy low, sell high." He didn't understand that what you want to do with dollar cost averaging—which is what you're doing with a 401(k)—is to buy low and lower and lower and *then* sell high. Michael had actually chosen a great fund to invest in, and since he had many years left until he retired, he should actually have been thrilled when it took a tumble. But no one told him that.

BUY LOW AND LOWER AND LOWER AND THEN SELL HIGH

With dollar cost averaging, you are taking the money you're investing and averaging the cost of the shares you're buying over time. Since you are investing every month, wouldn't you rather buy into your funds when the market is low, so you don't have to pay so much for your shares? Of course you would. When what you are buying goes down rather than up, that means you're paying less and are able to buy more. I always think of it as a mutual fund sale—getting what I want for less than others had to pay just a few months earlier. Michael got upset because the shares he bought went down in price over a few months. Had he stayed in for the long run, however, he would have made everything back plus more when his mutual fund started to climb again.

BE ON ALERT WHEN THE MARKET GOES DOWN

When I say you should be happy if your fund starts to go down as you're buying it, I mean be happy if all the funds that are similar to yours are also going down. You want to make sure that your 401(k) plan, and any other mutual funds you hold, are with a good portfolio manager (page 247), one who is able to do as well as or better than other comparable managers. If your fund is going down and the others are all going up, then you do need to take action; check with your human resources department. If the market starts to go down, just keep an eye on your funds to make sure they're not going down more than other similar funds. If your portfolio manager can keep your money from going down as much as the others in a down market, think what she'll be able to do when the market goes back up!

DOLLAR COST AVERAGING: BETTER THAN INVESTING ALL AT ONCE

Michael's plan was to invest $9,000 a year. What if he had invested the entire amount in January, when the market happened to be at its highest? He would have paid top dollar for that mutual fund. Let's see how this would have played itself out. If the mutual fund he wanted to buy was at $15 a share, Michael could have bought 600 shares for his $9,000. But now let's see what would have happened if he had just stayed in the 401(k) and continued to put his $750 a month in this mutual fund over time, rather than all at once.

MONTH/ CONTRIBUTION	PRICE PER SHARE	NUMBER OF SHARES BOUGHT
JANUARY/$750	$15	50
FEBRUARY/$750	$15	50
MARCH/$750	$12	62.50
APRIL/$750	$14	53.57
MAY/$750	$12	62.50
JUNE/$750	$13	57.69

JULY/$750	$12	62.50
AUGUST/$750	$11	68.18
SEPTEMBER/$750	$10	75
OCTOBER/$750	$10	75
NOVEMBER/$750	$9	83.33
DECEMBER/$750	$10	75
TOTAL INVESTED:	$9,000	
SHARES BOUGHT:	775.27	

The price of the mutual fund at the end of the year was $10 a share, which means that Michael's $9,000 investment would now be worth $7,753 (775.27 × 10), for a loss of $1,247. That's a 13.9 percent loss on paper.

But if you look at what happened to the shares, they dropped 33 percent in value from 15 down to 10. So here is a fund that went down 33 percent from the start. This is what Michael's loss would have been on paper if he had invested all at once. With dollar cost averaging, however, his loss was only 13.9 percent. Let's look at the actual dollars and cents of it. If he had invested the entire $9,000 in January, when shares were $15, he would have only 600 shares, not the 775.27 he would have had with dollar cost averaging. His fund on paper would be worth $6,000, not the $7,753 it could have been worth. Dollar cost averaging can really cut your risk. Michael lost money, but he didn't lose his shirt.

YEAR AFTER YEAR, IT GETS BETTER

Michael is investing here for the long term, not just for a year, and this fund is not going to stay down forever. Let's take dollar cost averaging through another year.

Let's say the market starts to rally, as it always does sooner or later, and he keeps putting in the $750 every month. Since the market is going up, by the end of the year he has been able to buy 685 shares, fewer than the year before; the fund ends up the year at $15 a share.

In total, he has put in $18,000 over the two years, in a fund that started at $15 and ended at $15 but was considerably down in between. He now owns a total of 1,450 shares, 765 from the first year and 685 from the second. But since the market was down so much of the time, what's the best you think Michael can hope for—that he broke even? He did better than that. At $15 a share his total shares are worth $21,750, which is a 21.7 percent gain on his money over the two years of market fluctuation. Not bad, huh? If you're not going to be cashing out for years to come, the more shares you accumulate the better. When the market does skyrocket, you will have made very good money.

This is not to say that if you buy stock that starts to go up, you should be sad—but here is a no-lose case, because you win in the end with a downslide as well. With dollar cost averaging you don't lose as much as you could have if you had invested in one lump sum just before the market goes down. If the market goes straight up from the time you started, you won't make as much, either. In my opinion, this is a really safe way to take risks—the best of both worlds.

TAKE THE LONG VIEW

Michael also wasn't trusting the principle that time creates money. The first thing you need to know about investing is that there has never, in the history of the stock market, been a ten-year period during which stocks have not out-performed every other investment out there, regardless of the day that you invested. Even if you had invested in a variety of stocks the day before the October 19, 1987, crash, when the market went down five-hundred points, ten years later—had you left the money alone—

you would have made far more than with any other investment. At forty, Michael had twenty-five years for the money to grow before he would turn sixty-five, well more than the ten it generally takes to watch your money really grow. I am always thrilled for myself and others when the market goes down and we have money available to buy more shares. The best investment advice I could give Michael was to go back into the 401(k) and take that $750 he wants to put into it every month. But this time he should diversify the money among two or three other good funds in the plan, be patient, and wait for time to touch his money.

This kind of investing is being respectful to what you have and respectful to what you want to have. It is not going out on a financial limb or taking a gamble with everything you have.

But you also have to watch over those things that whittle away at the money you want to create. You must also be respectful to the money you don't have.

DEBT

Your money is governed by how you treat it; it's that simple. It thrives when you are being responsible, respectful, and doing honorable things with it. For many of us, debt is too big a part of our overall money picture not to give it the respect that it is due. How we treat our debt and the people who are a part of that debt plays a major role in our path to financial freedom.

HAVE THE CREDIT CARD COMPANIES SEDUCED YOU?

Credit card companies are very smart and seductive, and they know exactly what to do to get you deeper and deeper into trouble. Have you ever noticed, for example, if you're one of the many among us who are susceptible to credit card debt, that you find that as your balance keeps creeping up and up, your "available credit" total keeps going down and down? Then, right before you have used up your total credit limit, all of a sudden, without even asking for it, you get a letter in the mail, saying that because you're such a great customer, they're raising your credit limit by $2,000. What a great company! With financial "friends" like this, who needs enemies? Before you even know it, you've used up that extra $2,000 limit, and you're in more debt than ever before. Not to worry. Those magic credit genies will extend your limit again, just in the nick of time. You are a great customer!

BREAKING THE CREDIT CARD HABIT

Credit cards can be as addictive and destructive as hard drugs, with the same ability to create a false sense of euphoria, give you a quick fix by satisfying temporary desires. Drugs are different in one respect, though. In most cases you have to seek out the drug dealer. Credit card companies seek *you* out. The more you use the cards, the more new cards, with enticing offers and promises, will come your way. In fact, all you have to do now is answer the phone. Credit card companies have taken to the phone lines to call you directly to see if they can get you addicted to what they have to offer.

ARE YOU IN CREDIT CARD TROUBLE?

If you can't pay off your credit card debts right now, today, then you're in credit card trouble, which can erode a solid financial foundation faster than anything. It's true that if you're in credit card trouble, you got yourself there, but it's also true that the credit card companies worked as hard as they could to help you along. I've seen this happen so many times and I've seen the damage debt can cause. If you are in credit card trouble, you have to get out of it—and stay out by learning to avoid credit cards like the plague.

WHAT DEBT FEELS LIKE

Debt feels like the heaviest burden of life. It weighs down your spirits, keeps your mind occupied with your burden, and makes you feel bound—because you are bound.

There are two kinds of debt, personal and institutional. Personal debt is money you owe to a family member, friend, or any other human being. Institutional debt is money you owe to a credit card company, a business, a school, the IRS, a bank, a credit company, and so on. When debts start taking on a life of their own, and start growing faster than you can pay them, the weight of the debt drains everything—the money you're saving for your future, your capacity to save and invest more, your ability to pay the debt as it keeps growing. My friends who are bankruptcy lawyers say that if your credit card debt is equal to your annual salary, you will never be able to get out of debt. You are in essence bankrupt.

FACING THE TRUTH ABOUT DEBT

When people start facing the truth about their finances, they'll often say, "Well, I owe my brother $5,000, but what I'm really worried about is that I owe $8,000 on my credit card bills." But I've seen money destroy personal relationships so many times, and I know what loaning money to, or borrowing money from, someone you care about can do to both of you. Remember: *People first, then money.* Personal debt is every bit as important as institutional debt, and I would much rather have a credit card company, with all its resources, tracking me down than watch as my best friend grew more and more resentful the longer I waited to pay her back the money she lent me in good faith and that is long overdue to her.

It's this simple: Whether it's personal or institutional debt or both, you must face your debt head-on. Otherwise the disrespect starts to take root in your soul. Even if you have permission from the person who loaned you money to take your time, it will still weigh heavily on your heart every time you think about it (which will be often) and fail to take action. It will be harder and harder to face people to whom you owe money in person. Remember: *Disrespect repels money.* Not paying your debts is a serious form of disrespect that makes it almost impossible to find new ways to create new money to pay off old debts. Not paying debts will not make them go away; instead, it will make your money vanish, and possibly your friendships, too.

THE RICH *CAN* GET POORER

This was a shocker to me, but the more people I started to see after I opened my practice, the more the numbers spoke for themselves. Most of the people who had major credit card debt were people you would consider affluent. It seemed as if the more money they made, the more disrespect they had for their money.

My associate, Janet, did an informal survey in our area, and out of the sixty people we talked to, all leaders in the community, all of them carried credit card debt. How much debt? Only eleven had debt below $1,000. All the rest had debt ranging from $6,000 to $45,000. When we started asking around among these people if they thought others like them carried debt as well, they all guessed wrong. They would say, "Absolutely not."

All these people made great money and were highly regarded in the community. Credit card debt is rarely created out of true need. It fills up, even if just for a moment, something else that is missing. If you hide it from others, as these people did, and believe you're alone in your debt, you create a secret as burdensome as the debt itself.

THAT SECRET CREDIT CARD

Another scenario that plays itself out often is when one spouse or partner has to admit to the other that he or she is hiding debt, usually credit card debt, from the other. That secret Visa card with the growing balance. The department store bill on which you keep paying the minimum balance due, but that never seems to go down. The big check you wrote against your Optima card and haven't been able to pay off. Cash advances here, cash advances there. You just sort of don't tell your partner for a while, and then it's too late to tell.

This terrible secret is a burden to you, if you're carrying it, and it's an unfair burden on your partner, who, if you share expenses together, is unconsciously also carrying the debt. Debts can't be kept secret forever. I've had blowups in my office. More than once I've heard, "Oh, so that's the secret. I thought maybe you were having an affair." Responses to the news vary. Some couples decide to deal with it together, some feel that the person who created the debt has to deal with it. But even if there's a blowup, the result of letting that secret out is always a relationship that's truer and more honest.

Please tell your partner if you're hiding debt. Your integrity and self-respect are more important than whether your partner gets mad at you. Get help if you need it. You're not alone. Non-profit credit counseling bureaus have been set up all over the country to help in cases just like yours; call one if you feel you need one. You can get out of debt. So many others have, and you can, too—and once you do, you'll create so much more money, without being drained by your debt and your secrets.

THE FIFTH LAW OF FINANCIAL FREEDOM:
You and Your Money Must Keep Good Company

In life we are very much influenced by the company we keep. If you have surrounded yourself with people who are healthy, eat well, exercise, and are well balanced, chances are good that you yourself live a vigorous and healthy life. If you surround yourself with people who drink, smoke, take drugs, and so on, I would venture to guess that your vitality level is not so high.

It works the same way with your money; the only way to keep it vital and make it grow is to keep it in a healthy environment. Credit card companies are never good company to keep, unless you've chosen one wisely, use it sparingly, for convenience, and pay it off in full every month, with only the rarest exceptions. Being respectful of your money also means being respectful of those to whom you owe money, and being respectful to yourself also means getting out of debt—as fast and efficiently as possible.

HOW CREDIT COMPANIES WORK

CARYN'S STORY

Caryn tried everything to get out of debt. But the credit card companies kept winning.

Every time I start to make a dent on my credit cards, something happens, and boom, I'm right back charged to the max. It's hard to move $15,000 of debt. For a while I was putting the odd $100 into a savings account and just paying off the minimum, but then I noticed that sometimes my finance charges were bigger than the amount I was putting away. So that was losing money. Before I save any more, I just want to get rid of this debt. It hasn't helped that my back is bad again, making it hard to work. Since I couldn't work, I decided to figure out everything there is to know about credit cards, all the fine print, and at least get the best deal I could. I had about five different cards, all with different interest rates, and I got obsessed—with getting a better rate, a bigger grace period, with all the new offers. I figured that some have to be better than others, right?

But it is hard to tell what's the best deal. They charge every which way. One card sent me a bill saying, hey, you can skip this month's payment. I thought they were doing me a big favor, but no. They charged interest on the money I should have paid. When the bill came the next month, it had grown by two finance charges. If I had known, I would have paid the money the first month. One time I thought I found a really good deal—5.9 percent. Turned out it was 5.9 percent on the balances I had transferred, but much higher on cash advances and new purchases. I would have been better off staying with the company that charged me 9.9 percent on everything. Then there was that so-called grace period. I learned the hard way there, too. I thought that no matter what I bought I would have twenty-five days to pay it off before I was charged interest on it. I was out with a friend and she wanted to buy an anniversary gift for her parents—we were at an art fair and she saw this wonderful sculpture she wanted to buy for them. She didn't have her credit card with her, so I said I'd use mine and she could write me a check and I'd just pay the bill when it came. Done. When I got the bill, I couldn't believe it. They began charging me interest on that sculpture the day we bought it. But they had told me there was a grace period. When I called them up they said no grace period for me because I carry a balance. Only if I paid off the card every month could I have the grace period. Also, no grace period on cash advances; I found that out the hard way, too. Cash advances cost the highest interest rate, plus a fee on top of that—about 5 percent of the amount I withdrew just for withdrawing it. I hadn't even thought of that. So I went back and checked. Already this year I had paid $220 in fees for cash advances.

I guess it's all there, in small type, but who can figure it out? How do you get out of credit card debt?

There's nothing like credit card debt to paralyze us. The sad part is that most of us don't have a clue how the cards we have really work. When you were reading Caryn's story, did you already know as much as she had found out about how the cards work? Probably not. The only thing most of us pay attention to is the interest rate they are charging us, and even then some of us don't take any action. Even though we know there are credit cards at lesser rates, we just don't want to deal with it. Grace periods, average daily balances, the forms we might have to fill out . . . most people would rather keep paying 18 percent or more just so they don't have to deal with it.

Throwing away hundreds of dollars in unnecessary interest payments every year is truly being disrespectful of your money. Caryn was so close to getting the formula right that I told her simply to keep obsessing about it—and acting on what she learned. She has, and little by little she is erasing her debt. She has also become something of a crusader and is starting a business creating a newsletter to keep people up-to-date on all the rates and scams: all she wishes she had known about before.

WHEN YOU SHOULD SWITCH CARDS

Credit cards really want your business, and if you're a heavy user, with good credit history, they will make it very easy for you to switch to the card they're offering. Caryn had discovered that you can switch your balance to an account with a lower (much lower) interest rate with a few phone calls and five minutes of paperwork.

And continued vigilance.

Too-good-to-be-true offers are usually just that: too good to be true. Open and read every credit card offer you receive in the mail. Ask and answer for yourself all the questions that follow. It may be that you have to roll over your debt two or three times a year to get the best deals. That's a few calls and fifteen minutes of paperwork a year, and it might save you literally hundreds of dollars. When can you stop being so vigilant? When your debt is gone and you've taken the steps to guarantee it won't go back up again.

WHAT YOU MUST KNOW ABOUT YOUR CREDIT CARDS

If you spend just a few minutes working on your debt as hard as you work on your job, you'll at least create intelligent debt—debt at the lowest possible cost. You'll also become aware of what you really owe, freeing up the paralysis you feel dealing with it. And with your knowledge, you'll be facing your debt from a position of power, instead of one of weakness. The credit card companies are expecting you to behave a certain way—to be ignorant of the real costs of your debt and too lazy to change it. They want your money. You have got to want your money more than they do, or they'll get it.

If you currently have a credit card or are considering a new card, here is what you need to know.

Which of the Two Methods Do They Use to Charge Interest?

One of the hidden costs of a credit card may be the way in which it computes interest.

The first—and the better way by far for you—is to charge interest on the average daily balance, including new purchases. The second method, which is much less favorable, is the two-cycle average daily balance, including new purchases. Even if you never carry a balance from month to month, keep away from a company that calculates interest this way. You never know when even you might need some emergency money for a few months, and this is an expensive way to get it. Always leave yourself the best option just in case.

Let's say you charge $1,000 on your credit card for that CD player you always wanted. Even though you have the money in your savings account, you think, Well, I might as well get those airline miles, or I might as well just use my credit card and pay it off when the bill comes in. When the bill arrives you're a little short, but you send in $980 against the $1,000 bill, thinking that a $20 balance is no big deal. Next month when your statement arrives, even though you haven't charged anything else, you see that you now owe $47.60, $20 from the previous balance and interest of $27.60. How can that be? It's because your credit card uses the two-month average daily balance method. Not so good, if you ask me.

If, on the other hand, your credit card charged interest on the average daily balance, you would have seen a bill for only $32.60—not chopped liver, but certainly better than $47.60. This represents a $20 carryover from the previous balance and $12.60 in interest: about 54 percent in interest savings. This can really add up if you charge and pay off more than $1,000 at a time. Of course, the numbers will vary depending on the interest rate you're paying and other factors, but no matter what, you must avoid the two-cycle method, especially if you tend to charge and just pay off your balance two months later.

What Is the Minimum Percentage That Is Required to Be Paid Every Month?

The answer to this will vary from 1.5 percent of your balance to up to 4 percent. Here, for once, you want the figure to be higher, rather than lower, because the lower your required payment, as the credit card companies well know, the longer it will take you to pay off the debt.

In fact, it is essential that you pay more than the minimum each month. (We'll talk about why later in this chapter.) But the higher the minimum is, the better.

If You Carry a Balance, Is There a Grace Period on New Purchases?

Most cards will charge you interest as soon as you make a purchase if you carry a balance, but there is one card I know of that does not, so keep your eyes peeled for others.

What Is the Cash Advance Fee Charge, and What Interest Rate Applies to Cash Advances?

This is where these companies can get you big-time. Even if your introductory rate is 5.9 percent, if you take out a cash advance, regardless of whether or not you owe a balance, many companies charge 2.5 percent (give or take) of the amount of each cash advance, up to a maximum fee of $20. Some cards will charge you less for cash advances or tell you to use the convenience checks they supply, but you have to ask, because many companies charge those exorbitantly high interest rates even when you use their convenience checks. "Convenient" for them.

Is There an Annual Fee?

The only acceptable answer is no.

Am I Penalized If I Don't Carry a Balance?

Most credit cards make their money three ways: from the interest you pay; from annual fees, if applicable; and from the discount they get from every merchant who charges them for the privilege of letting customers use their card. You would think this would be enough. Some credit card companies, however, are beginning to sneak in a little extra fee to those customers who don't carry a balance from one month to the next—the responsible customers. G.E. Capital, for instance, charges $25 to any customers who don't pay at least $25 in interest over the course of the year.

Because more and more people are defaulting on consumer loans (credit cards, home equity, and car loans), these companies are beginning to scramble to think of new ways to charge you.

Read all the tiny print every month, and watch for any undesirable changes in policy. When you spot one, switch cards.

Then there are the essential questions: What is the current interest rate? How long will this rate last? What does the interest rate go up to after the introductory period?

So many credit card companies are competing for your money that many very low introductory rates are offered. Again, you need to scrutinize them carefully—sometimes the rates for balance transfers and cash advances are higher. And their introductory rate may jump by 10 percent or more after a few months. Obviously you want the card with the lowest introductory rate, and the longer the low rate lasts, the better. In any case, you don't want a card whose normal rate is above 10 percent.

Take a look at the table that follows and you will see how much more you will pay and how much longer you will pay with higher interest rates. If you have a $4,000 credit card balance and are paying $100 every month:

AT THIS INTEREST RATE	IT WILL TAKE YOU THIS LONG TO PAY	AND YOU'LL PAY THIS MUCH IN INTEREST
5.9%	45 MONTHS	$465
7.9%	47 MONTHS	$658
9.9%	49 MONTHS	$874
12.9%	53 MONTHS	$1,257
15.9%	58 MONTHS	$1,736
18.9%	63 MONTHS	$2,362

GETTING CONTROL OF YOUR DEBT

First thing: All credit cards must be cut up! If you are not willing to do this right now, it's a sign that you need some serious help. It means that you still don't understand the implications of having debt of this kind—and that you are still being disrespectful to yourself and to your money.

People are often afraid not to carry credit cards, and if you feel this way, carry one for emergencies by all means, but lower the credit available to you by calling the company and asking them to lower it—a simple phone call. Pick the amount of credit you would like to have in case of an emergency ($500 or $1,000), and ask them to set it there. Or carry an American Express card, the one they offer that must be paid off in full every month or they'll be all over you like a cheap suit. You wouldn't stock the kitchen with cookies if you were dieting, would you? Why keep credit around that you don't need and don't want to use, if the temptation might get you into trouble?

TAKING STOCK

Now is the time to sit down with your debt, study your statements, face what you owe, and see what they're charging you to owe it.

Make a list of all the money you owe in descending order, starting with the highest interest charges first. List as well the phone number of everyone you owe money to. Please include personal debt. Debt is debt, and just because most personal debt doesn't inspire the fear of most corporate debt, on the scale of self-respect it weighs in pound for pound. List the amount you owe, the interest rate, the minimum monthly payment, and how they charge you this interest payment (average daily or two-cycle average daily). For example:

CREDITOR	BALANCE OWED	INTEREST RATE	PAYMENT	CYCLE
DEPT. STORE	$4,320	21%	$180	AVG. DAILY
VISA	$6,300	18.9%	$200	2-CYCLE
DEPT. STORE	$3,100	16.9%	$100	2-CYCLE
OPTIMA	$4,000	7.9%	$120	AVG. DAILY
MOM	$5,000	0	0	

If you're late with any of these payments, personal or institutional, call them up now and tell them why. All the entities to whom you owe money already know that you don't have the money to pay the bill or you would have, so don't be embarrassed. With your new truth from Step 3 in hand, pick up the phone and call. You're in debt, that's all. You're not a failure or a bad person. If someone is rude to you, be very kind and gentle in return. Explain your situation. It might be that you're late but will have the money in two weeks. Or it might be that you can only send them $25. In any case, call them before they call you.

If you're not late with your payments, call up the high-interest credit card companies anyway, tell them you're considering switching to a better value card, and see if they'll match a lower rate. You can negotiate with them, and often they will reduce your interest rate right on the spot. If they won't make good on your request, move the balance to a card that meets the criteria just discussed. If what they will agree to is not as good a deal as you can get elsewhere, you're out of there.

Offers keep changing from company to company, so keep up-to-date on the best offers by checking a current issue of *Smart Money* magazine (http://www.smartmoney.com) or *Kiplinger's* magazine (website http://www.kiplinger.com). You can also check via the Internet site www.bankrate.com or via my own website www.suzeorman.com in the Resources section.

If you have a blemish on your credit record, try to clean that up before you start switching companies. Credit card companies don't like it even if you've been just one payment late, and for that reason alone a better company could turn you down.

DIGGING YOURSELF OUT OF CREDIT CARD DEBT

If you're in big credit card trouble, don't panic. But you can get out of it, a step—or a month—at a time. I have found that most people are not aware of how very important it is to pay more than the minimum. Let's say you owe an average balance of $1,100 on a card that charges 18.5 percent interest. If you pay the minimum 1.7 percent every month, and you never charge another thing, it will take you twelve years and six months to pay off your debt. It will have cost you $2,480.94 in interest.

Same situation, but if instead you had paid $10 more than the minimum each month, you would have cut the payment period down to six years and cut the total interest payments to $676.37. That is a savings in interest of $1,805.57. Ten dollars a month is only thirty-five cents a day.

Remember, with many cards, the more you owe the longer it will take you. I have seen cases where just paying the minimum every month would mean that the debt would take forty years to pay off, to say nothing of the thousands and thousands in interest it would cost you.

Let's assume that you owe $4,000, which is the average credit card debt in this country, and see what a difference a few bucks will make at different interest rates. Once I showed my clients this chart, they began to see what a difference a little more money each month can really make.

ANNUAL % RATE	MONTHLY PAYMENT	DEBT PAID OFF	TOTAL INT. PAID
5.9%	$100	45 Months	$465
5.9%	$110	40 Months	$417
5.9%	$150	29 Months	$298
5.9%	$200	22 Months	$221
7.9%	$100	47 Months	$658
7.9%	$110	42 Months	$587
7.9%	$150	30 Months	$413
7.9%	$200	22 Months	$303

ANNUAL % RATE	MONTHLY PAYMENT	DEBT PAID OFF	TOTAL INT. PAID
9.9%	$100	49 Months	$874
9.9%	$110	44 Months	$775
9.9%	$150	31 Months	$536
9.9%	$200	21 Months	$389
12.9%	$100	53 Months	$1,257
12.9%	$110	47 Months	$1,101
12.9%	$150	32 Months	$739
12.9%	$200	23 Months	$528
15.9%	$100	58 Months	$1,736
15.9%	$110	50 Months	$1,494
15.9%	$150	34 Months	$968
15.9%	$200	24 Months	$678
18.9%	$100	63 Months	$2,362
18.9%	$110	54 Months	$1,986
18.9%	$150	35 Months	$1,229
18.9%	$200	25 Months	$842

A STEP-BY-STEP PLAN

These are the steps that many people, including quite a number of my former clients, have taken to get out of debt. You can do it, too.

1. Figure out the absolute largest amount you can afford to pay monthly toward your credit cards. Let's say that amount is $600 a month. You may think this is a lot, but when you carry a lot of debt on at least several different cards, this is probably not much less than what all your payments add up to.

2. Review the list of creditors you made up and total the cost of the minimum monthly payments, *plus $10,* for each of

them. If the minimum payment on one card is $150, write down $160, and so on; then take the total of those figures.

3. Subtract this total from the number you wrote down in step 1. Let's say the minimum payment plus $10 for all of your credit cards is $400. You've decided that in fact you can pay $600 a month toward eradicating the debt. Subtract the $400 you must pay from the $600 you can pay, and this leaves you with $200 extra to pay on your credit cards.

4. Now take the "extra" $200 and put it monthly toward the credit card that is charging the highest interest rate. When that card is paid off, call the company and close the account.

5. Now you start all over. Stick with $600 a month (unless you can raise it!) as your debt-paying allocation. Total all the minimum payments of your remaining cards, adding on $10 to each card. Let's say that this figure is now $300 a month. Subtract this from the $600 you have allocated a month, leaving $300. Pay that $300 to the card that is now charging you the highest interest rate. When this card is paid off, call up the company and cancel it and start all over again with the third card.

WATCHING YOUR DEBT GO DOWN

This whole process may take months or it may take years, but with each payment you will be closer to becoming debt free, at which time you'll be free to pay yourself more and more. Look at the statements each time carefully, keep transferring accounts for the best interest rate deals as necessary, and take pleasure and pride each time the amount due is smaller. With each payment you are that much closer to financial freedom.

BORROWING FROM YOUR 401(K)

You may be able to borrow from yourself to pay off your credit cards through your 401(k) plan at work. Many employers will let you borrow up to 50 percent of the money you have in your plan, up to $50,000, to buy a house or pay off bills or for other situations that qualify. Be careful in doing this, however, the supposed upside is that when you borrow money from a 401(k), you have five years to pay back the money (rather than the forty years it could take you by paying the minimum on some credit cards). In addition, the interest you pay goes right back to yourself—that's right. It's your money, you've borrowed it from yourself, and you're paying it back directly into your account; all the payments plus interest go to you. Usually you will pay yourself about 2 percent above the prime rate, which is the basic interest rate set by the government.

But the realistic downside is this: when you borrow money from your 401(k), you are losing out on the growth potential of the money. So it's a decision to be made cautiously and wisely.

Another consideration is that if you take out a loan on your 401(k), you are in essence paying back money that you have never paid taxes on with money you have paid taxes on, and then, when you go to take the money out sometime in the future, you will have to pay taxes on it again. That really makes no sense. So you really have to think about this carefully before you take out a loan from a 401(k). Not only are you losing growth on this money, but you are subjecting yourself to double taxation.

Another prospective downside is that if you happen to leave the job or get fired, the money you borrowed is due in one lump sum at that time. If you can't pay it back, you'll pay taxes on the money as if it were ordinary income; if you're under the age of fifty-five, you may also have to pay a 10 percent penalty on the amount you haven't paid back. If you are thinking of taking out a loan, and there is a possibility you may leave your current employer, you might want to reconsider your situation before you take out the loan; make sure you understand what you would have to do if you were to leave your job.

HOME EQUITY LOANS TO PAY OFF CREDIT CARDS

Another alternative, if you're really in credit card trouble, is to take out a *home equity loan* to pay off your debt. A home equity loan can have its advantages. The loan may be at a lower interest rate than your credit card, and often that interest is tax-deductible, so you'll have converted a high-interest, non-tax-deductible debt to one that has lower interest and is probably tax-deductible.

The amount of money that you can take out of your home with this kind of loan is based on a percentage of the equity that you have in your home. Equity is the difference between what your house is worth and how much you owe on your mortgage. In other words, if your house is worth $200,000 and you have a mortgage of $150,000, it means that you have about $50,000 equity in your home.

Can you then take out a $50,000 home equity loan? No, most banks will let you borrow a total of only 80 percent of the value of your house, including all current mortgages. If your house is worth $200,000, 80 percent of its value is $160,000. Subtract the $150,000 you owe on the first mortgage, and this gives you the amount you can get on a home equity loan if you qualify: in this case, $10,000.

PRIVATE MORTGAGE INSURANCE

Some lenders will let you take out more than this conventional 80 percent, but if you do, it can turn out to be quite costly.

Most mortgage companies that lend more than 80 percent will make you pay what is called *private mortgage insurance,* or *PMI,* which will add quite a bit to the loan—so it's best if you can stick to the straight 80 percent loans, which after all are based on what lenders think you can comfortably afford.

EQUITY LINE OF CREDIT

Another option is an equity line of credit, which enables you to borrow money as you need it against your house. Rather than a fixed interest rate, an equity line of credit usually has a rate that varies according to what interest rates are doing. Also, the payback period is not set—so be sure you're very disciplined if you consider this alternative. With this type of loan you do not have to pay back principal each month if you don't want to. You can just pay the interest if it better meets your needs. A home equity loan, on the other hand, works pretty much like a regular mortgage. You can get a fixed interest rate and pay back the loan over a fixed period of time, usually from five to fifteen years.

WHICH IS BETTER: BORROWING FROM MY 401(K) OR A HOME EQUITY LOAN?

Before we compare the numbers, think about whether you are disciplined or not—it may have been lack of discipline in most cases that got you into all this debt to begin with. With a 401(k) loan you don't have a choice. You have to pay back the loan in five years. Home equity loans, on the other hand, can go on for up to fifteen years. So you have to make sure that you don't let the loan drag on for fifteen years, that you stick to a maximum payback period of five years, just as you would with a 401(k) loan. If you will agree with yourself to do this, and if the interest rate is favorable compared to your credit card's interest rate, I would say in general that a home equity loan would be better.

Now let's look at the economics.

401(K) LOAN FEES VS. HOME EQUITY LOAN FEES

With a 401(k) loan, fees are variable: some employers will charge you for taking out the loan and some won't. Some make you pay a fee of up to $100 just to fill out the paperwork, and some charge a yearly fee while the loan is outstanding. The same is true of home equity loans: some can be gotten for no fees except for an appraisal on your home ($200–$350), and some will charge you fees up front to get the loan or do the paperwork, which can add another $100 or $200 to the bill. But if you look carefully, you should be able to find a home equity loan that can be gotten for no fees, no points, and a very small appraisal fee, if any.

With both kinds of loans, the application process is usually fairly easy. You may have to fill out a form, or you may be able to do it over the phone. However, loans from either source take time to process, so if you're desperate, ask your employer or lender how long each loan will take to process and when you will you have the money in hand.

Who Decides What Investment My 401(k) Will Come From?

If you take out a 401(k) loan, it will depend on your company's policy who decides which investments get sold. Some let you decide; others decide for you. Ask about how this works in your company. If you do have a choice, and if you have some of your money in a bond fund within your 401(k) plan, take your loan from that fund. Your equity funds will still have their full potential for growth, and since a bond fund is mainly giving you income anyway, it makes the most sense to take it from there.

Which Is Better?

This is a bottom-line decision. Consider the following chart:

	401(K) LOAN	HOME EQUITY LOAN
TAX-DEDUCTIBLE	NO	USUALLY
PAYBACK PERIOD	5 YEARS	5–15 YEARS
SUBJECT TO INCOME TAX IF NOT PAID BACK	YES	POSSIBLY
DUE/PAYABLE IF YOU LEAVE CURRENT EMPLOYER	YES	NO
GIVING UP POTENTIAL GROWTH	YES	NO
DOUBLE TAXATION ON PAYBACK	YES	NO

Now consider the actual numbers. Let's examine what it means to borrow $10,000 at 9 percent interest (assuming a 28 percent tax bracket). In both scenarios the payback period is five years.

	401(K)	HOME EQUITY LOAN
MONTHLY PAYMENT	$208	$208
NUMBER OF PAYMENTS	60	60
TOTAL PAID	$12,455	$12,455
TOTAL INTEREST PAID	$2,455	$2,455
TAX SAVINGS (AT 28%)	0	$687

On the face of it, the home equity loan looks better than borrowing from your 401(k). But there's one other consideration: What happens if over these five years the money in your 401(k) goes down rather than up?

At What Rate of Return Is the 401(k) Better?

Since we can't predict the odds of the market, all we can do is play them. And the odds still fall pretty much in favor of a home equity loan. An 8 to 10 percent tax-deductible home equity loan usually works out better as long as your money in the 401(k) does not earn more than 6 to 8 percent. The variation here depends upon how large this loan is, how much you are paying for your home equity loan, how much you would have paid for borrowing from your 401(k), what the market is doing, and what tax bracket you are in. Make sure you take your information to a financial type and work out numbers for yourself to make sure.

Remember, however, that this isn't a triumph of economics or a windfall. You are borrowing from Peter to pay Paul, and sadly enough, you are both Peter and Paul. This money is debt, debt to help you get out of worse debt.

CONSUMER CREDIT COUNSELING SERVICE

Even worse, you may feel that you are in a situation that is totally out of your control. Maybe you do not have a 401(k) to borrow from or you cannot take out a home equity loan. Maybe the creditors are calling you at home or at work all the time. Your interest rates are sky high. You've tried to negotiate a lower interest rate with your creditors. (I always urge people to call their creditors and try to negotiate a lower rate; it often works.) But your creditors have said no, because your credit report is not the best. When you are at your wit's end, you might want to check out a nonprofit organization that has been set up to help educate you on your money and at the same time, set up a payment plan with you so that all of your cards will be paid off within five years at most.

My favorite of them all is a group known as National Foundation for Credit Counseling (NFCC, formerly known as CCCS, or Consumer Credit Counseling Service). To find the office nearest you, please call 1-800-388-2227 or visit www.NFCC.org. Other companies, such as Debt Counselors of America, offer similar programs; it would be wise for you to check out these kinds of programs.

This is how they work: You hand over all your credit cards to them, and for about ten dollars a month, you will pay them one check and then they will pay your creditors for you. Most likely they will be able to get you a lower interest rate on your cards than what you are currently paying. They can do that because they have deals with many of the credit card companies themselves, so that they are able to negotiate a better interest rate with your current cards than you are able to. In fact, it is the credit card companies that help to fund most of these kinds of companies, for they believe that it is better to get some of their money back rather than none at all. Many people take advantage of organizations such as the NFCC, but they do have their drawbacks as well.

Below is an interview with Caryn Dickman, who is the woman in our story here and one of the heads of a local NFCC office. Please read it carefully; it will help you answer many of the questions that you may have about NFCC.

CD: Can you talk to us a little about what a debt management program is?

NFCC: A debt management program is when we negotiate with the creditors to reduce the interest rates or to eliminate them altogether. A lot of creditors, because they're going through NFCC, will go ahead and completely eliminate the interest rates. This is really great. In other words, if I, as Joe Consumer, were to call the creditors and say "Let me work out a payment arrangement"—sometimes what they'll do is say, "Okay, fine, we can do that and we'll lower your payment, but your account is going to continue to age." So you're constantly going to be behind. Most of the time when going through NFCC, you don't have a problem because we negotiate that by saying we don't want any of this in arrears, we don't want the person to be continually showing as behind. I want them brought up-to-date as of today. When we sign the contract, I want the interest rates either eliminated or reduced and this is what we do. Sometimes we have to get nasty with creditors.

CD: Then does the client pay NFCC every month or can they continue to pay themselves?

NFCC: Well, what happens is they give us the money; they're not actually paying us, they're actually giving us the money and we put it in a trust account. And it sits in the trust account until Thursday of every week. We make payments on Friday mornings. And we usually do it by ACH, so it's automatic. What we're also offering our clients now is, if they're comfortable with it, we're taking the money directly out of their accounts so they don't have to send in payments, they don't have to worry about going to the cash machine and getting their ATM swiped or anything else.

CD: In that respect, when you get a credit report it would say that the accounts are being paid by NFCC?

NFCC: A credit report will never show us because we don't report to the credit report agencies. Everything we do is confidential. It is between us and the client.

CD: What about the company that's owed money?

NFCC: Right. Now what the creditors will do sometimes is that they will put a line in the credit report saying paid through a NFCC. The reason why it's a good thing when this happens is because we really don't want the client to accumulate any more debt. And sometimes what will happen is, because somebody's habits haven't changed and their skills haven't developed yet, they will go and try to get more credit. In that case, having this line on their credit report is good because they know not to give them any more credit until it's paid off.

CD: And when it's all completed, then if they do want to reapply for credit, can they get it? These are the kinds of things that keep people from wanting to use your servces; they're afraid that they won't be able to ever get credit again.

NFCC: If they choose to reapply, that's not a problem. We have a pool of creditors that we work with that actually want to give credit back to our clients.

CD: My question is what is the point at which you advise people to go bankrupt?

NFCC: There is a point and quite frankly, sometimes—we never say you have to go bankrupt. What we do say is you may want to contact a lawyer; that is one of your options. Another one is that you can fight your way out of this situation and we can also show you how to do that.

Basically what happens is if somebody can't meet the basic living expenses, forget about the debts. If they can't pay the rent and they can't afford food and they can't manage their fixed expenses, then that's when we say to them you're going to have to look into some other way of taking care of this, because there's not enough money here to make it even with our recommendations. We try to explore all options like having people move in with their families. Maybe that's not even an option. Maybe there's just no other way. That's when we'll say it's time to go ahead and see a lawyer.

Sometimes, however, I have had clients say that's absolutely not acceptable. And I say, fine, let's figure out another way of doing this. Let's figure out how I can help you and what I can do. There are tons and tons of jobs available right now. Are you willing to work two jobs? Are you willing to go and get some training so that you can get a better paying job? We have this huge referral book and our counselors are really well trained—some of them have been doing this for years, so they know what's available.

CD: Is the training free?

NFCC: Sometimes it's free; it depends on the situation. If somebody, for example, is on welfare right now, we know we can go through the county and help them get the training for free. If they've been downsized, there is usually a way we can figure out how to get it for free or at a very low cost.

CD: Maybe we should talk a little bit about the fees.

NFCC: Sure. All the classes are free. The educational material is free. The counseling session is free. For the debt management plan, it's $0 to $20 and it depends on your debt load. It is 6.5 percent of your debt up to the maximum, which is $20. You'll never be charged more than $20. However, let's say you're in that situation where you just don't have anything left over; we're just not going to charge you. Obviously we want to get you onto the program; sorry, you're going to need $20 more a month—I mean that's just ridiculous. So what we try to do is keep it as low as possible. I think the average is $15 a month, which is a little bit higher than last year and that's only because people's debts have increased. We've seen debts increase. Last year the average was about $18,000 and this year it's $24,000.

CD: Another question I wanted to ask is how is coming to NFCC different from collection agencies?

NFCC: Collection agencies work for the creditor. We're working for the client. That's the biggest difference. And basically what we do is we're not trying to get the creditor's money back. That's not our purpose. Our purpose is to help you by giving you the tools that you need in order to gain control so that you can sleep at night, so that eventually you can start saving money, so that you can get out of debt, so that you can have an emergency fund, so that you don't have to constantly be worrying about this same problem over and over again. A collection agency's primary purpose is to get money back; they don't care how it's done.

CD: Who pays them?

NFCC: They get paid by the creditor. What happens is most organizations have their own internal collection agency. And basically the way they work is that they're paid a salary, for example, $24,000. Then, of course, they get commissions on top of that $24,000. So they get paid by collecting money from you. The more they collect, obviously, the more money they make.

CD: Okay, so when you go to a creditor and you say you have a client who wants to pay it off, just get rid of all the interest, why would they choose to let that happen as opposed to letting their own collection people go after them?

NFCC: Well, because a lot of times what happens is their own collection people have tried and failed. That's usually what happens. Basically, there are a couple of reasons why. One is that our program has been more successful than their collection departments. The reason why it's generally been more successful is because we're on the clients' side. Also the creditor would rather get some money back than none at all. Many people come here distraught; they're at that point where they're on the verge of bankruptcy. Also, we do get money from the creditors. About 75 percent of our funding does come from creditor contributions. But please remember they are contributions. We're not getting paid. It's also cheaper for them to use a nonprofit organization because it's tax deductible and it's voluntary. They have to pay their employees; that's not an option.

A question I hear fairly often is "Is this going to go on my credit report?" And basically the answer is it's up to your creditor. Usually it's that line that says paying through NFCC. Is that negative? Some people look at it as negative and some people think of it as something positive because you're doing something about it and taking control.

CD: Another question you must get a lot is "When I walk in here are you going to rip up all my credit cards?"

NFCC: When you walk in here, no. If you choose to go on the debt management program, then what we will ask you to do is cut up all your credit cards.

CD: Every single one of them?

NFCC: Every single one of them. However, if you have your own business or if you have an emergency or there may be an exception, sometimes we let you keep one.

CD: What is the average amount of time that people stay on the program?

NFCC: Basically, we don't like people to be on the program for more than five years. We want to get them out of debt in five years. That's our goal. The average length of time is three and a half years with an average debt load of $22,000.

CD: I keep coming back to this question. How long does the fact that someone has been using NFCC stay on their credit report?

NFCC: Generally, things stay on your credit report for seven years. Now what we have done is with those creditors that work with us, they are usually really great about just going ahead and taking it off and showing it as a zero balance and that's it.

CD: How often do you have "repeat offenders"?

NFCC: The rate is not high. Unfortunately, we don't have solid numbers. What I really find is the number-one reason why people have so much debt is because they don't have the skills or they didn't implement them. So, in other words, they're not tracking where their money is going. They don't have a spending plan. And they don't have their goals. It's like they're driving around and they've got no map and they have no idea where they're going. You need to do all this planning and preparation.

AFTER THE DEBT

Once out of debt, you'll find the pleasure of not creating debt far exceeds the momentary thrill of buying something on credit that you really don't need, can't afford, and won't really care about much beyond the time you get it home. What is more, all the money you've been pouring into interest charges can now go instead toward creating wealth, investing in yourself and your future.

FOUND MONEY

If you saw a quarter on the street, would you stoop to pick it up? Of course you would—we all would. Would you throw a dollar on the street for someone else to pick up? I doubt it. Yet without even knowing it, you may be throwing away hundreds or thousands of dollars in found money for you and your future just by the way you're dealing with your financial life.

Most people try to set up their lives for convenience, to make things easy. But easy can be costly. Respecting yourself and your money means wanting to put every penny you can to work for you. Respect attracts money, remember? You might have "found money" right now, a few hundred dollars a year here, a few hundred there, or more. Wouldn't you like to find it? You can if you are just willing to look. If you're willing to rearrange the pieces of your financial life just a little, you'll be able to see the solution to the puzzle—and find the money.

YOU MUST LET YOUR MONEY EARN THE HIGHEST WAGES POSSIBLE

ROB'S STORY

"I suppose I could be making more money on my money," said Rob. "I guess I'm just too lazy to figure out how."

I do work in landscape design and make pretty good money at it. Last year I made about $60,000. I'm getting better at the building side of it—making walls, building arbors—so this year I should do even better, maybe $70,000 or $75,000. But the money I earn is seasonal. Maybe in February, someone will come and ask me to design something, so that's when it starts. I'm busy all through the summer and into the fall. By Thanksgiving I'm usually through, then a few months of downtime. The thing is, all my money comes in all during the season for me to live on all year. I pay taxes, I put some into a SEP-IRA, but the rest is just in my checking account. This way, I can always see exactly what I have. I've got about $10,000 in there now, and just got my first call about next season, so I'll

have enough. I know that $10,000 should be earning more
than 2 percent interest, but I haven't taken the time to figure
out how.

You and your money must keep good company, remember? If
there is a company, bank, brokerage firm, credit union,
mutual funds company, or anywhere else that's offering you a
higher interest rate or lower fees than where you are currently
keeping your checking or savings account, it is your duty to
yourself to transfer your money into a higher-paying account.
You put time and energy into finding the lowest rates for your
credit cards, right? That same kind of energy needs to go into
finding the highest rates for your cash. Going through Rob's
checking account statements for one year showed me that for
four months during that year he had $45,000, give or take, in
his checking account. Talk about throwing dollars on the
street! During those four months alone, had he kept the bulk
of his money in a money-market account earning, say, 5 percent (and these accounts often earn more), his money would
have earned $750. Over the course of the year he was losing
much more.

Rob's case is unusual, in that his money is seasonal, but not
unique—I've had plenty of clients who receive bonus money,
sizable tax refunds, and big checks and simply deposit them
into their checking accounts, or savings accounts where the
interest isn't all that much better, then just leave it all there until
it dwindles away. I also have had clients who keep a lot of
money in their savings accounts so that they'll have free checking at the same bank, when they could be making much more if
they moved their savings to a money-market fund. By saving
the checking fees, they are giving up much more that their
money could be earning for them elsewhere. And I have had

clients who keep huge balances in checking accounts, just "so they can see their money at a glance."

I tell them what I told Rob: You can see your money just as well in a money-market account. There, you'll also see it grow.

WHAT I LEARNED FROM MY RICH CLIENTS

Money-market funds were still a new concept when I first became a broker at Merrill Lynch, whose money-market fund was (still is) called their *CMA account—cash management account.* You could open the account with $20,000 minimum, but after the account was opened, you could keep whatever you wanted in it and still keep the privileges of the account. Those privileges were many. The first was that the account paid the going interest rate—around 18 percent at that time, in 1980; comparatively, most banks at that time paid no interest at all on checking accounts. You could write as many checks as you wanted per month and were given a debit card as well; you could withdraw from your account through any bank in the world: no fuss, no checks necessary, no fees for these withdrawals. This was great for travelers, who didn't have to tie up interest-earning money by withdrawing large sums of cash or traveler's checks.

If you wanted, you could also use this account as a catch-all for other investments you wanted to make or already had. For instance, let's say you happened to own XYZ stock, which you kept in your safety-deposit box and which sent you dividends in the mail every three months. Most likely that dividend check sat around the house for at least a few days until you either mailed it to the bank or took it there to deposit it. Probably this process took one or two weeks or more. If you had held those shares of XYZ stock in your CMA account instead, the dividend would automatically have been deposited directly into your account the day it was issued and would have begun earning the 18 percent interest at once, or you could have withdrawn it at once.

Merrill Lynch charged a yearly fee of $100 for operating the account. But even with that fee you came out way ahead of the game. Back then, most banks not only paid no interest, but also charged a service fee of $10 a month, which sometimes went higher if you wrote a lot of checks. Thus the service fee alone would be $20 a year more than Merrill was charging for its CMA account, with all those privileges. Most people would have made far more on 18 percent interest than the $100 to do so cost them.

Money-market accounts still work more or less this way. But back then they were still new. To inspire us to sign up clients for the CMA accounts, Merrill Lynch held a contest among all of us brokers: Whoever opened the most CMA accounts would win a trip to Hawaii. They had to offer us something, because it was not to our advantage if clients opened a CMA account—we received no commissions on them. We made money only if our clients bought or sold stocks or bonds or the other investments Merrill offered.

I didn't win the contest, but I tried to. As I was working on my tan-to-be, though, I learned something about human nature. Those of my clients who had tons of money opened one of these accounts as soon as they heard about it. Those people who weren't as rich, but who still easily had the $20,000 to open the account, all said, No, I don't think so. They said they felt safer with their money where it was. They all would have picked up that quarter from the sidewalk, I'm sure, but even when I showed them the hundreds or thousands of dollars they were leaving on the sidewalk, so to speak, they refused to pick it up.

ASK YOURSELF THESE QUESTIONS ABOUT YOUR MONEY

Your money needs to be in the holding place where it will earn the most it can for you; it's that simple. Otherwise, like Rob, you could be losing thousands of dollars a year.

So wherever your money is now, ask yourself the following questions—and if you don't know the answers, find out:

❧ How much is the money in your checking and savings accounts earning?

❧ How much do they charge you for your checks or as a service fee?

Now you need to find out whether you can get a higher interest rate somewhere else, whether you can be charged less in fees, and whether you can establish an account that is just as safe and just as convenient. The answer is probably yes.

MONEY-MARKET ACCOUNTS

A *money-market account* can be had through a bank, a full-service brokerage firm, a discount brokerage firm, a mutual funds company, or through a credit union. It works like a bank account. You keep your money there, can write checks against it; there are various restrictions, but you can always find a money-market account to suit you. When you put your money into a money-market account, you are buying shares in a money-market investment fund. The share price does not fluctuate in value, the way it does with stocks or mutual funds. Money-market shares are priced at $1 a share. How is a money-market account different from a bank account? In the interest it pays, which can add up to more—sometimes far, far more—than you'd get from almost any checking or savings account, as well as the ways in which the money is protected.

One of the main reasons many of my clients back then were nervous about opening a money-market account is that the funds aren't insured by the Federal Deposit Insurance Corporation (FDIC). Even so, funds in a money-market fund are extremely safe. Essentially, every money-market fund has a manager who oversees the money that people like you and me deposit into the fund and lends it out to different entities—the federal government, state governments, or various large institutions or corporations. These are all short-term loans, usually for about thirty days, and they have a nice interest rate attached to them. Because the payback is so quick, the risks are minimal, and as soon as these loans are paid back into the fund with the interest, that interest is passed on to you.

Treasury Money-Market Account

If you still feel uneasy with the idea of money-market accounts, you might consider money-markets that invest (which is to say lend) all their money in U.S. Treasury bills. Treasury bills are guaranteed and backed by the full credit of the government, which means that if the government can't pay back the money when it is due, they will be forced to raise taxes to do so. When I was training to be a broker—and this still holds—the only time I was allowed to use the word "guaranteed" was when I was talking about a U.S. Treasury bill, note, or bond. In short, even though these kinds of money-market accounts are not insured by the FDIC, they are backed by the taxing authority of the U.S. government, which in my opinion is certainly as safe as, if not safer than, FDIC insurance. U.S. Treasury money-market accounts will not pay as much in interest as regular money-market accounts, but you will still do better than you will with most savings accounts.

Other Money-Market Accounts

These include tax-free money-market accounts and those that invest in U.S. government–backed securities (which are backed not by the taxing authority of the government, but by its moral obligation). Again, not as safe as FDIC-insured money, but to my mind not worth splitting nickels over. In any case, there is definitely a money-market account to match your level of risk tolerance.

Where There's a Will, There's a Way

Another reason many people were reluctant to think they couldn't take advantage of a money-market account is that they thought they didn't have enough money to open one or that they wouldn't always have the minimum it takes to keep one open. Not necessarily the case. Many funds don't require all that much to open them, don't charge high fees if your balance drops, and don't require a minimum balance. They're smart. They know that just by opening the account, you're on your way.

When I first became a broker, most of—in fact, all—my clients had far more money than I did. It felt funny to me sitting there, with my $2,000 of Macy's credit card debt hanging over me, telling people what to do with their money. But I decided that since they had so much more than I did, I should listen to them as much as advise them. My dad always said, "Suze, when in doubt, do what someone who is successful does." So when this CMA account came along, and I had never seen so many rich people jump on something so fast, I thought, Okay, I need to get myself one, too.

But who had $20,000? None of my friends did, but when I told them about the account, they all wanted one as much as I did. So we came up with a scheme. We needed $20,000 to open the account (today you can find other great ones for far less, as noted on page 221), so we decided to pool all our money to come up with about $1,000 more than the minimum needed. First one person would take all the money to open an account, then one week later withdraw all but maybe $100 (once opened, there's no minimum balance, remember?). Then the next person would do the same thing, and so it went, all the way down the line. When the last person had her account, all the money was given back to its rightful owners and deposited into our correlating money-market accounts.

We were all so proud. Most of us had gone in with about $3,000, and we knew that the $100 fee was nothing to pay to get all the advantages and the 18 percent interest rate back in 1980. Most of us still came out $440 ahead that year, and that was a lot of money. (If I had known better back then I would have had everyone sign a promissory note or some documentation showing what belonged to whom, in case something happened to the one who had all the money.)

Determining the Best Money-Market Account

Here are the questions to ask to determine the best money-market account for you:

⇥ *What is the minimum deposit I need to open up the account?* You can open a great account for about a $5,000 minimum.

⇥ *What is the minimum balance, if any, required to keep it open?* "None" is the answer you want to hear.

⇥ *What is the yearly fee to have this account?* The answer should be "Nothing."

⇥ *Does this amount apply even if I drop my balance down to $1?* "Yes" would be a great answer, but if the answer is "No," the fees should not cost more than $60 a year.

⇥ *Am I required to purchase securities in order to maintain the account? If I don't plan to do so, will you charge me a fee eventually?* Some money-market accounts require you to make a transaction—buying a stock, buying into a mutual fund—in order to maintain the account or at least to maintain it for free if you don't keep your balance above the minimum amount needed. Others don't. This is not a big deal and may encourage you to test the investment waters (page 243), but if it makes you uncomfortable, the answer you want to hear is "No."

⇥ *Do you issue a debit card?*

⇥ *Do you issue an ATM card?* The answers should be "Yes," or that you can use your debit card at ATMs.

⇥ *Are there fees if I use the ATM card?* If so, they should be not more than a few dollars per transaction.

⇥ *Is there a maximum number of checks I can write every month?* There shouldn't be.

⇥ *Is there a minimum amount for which checks can be written?* The answer should be "No."

⇥ *Do you return my canceled checks or simply send me an itemized statement every month?* Either way is okay, but most will just send you an itemized statement.

⇥ *At the end of the year, do you give me a summary of every check I've written?* "Yes" is the answer you want.

⇥ *What interest rate are you currently paying, or what is your seven-day yield, or the amount in interest they have paid for the past week?* The higher the better.

⇥ *How do you credit this interest?* "Daily" is the answer you want to hear.

Where Is the Best Place to Open a Money-Market Account?

My favorite place to establish a money-market account is at a discount brokerage firm, but many discount firms don't like it if you write more than fifteen checks a month; some, on the other hand, could not care less. If you write more than fifteen checks each month, you may find that it is just as cost-effective to keep your checking account where it is and to move only your savings to a money-market account. There may be other rules governing the account—minimum balance, minimum you can write checks for—so keep your needs in mind and ask the questions just listed before you set up the account.

Almost every major brokerage firm, including the discount brokerage firms like Etrade or Charles Schwab, offer a money-market account. Usually the difference between an account at a full-service firm like Merrill Lynch and a discount firm is the minimum needed to set up the account and the amount of the yearly fee they charge to keep the account. At Schwab you can set up a money-market account for $5,000. If you keep $5,000 in the account at all times, it's free; otherwise they'll charge you $5 a month, or $60 a year, unless you make two commissioned trades in the year, in which case there's no fee. This is better than an account at a full-service broker, which has an entry fee of $20,000 and charges $100 a year.

Yearly Fees

One hundred dollars a year might not seem like much— under $10 a month. But if you're in your early thirties and open your account at a discount brokerage firm, saving that annual fee year after year will pay off big. If you keep your savings in there for fifty-five years just growing and growing, that savings of $100 a year at a rate of return of 8 percent will grow to $84,892.32. From just $100 a year.

A quarter on the sidewalk here, $84,892.32 there . . . it's all the same principle. Money creates money, if you house it well and give it time to grow.

FOUND MONEY: OTHER SOURCES

There are lots of other ways we leave quarters on the sidewalk. Here are ways to pick up that found money.

PAY TAXES QUARTERLY RATHER THAN MONTHLY

If you are self-employed or retired and getting a pension check, did you know you don't have to have taxes taken out of your checks each and every month? The interest that this tax money could earn could be about $100 or $200 a year, which invested yearly over forty years at 8 percent could net between $25,906 and $51,811.

If you can, pay your taxes by using an estimated tax payment schedule, which means that four times a year (April 15, June 15, September 15, January 15) you need to send in an installment payment of the taxes that you will owe. Here, too, you have a choice. In these four installments you need to send either 100 percent of what last year's tax liability was, or 90 percent of what this year's is projected to be. For 2002 estimated payments, you will have to pay in 112 percent of the 2001 liability, or 90 percent of what this year's is projected to be. For 2003 and later, it goes back to 110 percent. (States all have their own rules for estimated taxes, so it would be wise to check.) You would naturally choose to send in whichever was less.

Let's say last year you owed $8,000 in taxes, but this year you took a large sum of money from your retirement plan and, as a result, you will owe about $18,000 in taxes. Your choice is to send in 100 percent of last year's taxes, which totaled $8,000, over those four installments at $2,000 each, or pay 90 percent of what you expect this year's tax liability to be—in this case 90 percent of $18,000 = $16,200.

Who wants to part with money, particularly to the IRS, before they have to? You would pay the $8,000 on time, in four installments of $2,000 each, and keep the remaining $8,200 you owe in a money-market or interest-bearing account of some kind. Instead of letting the IRS earn interest on your money, you're doing it. And it can add up to a nice sum.

PAY OFF YOUR THIRTY-YEAR MORTGAGE IN FIFTEEN YEARS

Let's say that you buy a house with a thirty-year mortgage of $150,000 at 8 percent. You will be scheduled to make 360 payments of $1,093.35, paying a total of $393,606 by the time your house is paid for. That interest can sure add up, to the tune of $243,606, over time. However, if you pay off this thirty-year mortgage in fifteen years, you will pay far less in interest. Your payments would be higher, $1,423.98 a month rather than $1,093.35, but since you would be paying them for only half the time, you would have shelled out a total of $256,316 to own your house free and clear, or $137,290 less than if you did it over a thirty-year period of time. That's quite a savings.

If this is something you're thinking about doing, please make sure you consult a financial professional. There are other factors to consider—the present tax deduction on the interest from a primary-residence mortgage; what the $330.63 difference in monthly payments would add up to if you invested it well instead (and whether you would be disciplined enough to do it). This is an emotional decision, too, as well as a financial one: if you bought a house with a thirty-year mortgage at age forty, how would you feel knowing that those monthly payments would cease when you were fifty-five? Or when you were seventy?

Several other options are available to you as well. Sending in one extra mortgage payment per year, for example, and specifying that it be used against the principal will start to reduce a thirty-year mortgage. If you do this, it will reduce a thirty-year mortgage to twenty-two years and a fifteen-year to twelve, depending on your interest rate. Beware, however, of banks that offer to do this service for you (deduct from your account bimothly) and charge a one-time $300 fee. You can accomplish the same goal by simply sending in an extra payment.

DON'T APPLY FOR A THIRTY-YEAR MORTGAGE WHEN YOU INTEND TO PAY IT OFF IN FIFTEEN YEARS

Did you know the interest on a thirty-year mortgage is usually higher than the interest on a fifteen-year mortgage? The 8 percent you're paying for your thirty-year mortgage in the previous example would most likely have been only 7.75 percent, or .25 percent less, if you had applied for a fifteen-year mortgage to begin with.

You need to give thought to this before you apply for your mortgage. If you are planning to pay it off in fifteen years, why would you apply for a thirty-year mortgage in the first place, the way so many people do? For a safety net, right? You figure that if money gets tight, you can always go back to paying it off with less expensive monthly payments over a longer period of time.

Your safety net, based on the difference between 7.75 percent and 8 percent, is costing you $21 a month, which at 8 percent interest adds up to $7,093 over the course of the fifteen years. Another way of looking at it is that you've just left 28,372 quarters on the street.

DON'T HAVE THE MORTGAGE COMPANY WITHHOLD YOUR PROPERTY TAXES AND INSURANCE PAYMENTS—PAY THEM YOURSELF WHEN THEY COME DUE

Wasn't it nice when you signed up for your mortgage and the lender said, "Why don't we just go ahead and add your property taxes and insurance to the bill every month, and we'll pay it all for you?" Sure it was nice. For them.

Property taxes and insurance both come due twice a year, but by saving yourself the hassle of writing four simple checks a year, you're paying them every single month—and losing out on the interest the money could be earning. It is not farfetched to think you could have earned $240 a year on the interest from your insurance and property taxes. Let's say you did. Over forty years (which is about how long people really pay mortgages, by buying a house, selling it, buying another house, and starting the mortgage process all over again) at 8 percent, you could be paying your bank $62,173 in lost interest and earnings just to be your personal secretary and write those four checks for you. Over thirty years you could have lost out on $20,187; over fifteen years, $6,517. And if you're carrying two mortgages, your savings will more than double.

DON'T PAY CREDIT CARD FEES WHEN YOU DO NOT HAVE TO

The fees are usually $25 a year, and you're thinking that it would be a hassle to switch credit card companies, and anyway, $25 a year is not that big a deal. How long do you plan to have your credit card? Probably for the rest of your life, let's say until you're eighty-five. At 8 percent interest that $25 will add up to $6,476 if you're forty-five today; $14,344 if you're thirty-five today; and $31,330 if you're twenty-five today. To me, that's found money.

DON'T PAY FULL-SERVICE COMMISSIONS WHEN YOU CAN GET WHAT YOU WANT FOR LESS

Often I encounter people who tell their brokers exactly what to buy or sell, yet they are still paying full-service commissions on their trades. When I ask them why they don't switch to a discount broker, the answer is usually: "Well, we're settled where we are, so why change?" Or, "Well, he's a great guy." (Or, "He's done so well for us," which is curious, since they're the ones making all the decisions!) Even if you're forty-five right now, if you save just $300 a year on commissions and invest the money at 8 percent over the next forty years, that adds up to $77,717. Will you still be making investments in forty years? If you're alive, you will. Are you sure you like your broker that much?

NEVER BUY A LOADED MUTUAL FUND WHEN YOU COULD BUY A NO-LOAD FUND

Let's say all you ever invest is $2,000 a year in an IRA, and you put that money in a loaded mutual fund with a 5 percent commission. (The difference between loaded and no-load funds is explained in Step 6.) Five percent of $2,000 a year is $100. If you start your IRA at the age of twenty-five, by the time you turn sixty-five that $100 that you did not need to spend invested at 8 percent a year would have added up to $25,905. It seems to me that the one who will eventually be loaded is that broker who is selling everyone these funds.

By the way, this calculation does not include the charges incurred every time you sell the loaded fund you've invested in in order to buy another one. If you were to do this just once every ten years for the next thirty years, assuming that your funds grew at the rate of 10 percent, you will have paid another $15,593 in commissions on just the principal, not including the $25,905 you could be saving on those commissions. Over $40,000, and you did not think it was such a big deal?

DON'T PAY A $25 ANNUAL FEE FOR YOUR IRA

If you start an IRA at twenty-five and keep it until you're eighty-five invested at 8 percent, that little fee will add up to $31,330. (For investments with no annual fees, see page 252.)

USE SELF-SERVICE GAS PUMPS RATHER THAN FULL-SERVE

Next time you pull up to the gas pump and say "Fill it up," think what it's costing you over time, at today's gas prices, to spend that extra $.18 or $.25 a gallon.

If you drive enough to fill up your car once a week, at $.18 a gallon for a full tank of eighteen gallons, the difference is $13 a month; at $.25 a gallon the difference is $19 a month. No big deal? Over forty years the $.18 a gallon would have earned, at 8 percent, $41,894; at $.25 it would have earned $58,007. Isn't it worth it to get out of the car and pump your own gas?

USE COINS, NOT YOUR CALLING CARD, IN PAY PHONES

One convenience call per day can cost you dearly. You're out and about and you need to make a call. There's a pay phone. You punch in the number of the person you're calling, then you punch in your convenient calling card code. No big deal. Who wants to carry around a lot of change anyway? Seventy-five cents a day, the average calling card charge, over forty years will cost you at that 8 percent $74,746. Isn't it better to pick up the quarter?

DON'T GET A TAX REFUND AT THE END OF THE TAX YEAR

Would you lend me, every year for the next thirty years, a few thousand bucks interest free?

Well then, why would you make that loan interest free every year to the IRS?

This drives me crazy. Every year at tax time I used to get a few new clients all excited because they had just gotten their refund back from the IRS. Well, they could have begun investing it months before and, on a $4,000 refund, could have already earned a good bit of interest. The IRS takes your money, but know that it doesn't give any back with interest—these refunds have been earning interest for the IRS, not for you. Make sure you send them your fair share of taxes when they're due, but not a penny more. No refund is what you want. Let your money work for you instead.

ON BECOMING RESPECTFUL

When someone says to me, "Oh, I don't know, I guess I just don't really care about money," I always say, "But if you don't care more about your money than anyone else, who is caring about it on your behalf?" When someone else says, "Well, I just don't think about money," I say the same thing: "But if you don't think about your own money, who will? You must think and care about your money until you've taken the necessary steps to know that you have done everything you can to show respect for your money, which is a way to show respect for yourself." Then your money will think and care about you in return.

That's what this step has been about: respect.

With this step, the path to financial freedom is coming into view. You're almost there, you're on course. Now you can clear out the debt that's cluttered up your present and weights you down in fear. The future looks clearer, too, now, doesn't it? Now you can see that you can create enough for tomorrow once you've acted today. You have to count every penny to make every penny count. When you have done that, you can begin to create money, more and more money.

Respect for your money and respect for yourself are linked. Building one builds the other. With the next step, you will learn how much you already know deep inside you. We all have a wisdom within us that will tell us, if we listen, how to act, with our money and with every other aspect of our lives. To get in touch with that voice from the core of our being is not only a step toward financial freedom. It's also a step toward spiritual serenity. That they go hand in hand is not as curious as it may seem at first glance. When you can create money, you are suddenly free to live a life rich in all kinds of ways.

STEP 6

TRUSTING YOURSELF
MORE THAN YOU
TRUST OTHERS

WHEN I WAS A STOCKBROKER, it never ceased to amaze me that when I could buy the exact same stocks for my clients, some would always make money and some would never make money.

When brokers find stocks they like, they try to do what is called *building a position* in the stock—buying lots of it for their clients. For instance, if I liked widget stock, I'd call every single client I had to tell them all about widgets.

Then I'd say: "How many shares would you like, five hundred or one thousand?" I was taught in stockbroker training school never to ask a "yes" or "no" question when trying to make a sale. By asking whether clients want five hundred or one thousand shares, you leave the client only with a choice of how many they want, not whether they want them.

I was a good salesperson, so most of my clients would buy widgets at, let's say, $85 a share. Now let's suppose all of a sudden Widget cuts its dividend, and before you know it, the stock is down to $40 a share—and my phone begins ringing off the hook. Some people would invariably say, "Sell, sell, I don't want to lose more than half my money!" In those cases I had no choice but to sell their stock. Some of my other clients, in for a longer haul, even though they might not have been happy that the stock was down to $40, still knew that this was a good company and that in time it could come back. Often they would buy more shares at the lower price. Before you knew it, widgets were at $120 a share. All of my clients had bought the same stock. Some had made money, and some had lost it. By the way, if you think I'm exaggerating the way stocks move, I'm not. Something very much like this happened with IBM.

It also worked the other way around. Let's say this time I was building a position in lobster pots, and all my clients bought it at $6 a share; before long, it went up to $12 a share. Big increase. I'd call my clients and some would say, "Okay, sell it," and others would say, "Let me think about it," then call back to say, "No, let's see if it will go a little higher." All of a sudden something happened and the stock fell, to $4 a share. All the people who didn't want to sell it at $12 now got frightened and sold at a loss.

Over the years I started to notice that the people who lost money in either of these ways were always the same ones. They'd sell too soon or too late, but they always lost money. In the business, we called them clients with the "kiss of death" when it came to their investments.

It bothered me when my clients lost money, and I began to think more about it. Finally I realized that it wasn't a matter of luck, but a matter of, well, spirit, for lack of a better word. It was the attitude, the instinct, with which the client went into an investment that helped to determine whether he or she would make money or lose money. Of course there are good investments and bad investments. But however solid the investment, the investor has to be solidly behind his or her investment as well.

I began to see, too, that the questions I had been taught to ask as a broker worked very well for me—I was rich in commissions—but often worked less well for my clients. I changed my approach. I began really talking to my clients about how they felt about investing in the stock market in the first place. The ones who invariably lost money said that it made them nervous, that they didn't like it. I asked them why then they invested in stocks, when there were so many other excellent places to put their money, and their answer changed my life: "Because you told me to, Suze." They were trusting me more than they trusted themselves.

From then on, my heart just wasn't into selling stocks the way it had been. I can date the beginning of my financial advisory practice from the moment I asked my first client, then the second and third, how they felt about buying a stock, rather than asking whether they wanted five hundred or one thousand shares. If there was any hesitation whatsoever, I began to suggest that clients pass. I suggested that they pay attention to that little voice inside them, because what it was telling them was what was right for them to do. In 1987 I left the corporate brokerage world to start my own firm, where I could really give advice that was good for my clients, not just good for me. Now I give advice in my books that is good for anyone with financial concerns.

THE SIXTH LAW OF FINANCIAL FREEDOM:
Inner Trust First, Then Outward Action

There are many ways the universe offers us guidance to protect ourselves, but we usually just turn our backs on this guidance because we don't recognize it as such. The little voice inside you is actually a powerful signal—I believe it's the voice of God—and if you listen to it, and take action based on what it tells you to do, it will keep you safe and sound. This sixth step to financial freedom is about finding that voice inside you—and learning to listen to what it has to say.

FEELING YOUR FINANCIAL PULSE

JANET'S STORY

It was Janet's first time ever buying a stock, and she just felt it was right. So why did she end up listening to everyone else?

I got this discount broker and told him to buy me one thousand shares of Atari. When I hung up the phone, I felt terrific about placing this order. Atari was around $4 a share, and I had read these articles about how they had all these great things going for them—and I have to admit I loved playing those games on the TV set when they first came out. I just thought, Go for it. I had this extra money that I was saving to invest, and I was so excited. I told all my friends before I did this, and everyone tried to talk me out of it, even this one adviser friend I have who said, "I wouldn't do that if I were you." But I went with my gut feeling.

Within two weeks the stock was at $8! I couldn't believe it; I had doubled my money. When my friends heard this—of course I called them all up—they were so sorry they didn't listen to me. In fact, a few of them decided that maybe it would go up more and bought some. Even my adviser friend started to buy it for his clients. It stayed at $8 for a little, and then I started to get this feeling that I should sell. So I called my adviser friend again—why, I do not know—and asked what he thought. He had just bought it at $8 for all his clients, and what could he think? That it would go up some more. I stayed for a few more days but still feeling I should get out. It went down to $7, but everyone kept saying not to worry, they would announce a deal or something and it would go through the roof. My husband needed a new car, and I kept thinking, Well, just cash in, we'll have enough for a car. But I didn't. To make a long story short, Atari did announce this new deal, and before I knew it, back it was at $4. So why did I end up listening to everyone else?

If Janet had listened to that voice in her gut, she would have doubled her money. If her friends had listened to their own voices inside them, they wouldn't have lost money. If her adviser friend had listened to *his* own inner voice, he wouldn't have lost money for his clients and himself, if he had invested, too, although it's worth knowing that many advisers don't have the money to invest in their own advice, nor are they obliged to. That little voice inside each of these people, perhaps dozens of people all told, was trying to protect them. None of them trusted themselves more than they trusted others. As a result, they all lost.

YOUR EXERCISE

Remember how, when taking multiple-choice tests, you would read the question and, without any hesitation, choose answer A? Then you would start to doubt yourself and begin to think that maybe the correct answer was D. You'd change your answer to D, even though your gut feeling was still A. You'd be wrong. When the test came back, you'd see that you were right the first time. The correct answer was A.

When it comes to every financial decision you will make for the rest of your life, you will choose correctly if you go with the answer that reflects your instinctual response. That answer will always be the right answer for you, the answer that will empower you to make money for yourself.

Please go into a quiet room by yourself. Sit there for a moment in silence—no TV, CD player, phone, children. Place your hand exactly on that part of your gut that tells you when you're nervous about anything; you know the place. As you contemplate the following scenarios, take careful note of your very first response, how nervous or confident you feel about each answer that comes to you right away, before you start to rethink it. You should begin to see how you feel emotionally about investing and about planning for your future and how much you trust yourself.

⇥ Your best friend, who's smart but has never been known for financial expertise, comes to you all excited. He's heard about this up-and-coming technology stock from another friend of his: a sure bet, he says, a once-in-a-lifetime thing. He's investing everything he has, and he just knows he'll see a payback in a month. Would you like to join him?

⇥ You've helped your sister find a new apartment. The rent is fairly high, and because she's just out of college, the landlord wants you to cosign the lease. Would this be a good idea?

⇥ Your parents just gave you one thousand shares of a stock they bought years ago, in a company that has done well for them all this time. Your own financial adviser wants you to sell it and invest in a company she likes better. What would you do?

⇥ Your company has just put into place a 401(k) plan for the first time, and you're presented with choices about how you want to invest your money—conservatively, with a modest but guaranteed return; or aggressively, with higher-risk investments but a greater chance for real growth. You must decide by tomorrow.

⇥ You are self-employed and you have all your retirement money in a SEP-IRA in a respectable mutual fund. You read in the newspapers that the manager of your fund, which has done well for you, is leaving the company under mysterious circumstances and starting up another fund of his own. The stories seem to suggest that maybe you should transfer the money to this new fund. What do you think?

⇥ Your new brother-in-law is a financial adviser, and a successful one at that. Your money is doing well in a mutual fund, but he says he can make it do better by playing the stock market, if you trust him with it.

⇥ You are offered a job with a new company that's just starting up, and you like the people a lot. The salary is about the same as you're making now, with room to grow as they do, but you wouldn't be getting all the benefits you have with your present company—no 401(k), no insurance. You feel there's such energy behind these people, and they really want you. But you're old enough that you are really beginning to think seriously about the future, and you also feel safe where you are. What should you do?

There are no right answers to these questions and no wrong answers. Instead, the exercise is about getting in touch with your inner voice so that you can begin to listen, really listen, to what it has to say, because this voice will tell you what's right for you to do. All the brilliantly conducted research in the world about an investment, all the enthusiasm and salesmanship of a broker, all the hype in the press about this company or that one, none of it means a thing if the pure voice inside you says it's wrong for you to do. You are far better off taking no action than taking an action that feels wrong to you. Sure, it's fine to ask around and learn what others are doing, but to be able to act upon what your own feelings and thoughts tell you to do is a priceless gift that only you can give yourself. This kind of power comes from trusting yourself more than you trust others.

HOW IT FEELS TO BE A STOCKBROKER

There are some great brokers out there as well as some who aren't so great, but if you're in awe of brokers (who now often call themselves financial advisers, figuring, I guess, that broker isn't the most confidence-inspiring title), or if you believe you can't possibly take any investment action without one, I want you to know how it feels from the other side. I was a very good stockbroker, but I had no mystical insights, no inside sources, no information I could learn that you couldn't learn, too. And a good many brokers out there probably feel like the Wizard of Oz hiding behind his curtain. It can be a scary business, investing other people's money.

There is not one adviser out there who wants to lose money for you, I can promise you that. The good ones would probably rather make more money for you than they do for themselves. It's also true that financial advisers are real live human beings with feelings, insecurities, bills to pay, dreams of their own, pride, and ego.

Imagine the pressure. Most people don't want to deal with their own money, so try to think how it feels to be responsible for dozens of other people's money, their livelihood, their futures. Think how an adviser feels if she recommends an investment to you that she can't afford to invest in herself. Is she telling you the right thing to do? Think how she feels if she's also investing in the stock herself—will it cloud her judgment? The pressure, particularly if the broker is a caring person, can lead to what I call the jitters, which is not a good state in which to make important financial decisions.

The jitters occur when raw nerves take over and important decisions about money, which after all are decisions about people's lives, are made from fear and nervousness, rather than from that pure inner voice and true knowledge.

Suppose an adviser has built a tremendous position in XYZ stock. As he sits at his computer terminal, he watches every time XYZ moves up and he watches every time XYZ moves down. With every tick down, his phone rings and it is a client asking about XYZ; with every tick up, he awaits the next tick down, he gets jittery; the notion hits him that maybe it's time to sell.

Now he starts punching in the symbol of that stock over and over again to get more detailed information than what the screen normally tells him. He watches the volume: What do others who are selling know that he doesn't know? He looks at the bid, the ask, the research reports. What do they really mean? He calls a few of his friends who also have a position in the stock, to see what they think. Even if none of these people had been thinking sell, even if they reply, "Well, I really still like the stock," something happens. Doubt has a domino effect; I've seen it.

Meantime the supervisor walks by to remind the adviser, who works on commission, that he hasn't met his sales quota this quarter. To do so, he must buy some more stocks on his clients' behalf or sell some more. Then his wife calls. They need a new furnace. Then the woman at the next screen starts jumping around with joy—another stock she has built a position in has just gone through the ceiling. She begins making excited calls to tell her clients the great news. Then our adviser hears a tick and looks at the screen: XYZ is down another one-half point.

After a few hours of this, the adviser makes the decision, calls his clients, and sells the stock. End of jitters? No way; now the real test begins. If the stock starts rising, the phone begins ringing with clients wanting to know why he sold so soon. It's almost harder not making as much as could have been made in a stock than it is to lose some and feel relief at not having lost everything. The whole experience goes into our adviser's jittery memory bank and is automatically recalled the next time he thinks about buying or selling.

It takes an extraordinarily disciplined person to overcome these jitters and to make continually intelligent decisions based on his or her pure inner voice and what can be learned about a stock. It takes even more discipline to believe what you know when the jitters of other people who happen to own the same stock as you are spreading through a brokerage firm like the flu.

If you decide you want to go with a broker, fine. If you already have a wonderful broker who has so far done very well for you, even better. Best of all is if you decide to handle your own money and feel powerful and confident about doing so. In any case, though, it is your money—and it must be guided by what your inner voice tells you to do.

TESTING YOURSELF, TRUSTING YOURSELF

YOUR EXERCISE

With most of us, decisions come, decisions go—we make them and deal with the consequences when we have to. But we all make decisions about our lives, financial and otherwise, all the time: What kind of a car do I think I should buy? When do I think I should buy it? Where should I send my child to school? What color should I paint the bedroom? Do I really want to go to dinner at the Wentworths' on Saturday night, with such a busy week ahead and my proposal due at work on Monday? Is such-and-such an issue worth the fight it's going to cause if I bring it up with my partner? Might this or that stock that I keep reading about be a good stock to buy?

Such decisions come up every day, and always that inner voice is there to guide us in making them wisely—if we let that voice have its say. When these decisions come up, I am asking you now to start keeping track of them: What was the decision that had to be made? What did your inner voice, your first instinctual response, tell you to do? What did you actually do? Please write down the answers and keep them wherever you keep the monthly bills. Now see how the decisions played themselves out, depending on whether or not you followed your voice. Should you have painted your bedroom that ivory, which was your first impulse, instead of the yellow? Should you have bought a new car when you knew you should have, before the old one collapsed for good? Did the stock you were thinking about in fact go up? Didn't you really know deep down inside that little Jenna would be better off at a school that was less competitive?

You will see the results for yourself. Testing your voice will enable you to trust it. It's your voice, and when you begin to take action based on what you yourself truly believe, you'll begin to feel power over your life—and over your money.

DO YOU HAVE WHAT IT TAKES TO DEAL WITH YOUR MONEY YOURSELF?

When I started as a stockbroker, the financial world was quite different from the way it is today—and it's still changing fast. You might think that this means it's all the more important to have a financial adviser, or a Certified Financial Planner® professional like me, look after your money for you, but the opposite is true. The changes in the financial world are actually making it much, much easier, and much, much safer, for individual investors to invest and look after their own money.

When I first started out at Merrill Lynch, money-market accounts were just beginning. Mutual funds numbered in the low hundreds and hadn't yet been embraced by a wide range of investors, much less changed the way millions of us now invest for our futures. Discounted ways to invest were just starting, which meant that the most common way into the stock market was through a full-service company like mine. With a full-service brokerage firm you're paying full-service prices: you're paying for their real estate, their overhead, their business lunches, their advertising, their commissions on all kinds of brokers. These firms are reputable, certainly, and once you read the rest of this chapter about the language and workings of investment, you may even decide that the way you wish to be respectful to yourself and your money is to have an adviser at a full-service firm, fees notwithstanding. As for the discount firms, they're thriving. Why? Because smart consumers always flock to where they'll get the best deals for their money. On their way, they stop to study what they're buying and where they're buying it.

THE LANGUAGE OF MONEY

Do you play tennis? If so, you've had to learn a few new terms and concepts to play the game—set point, double fault, and so on. If you play golf, same thing—par and eagle. To cook, you need to learn about basting, sautéing, reductions.

There's also a language of money, and by the time you finish this book you will know it.

If you have ten years or longer before you need your money, you *must* invest, whether in your 401(k) or on your own. And the more you invest, the better. After you finish reading this section, by trusting yourself, you will know which kinds of investments are right for you. Those investments don't have to be in the stock market; you can invest in Treasury notes and bonds or in your house. You can decide whether you want to invest on your own or whether you want to go with an adviser. Again, these are decisions you will reach by trusting yourself.

My own opinion is that most people have more than it takes to invest on their own. If you are computer literate, the information sources on the Web are extensive and accurate. If you've never tried it, I urge you to explore the financial networks on the computer just to see what you can find: chat rooms about investing, message boards where people post investments they've made and how they've done, featured interviews with various managers of good mutual funds, and much more. You can learn a lot this way and, just as important, really begin to feel much more comfortable in the world of money. The point is, you must learn the language of investing and have the knowledge to decide what kind of investing is best for you.

If you don't have a computer, this book will help for

starters, and there are plenty of general-interest money magazines out there. Even the newsweeklies have personal finance columns, and in most cities there are financial shows on the all-talk stations. Eavesdrop on the world and language of money, and pretty soon you'll know you belong.

The price of admission to the world of money is lower than you might think and, especially with the onset of mutual funds, the easiest and safest way to create your own fortune. Here's what they talk about inside.

WHAT IS A MUTUAL FUND?

A mutual fund starts out as a pool of money that many investors just like you have put their money in together—mutually. The manager or managers of the fund take all this money and put it into different investments. The manager is typically the one who decides what he or she wants to buy and sell, based on his or her judgment and the research of many others in the mutual fund company, but sometimes these decisions are made by a team of people.

The goal of each mutual fund is different and, as a result, each fund invests in different kinds of stocks, bonds, or other investments. Some funds invest for long-term growth, some for income, some for a combination of the two. (Growth funds typically invest in stocks of companies that are growing rapidly and whose price per share may increase dramatically in value. Income funds invest in bonds and have a smaller chance of making a lot of money; they generate present-day income—retirees might own these, for example, after they've seen their money grow during their working years.) Some invest in stocks just in the United States; some, those known as international funds, invest only in stocks overseas; funds called global funds invest in both. The variations go on and on, but if you have a specific interest, I guarantee that you can find a mutual fund that addresses it. When you invest in a mutual fund, basically you own a tiny fraction of each share of stock or whatever they've purchased, so even if you own just one mutual fund, your money is still quite diversified, because you own a little of everything they've invested in.

If you had a financial adviser at a full-service brokerage firm like Merrill Lynch, he or she would have to consult you before making any transactions, and you would have to pay a commission almost every time you bought or sold anything. That's not the case in a mutual fund, where the manager has free rein over the money in the fund and you're not charged a commission when transactions are made. You will receive a prospectus and information with a breakdown of what the mutual fund has been up to, but you're not notified day to day. By buying shares in the fund, you have made the decision to trust the fund manager.

A good mutual fund is a great way to invest money, particularly small sums of money: You achieve diversification, commission-free trading within the account, and a professional manager or team of managers who are buying and selling and doing what they think best.

OPEN-END FUNDS

Once a fund starts to do well, the word gets out and it seems as if everyone wants to invest in it. A fund that continues to take on new investors' money and keeps getting larger and larger is known as an *open-end mutual fund*. This means there's no set limit as to how much money the managers will permit to be invested in the fund. At their discretion once they've taken in more money than they feel is manageable, the manager and others in authority may sometimes close the fund to new investors, but this is a decision they can make anytime, as they go along.

How Is an Open-End Fund Priced?

At the end of each day, the manager totals up the entire value of the portfolio that constitutes this mutual fund. He divides that total by how many shares are owned by the investors. This figure, whatever it comes out to, is called the *net asset value,* or *NAV.* It is what each of your shares is worth. If you are a new investor and want to invest $1,000 into this mutual fund, and the NAV that day was $10 a share, you would own one hundred shares of the mutual fund. If the fund's value goes up by $.25 a share, you will make $25. The more shares you have, the more you make—and the more you lose if the fund goes down.

CLOSED-END FUNDS

There is another type of mutual fund, known as a *closed-end fund.* This is where from the very beginning the number of shares that can be sold to the public is decided ahead of time; once the shares are sold, the fund is closed to new business. It won't issue new shares, the way the open-end funds will. New people can buy into a closed-end fund only if someone who owns it wants to sell it. Essentially it's priced and traded just like a stock—so the value of its shares may not correspond exactly to the value of its holdings.

For our purposes here, though, we're dealing with open-end funds. These are the ones you usually hear people talking about, and these are the ones commonly offered in 401(k) and 403(b) retirement plans.

WITH THOUSANDS OF MUTUAL FUNDS AVAILABLE, HOW DO I CHOOSE?

You can buy mutual funds that invest in almost anything you want. Once you decide on your goals, you now have two other choices: Do you buy a managed mutual fund, or do you buy an index fund?

MANAGED FUNDS

A *managed fund* is run by a manager who decides what he or she is going to buy and sell with all the money the investors have deposited into the fund. If you know what kinds of things you'd like to invest in, you find a like-minded manager and choose that fund, if its track record stands up to scrutiny. When you buy a managed fund, you're actually investing in the manager who's in charge of the fund. A good manager buys and sells wisely, so that the NAV or the value of your shares goes up and you make a profit. A mediocre manager could lose you money. Thus it's important to keep track not only of how your fund is going, but also of the manager who's responsible for your return.

Rule of thumb: Before you ever buy a managed mutual fund, look to see how long the manager has been in charge. Is the current manager the one responsible for a fund's good track record, or has that person moved on, leaving someone new in charge? It's the manager's track record you want to know about, in other words, not the fund's, because the manager is the one who creates the fund's success.

A number of publications monitor the funds—how they're doing, who is moving on—but the one I like best is called *Morningstar*. You can subscribe to it directly, find it at the library, or access it on the Web or in the Personal Finance section of America Online.

INDEX FUNDS

When you don't know which mutual fund to buy, and don't want to learn all this stuff about managers, you have a great option: You can buy an index fund.

There are several indexes that track the values in the stock market. You hear about these every day when you listen to the news and constantly hear the newscasters quoting the Dow Jones Industrial Average. You know how they'll say, for instance, "The Dow Jones is up twenty-three points today and closed at 11,000." The Dow Jones average is an index based on thirty stocks. If these thirty stocks happen to go up, so does the Dow Jones average, and if they go down, same thing. I always found it fascinating that so much seems to rest on just thirty stocks, but it's used widely.

To my mind, a far better index, and one that's also widely referred to, is the Standard & Poor's index, the S&P 500. This index tracks five hundred stocks, which is a lot more than thirty, of good-size companies that are traded on the New York Stock Exchange. You will often hear this index quoted right alongside the Dow Jones, and when you do, pay attention. This is also a great index because so many people use it to measure the market—which means that many, many experts are keeping tabs on it every single day.

Another very popular index is the Nasdaq. This index currently tracks about 5,000 different stocks, mainly in the technology area. Since its inception in 1974, The Nasdaq index market has been the industry innovator. It was introduced as the world's first electronic stock market. With the boom and bust of the dotcom stocks, most of you by now have heard of the Nasdaq, and the truth is, as time goes on, you will hear more and more about it.

There are other indexes that track the American and overseas stock markets (as well as indexes that track the bond market, but we are focusing on stocks here); they aren't quoted as much as the Dow Jones, Nasdaq, or S&P, but they're also used to track how everything is doing overall. Among them:

⇥ The Wilshire 5000 equity index. This index tracks thousands of stocks of companies of all different sizes, large and small. It's also outgrown its name—it really follows almost seven thousand stocks. Even though it's not widely quoted, it's one of the best.

⇥ The Russell 2000 index. This index tracks two thousand stocks that are traded on the OTC (over-the-counter) market.

⇥ The EAFE index. This one ranks the stocks in Europe, Australia, and the Far East.

Managed mutual funds constantly compare their performance to that of the various indexes. A fund will boast of "outperforming the S&P 500" over a certain period of time, meaning it increased in value by a greater percentage than did the S&P index. (Of course, many funds *underperform* the indexes, too.) So one easy and effective way to invest is to buy what's called an *index fund,* which simply *mirrors* an index, by buying all the stocks in the index it is associated with. Its performance will, by definition, match that of the index exactly, whether that's the S&P 500, the Dow Jones, or the EAFE less the expenses of the index fund. Many mutual fund companies offer S&P index funds, as well as growth, international, and bond index funds, and it's easy as can be to sign up with one of them.

WHICH IS BETTER, A MANAGED FUND OR AN INDEX FUND?

The mutual fund industry is thriving, but it is still growing. Of the 9,000 and counting mutual funds available today, there are still more that have not been around for the past ten years than have been. In the late '90's, the Vanguard S&P Index fund had a higher return than almost 72 percent of the managed mutual funds that were out there. When it comes to mutual fund investing, it is true that there are some geniuses out there, certainly—those who can consistently outperform the S&P index, but the key word there is consistently. With the newer funds we just don't know yet, because the funds haven't been in existence long enough to determine a long-term (ten-year) track record. Remember, when you are investing for growth, you hope to leave your money right where it is for at least ten years. Only time will tell which would have been a better way to go, but if I were a betting woman, I would just stick with index funds if I did not want to be actively involved with watching everything about the fund I was in.

Index funds do not have the management fees, the manager changes, or the end-of-the-year capital gains tax (see page 251) that many managed funds have. All this in the end adds to your overall return.

Expense Ratio

Another reason the S&P does so well is that it isn't a managed fund—and no manager means no manager's salary. When a manager is hired to manage a mutual fund, he or she is getting paid—by you, if you're one of the investors. Most managers get a percentage each year to manage a fund's assets. The average is about 1 percent of the invested capital a year, which I think is quite high. In addition to the management fee, the fees for operating the fund also come from the investor. All these fees together add up to what's called the *expense ratio* of the fund. I've seen them as high as 2.75 percent. Whatever the expense ratio, it will definitely affect your rate of return. Let's say that one spectacular year the manager of your mutual fund makes a return of 20 percent. Do you get that 20 percent? No. Before you get your money, the fund subtracts the expense ratio. If the expense ratio is 2.75 percent, your return will be 17.25 percent.

One of my favorite index funds, on the other hand, has a

total expense ratio of .20 percent and does very well, thank you. Why in the world would you want to pay someone to manage your money for you if that manager couldn't consistently outperform the index that it's comparing its performance to? You wouldn't.

Capital Gains Tax

The other advantage of an index fund over a typical managed fund—and this can be major—is that most mutual funds are set up so that if there's a capital gain when they sell a stock, that gain is passed through to the investors. At the end of the year the fund will pay you (or reinvest in the fund, your choice) all the realized capital gains they've acquired that year. Whenever a mutual fund has a capital gain distribution, it also reduces the NAV by the price of the capital gain. Let's say that you've invested in a mutual fund with a NAV of $10, which itself has a capital gain distribution of $1. If you have chosen not to reinvest capital gains, you'll get $1 for every share you own, and you'll have to pay tax on it. If you have decided to reinvest the capital gains, then the fund will buy you as many shares as that capital gain allows, but you'll still have to pay tax on this amount. In addition, in both cases the NAV of the mutual fund has now been reduced to $9 a share.

Maybe this doesn't sound so bad, but depending on how much money you have in the fund, you may be unpleasantly surprised to see what this capital gain distribution does for you if it happens to come in a year when you're in a high tax bracket to begin with. It's definitely a drawback in a managed mutual fund that you have no say or way to plan in its decision whether or not to take a large gain in a given year. All that fund cares about is making the greatest return for you, which is fair enough. They don't care whether it's a convenient year for you to pay taxes on a capital gain.

Happily, this isn't as big a problem with an index fund. Since index funds buy the whole index, they do not in general distribute capital gains. Why? Because they don't sell with such planned regularity. They buy and sell when only one of the stocks of the index is removed and a new stock takes its place. Since a fund that matches the S&P 500 index is meant to track the stocks in the index, it has to make these appropriate changes as necessary. But these trades occur with nowhere near the frequency they do with a managed fund. So if the idea of paying taxes on unexpected capital gains worries you, this should be taken into consideration before you decide on a managed fund or an index fund.

Remember, it's not how much you make that counts. It's how much you get to keep.

LOADED FUND, NO-LOAD FUND: WHAT'S THE DIFFERENCE?

The difference is about 4.5 percent, give or take, out of your pocket.

In addition to the expense ratios that all funds carry in order to pay the people who work at the fund, if an adviser suggests you purchase a fund and you do so through him or her, you will also pay the adviser a commission. The commission can cost anywhere from 2 percent to 8.5 percent; the average commission is about 4.5 percent. The commission is known as a *load*. Think of it as a burden on your money.

A *no-load fund,* on the other hand, is a mutual fund you buy directly, without an adviser, and therefore there's no commission attached to it. In my opinion, no-load mutual funds are the only way to go. Think about it. If you were to invest $10,000 in a no-load mutual fund and decided, two seconds later, that you wanted to withdraw your money, you'd get all

$10,000 back, assuming the market didn't move. Loaded funds, on the other hand, would cost you.

The Price of a Load

There are two kinds of loads, a front-end load and a rear-end load (also known as a 12[b]1 charge). Sound confusing? It's meant to be. The people making this money, your adviser or broker, would rather you didn't know how much you were paying.

Front-end loaded funds charge a load up front. They are also identified as A share mutual funds. When you see the name of the fund spelled out anywhere, if it has an "A" or says "A shares" after the name, then you know it's a front-end loaded fund. If you invested $10,000 in a 5 percent loaded fund, and decided two seconds later to withdraw your money, you would get back only $9,500—the adviser got that $500. This fund would have to go up more than 5 percent in value just for you to break even.

Rear-end loaded funds are even worse.

When mutual funds first came onto the scene, you could buy one only through a broker, so they were all loaded funds. Over the years, though, many mutual fund companies came out with no-load funds, and slowly but surely investors began seeing their value and investing. This migration was putting a big dent into the profits of brokerage firms that sell only loaded funds, so they came up with a way to make you think you could buy a no-load fund through them: It's called a *12(b)1 fund*.

A 12(b)1 fund is a mutual fund usually sold to you by a financial adviser. Some of these advisers sell you these funds under the pretense that you are not going to pay a load to be in the fund as long as you stay in it for five to seven years. If you cash out before then, there will be, the adviser will explain, a "surrender charge" starting at around 7 percent and going down by 1 percent each year until it reaches 0 percent. (In a true no-load fund you can cash out the same day without paying a penny.) Not too bad, you might think, since I plan to leave the money in there for a long time anyway, so it won't really cost anything. Wrong. You will also be paying an extra .75 percent to 1 percent a year in 12(b)1 expenses year in, year out. What this means is that if your fund makes a return of 10 percent, you would get only 9 percent after the 12(b)1 charge, and you'll continue to pay that percentage in some funds for as long as you stay in the fund, even after the seven years are up. In fact, if you stayed in the fund for fifteen years, and were paying 1 percent for the privilege of owning your 12(b)1, you would in essence have paid a 15 percent sales commission. You would even have paid about 10 percent more than what a front-loaded mutual fund would cost. And, of course, you would have paid 15 percent more than what a good no-load fund would have cost. Please note that in recent years certain mutual fund companies that offer 12(b)1 funds automatically convert your B shares over to A shares without any costs after the surrender charges are up.

This 12(b)1 fee is in addition to the other fees as well. You'll also have to pay the management fees and other expenses of the fund, just as you do with a no-load fund. So the 12(b)1 fees are put in place to pay the adviser's fee for having sold you the fund. How it works is that you buy the fund, the brokerage firm advances the broker's commission to him the day you buy it, and you keep paying and paying so that the firm will get back the money they paid to the broker. Your 12(b)1 fee is how they get the money back. If you close the account early, your surrender charge is what guarantees the company it will get back more than it paid the broker: a no-lose proposition for the brokerage firm, but you lose all around.

In other words, 12(b)1 mutual funds are a rip-off. If you see a "B" or "B shares" after the name of a fund, or if your adviser says you have to stay in a fund for X years or pay a surrender charge—you have a 12(b)1 fund.

Why Would My Adviser Sell Me These Funds?

Because that's how he or she makes a living, and you've not chosen an adviser wisely. True financial advice is to tell the client how to get the most bang for the buck, even if it means the adviser won't make a lot of money with the transaction. Advisers are there to help you get rich, not to get rich off you. It's the adviser's fiduciary responsibility to tell you if there's a less expensive way for you to make money—and give you the choice of what you want to do after explaining how much each of your options will really cost you.

But no-load funds can be purchased without the help of an adviser—no middleperson, no commissions, no hidden costs, just smooth sailing to greater and greater wealth over time. Do you need an adviser? If after reading this next section you feel you do, then you do, for your own peace of mind. But you may just want to test the waters yourself.

TESTING THE WATERS

MY MOM'S STORY

Whether you want to believe it or not, you and you alone have the best judgment when it comes to your money. Here's a story about me and my mom:

A few years ago, I had a terrific hunch about a particular stock. I just knew it was a great buy, especially priced as it was at around $1.50 a share. So I told the person that I love most in the world, my mom. My mom has always lived really, really frugally and, since my dad died, has managed to have enough to live comfortably on, but she has never been a great risk taker in the stock market; in fact, she still worries about me when I buy or sell stocks. This time, to my amazement—maybe she caught the excitement in my voice—she said she also wanted to invest in the stock I had chosen—$5,000. Eighty-three years old, and now she decides she wants to jump into the market!

Now—again to my amazement—I began to caution her. Did she understand that any stock that was selling for only $1.50 a share was totally speculative? Yes, yes, she understood that perfectly well. Did she understand that she could lose the entire $5,000? Yes, she understood. She felt the worst-case scenario was that if she lost it all, she would have $5,000 less to leave me when she died. Was I willing to take that risk? (I hate it when she outsmarts me at my own games.) I was willing, so my mom and I invested in the stock that same day, each of us putting in $5,000.

Everything was holding steady pretty much until a few months later, when the stock started to go down and down and down. My mom, who by now was really into this, began calling me up every day and saying, "What do you think we should do?" I would say the same thing I would have said to my clients, "What do *you* think you should do?" and, satisfied, she'd say, "Let's just hold it." That was how I felt, too, until the day the stock hit twelve cents a share, which made me begin to doubt my own inner voice. Five thousand dollars is a lot of money, and this was my very own mother.

That was the day she called up to say, "Let's buy more." I couldn't believe it.

I said, "What did you say?" and she said, "I just have this instinct to buy more."

When she said this, I'm sorry to say I did not encourage her to follow her instincts. Instead I said something to the effect of,

"Mom, are you crazy? This stock is almost belly-up and we can't throw good money after bad." I'm also sorry to say that now she began to mistrust her own instincts as well and simply agreed with me. We left our money where it was, but our hopes fell and now we both trusted less in what we had believed about the stock.

To make a long story short, the stock fluctuated between twelve and twenty-five cents a share for almost a year, then: boom. It started to skyrocket, and soon after that we had both tripled our money. One day, while the stock was still at this high, my mom called again. "Suze," she said, "I've decided that it's time to sell." This time I didn't stop her from listening to her inner voice. I said, "Go for it." She made three times the money she put in, and she was perfectly happy about it.

Even so, my mom would have made ten times, not three times, her money if I hadn't drowned out her inner voice and made her doubt what she knew to be true for her. If that spark of instinct had been guiding her actions, she would have been far better off than she was by letting my doubts get in her way.

The moral of the story is that—whether you want to believe it or not—you and you alone have the best judgment when it comes to your money. You must do what makes you feel safe, sound, comfortable. You must trust yourself more than you trust others, and your inner voice will tell you when it is time to take action.

I'm not in any way suggesting that if you take your nest egg and go out and find a speculative stock to invest it all in, you'll get rich. You won't. You'll be a sitting duck if you do that. What is more, I doubt your inner voice would guide you in that direction anyway.

Nor am I suggesting that you shouldn't listen to others or learn about what you're planning to invest in. You need information to make good decisions. But your inner voice will help you weigh that information properly. What I am suggesting is that you test the waters before you jump in with everything you have and that you practice listening to that inner voice. As soon as you see how easy it is to stay afloat, and get used to the investing temperature, so to speak, you very well might want to go in deeper.

GETTING READY TO GET STARTED

It doesn't matter if you have a large lump sum you want to invest or if you're just starting from scratch and want to put in a little here, a little there, as you can. Rule number one is that to invest in the stock market (through mutual funds, index funds, and the like, not just by buying and selling this stock or that one, the way my mom and I did), you must invest only money that you will not need to touch for at least ten years. Why? Because, as we've seen, there has never been in the history of the stock market a ten-year period of time where stocks have not out-performed every other investment you could have made.

Not that history always repeats itself, but this is a spectacular indicator. However, if you do not give your money ten years, you will be taking a significant risk. If you don't have the time to leave this money sitting there, it is possible that when you do need to take it out, that need will arise at the worst possible time. Let's say you invested in 1999 and were planning to withdraw the money to buy a house within the next four years. You decided, Okay, I'll just invest in the market, make all I can, and then have more money when the time comes to make the down payment. One year later you find the house you want and make the offer, which is accepted—on April 14, 2000, a day the market goes down considerably, and the day you had decided to sell, for you need your money. You will most likely take out far less than you initially put in. If you could have just waited—but you could not, for you needed the money to buy your home. So time is everything.

Remember dollar cost averaging (page 175)? This is the technique that works so well for long-term growth, in which you are investing wisely by limiting your risk. If you are investing that $50 or more a month, or if you have a huge stash of cash in a savings account that you now feel right about testing the waters with, this is your method of investing, because with dollar cost averaging you raise your chances enormously of ending up a winner.

I am not talking here about you turning into one of those tycoons in B-movies who is always shouting, "Buy, buy, buy," or, "Sell, sell, sell," into the half dozen phones on his desk. Instead I'm talking about you venturing into the market in a safe way, spreading your money among dozens or hundreds of stocks, via mutual funds that gifted professionals spend their lifetimes watching and guarding, and having time and the market touch your money with magic. These days the richest and savviest investors may like to shout, "Buy, buy, buy," or, "Sell, sell, sell," into a phone from time to time for the thrill (and potential payoff) of playing the market on a hunch or a tip. But these same investors have most of their money exactly where I am going to tell you to put yours: in a safe place, where over time it will grow and grow.

If you are reading this and still feeling your inner voice say, *No, I can't do this, it's not right for me,* then listen to that voice and read on, because I will also tell you how to choose an adviser for your money, if that's what makes you feel best.

But if you can, try testing the waters on your own first. Most people, I find, discover they truly love dealing with their money once they understand how to do it. Just remember: Give your money ten years to grow.

IF YOU HAVE A LUMP SUM TO INVEST

Let's say you have $20,000 to invest. Maybe it's sitting right now in a retirement account at work, and you think you might want to be more aggressive with the way in which you invest it—or some of it. Maybe you've just gotten an inheritance or a huge raise at a new job. Maybe you've just had this money sitting in a savings account, have felt for a long time that you could do more with it than leave it in that savings account, and suddenly decide: Now's the time. Whatever the case, let's say it's $20,000, but it can in reality be more or even much less. Let's see how to invest it.

So that you can get used to the investment waters, rather than investing 100 percent of it all at once, I want you to divide it up and start investing slowly over the first year, to see how it makes you feel. The chances, I think, are good that by the end of the first year you'll be ready to plunge in.

Take 80 percent of what you have to invest, which in our example is $16,000, and put that money in a Treasury bill or note, or just leave it in your money-market fund, anywhere it will be kept safe for you for about a year. After that year is up, it will be up to you if you want to keep investing it so safely, invest more on your own, or if you want some professional help in investing it. Your inner voice will tell you which is best for you. Trust yourself.

If these are not funds you are investing within a retirement account, the best way to buy a Treasury bill or note is by contacting the Federal Reserve office nearest you—or by calling 800-722-2678 or visiting www.treasurydirect.gov and setting up what is called a *Treasury direct account*. This is where you buy your Treasuries directly from the Federal Reserve absolutely free of charge. You could also, if you wanted, buy your Treasuries from a broker, either a discount or full-service broker; but this would cost you about $30, and why spend $30 if you don't have to? The other reason to buy your Treasuries directly is to get used to them and the way they work (they're simple!). When it comes time to stop investing for growth, many people transfer some or all of their money from the market into Treasuries and draw the money they need to live on from the interest. This might be part of your overall plan, too, and it's a great idea to become familiar with how they work right now.

So $16,000, or 80 percent, goes into Treasuries or is just kept safe. The other 20 percent, in this case $4,000, is what you're going to invest in the market.

When Do I Buy?

Now you have $4,000 and you're ready to invest. If you were asking me for advice right now, I'd tell you to join a fabulous organization called the American Association of Individual Investors (AAII, PO Box 11092, Chicago, IL 60611-9737 or visit their website www.aaii.org). This entity has been around since 1978, now has about 175,000 members—independent investors like you—and costs $49 for paper membership or $39 for electronic membership. They will send you information that—believe it or not—you will enjoy reading; their information is always thorough and good.

You are not going to plunk down this $4,000 all at once, remember; you're going to use dollar cost averaging. Divide the amount you have to invest by 12; in this case, your figure would be $333.33.

Now you're going to take this monthly sum and, on the same day each month, put it into a good no-load mutual fund month in and month out for the first year, using the dollar cost averaging technique.

You can choose either a managed fund or an index fund;

and with dollar cost averaging the beauty is that when the market goes down, you'll simply be able to buy more shares. So don't be afraid. You have plenty of time to let that money sit. Buy, too, when the market is up, because next month— who knows?—it might be up even more. Just buy, each and every month.

After the year is up, you will have a sense of how you felt about investing, whether it felt right to you or not. I have to tell you that nearly everyone I've dealt with feels truly powerful once they take the financial reins of their lives in hand in this way; in fact, most people say that if they'd known it was this easy, they would have done it long ago. When the year is up, they usually invest all the rest of their money as well, or whatever percentage they feel comfortable with. Before you know it, using AAII, other publications, and the Web, they have invested in other mutual funds they like, which means they have a diversified portfolio. They're off and running.

What Do I Buy?

What you will buy will depend in part on how much you have to invest, because some funds have a very small minimum, while with others you need more to invest. The minimum will also vary depending on whether you're investing in a retirement account or on your own in a regular account. Vanguard, for instance, which is one of the great mutual fund companies, has a minimum of $3,000 if you just open a regular account with them. If you open an IRA at Vanguard, the minimum drops to $500. Most mutual funds work more or less the same way, although a few good ones will let you invest with minimums as small as $25 to $100, if you allow them to deduct that much from your bank account each month. They're smart; they just want you to start, and continue to save. These include:

Min	Family Fund	Telephone	Web Address
$25	TIAA-CREF	800-842-2776	www.tiaa-cref.org
$50	Fremont Funds	800-548-4539	www.fremontfunds.com
$50	Heartland Funds	800-432-7856	www.heartlandfunds.com
$50	Invesco	800-525-8085	www.invesco.com
$50	Strong Funds	800-368-1030	www.strongfunds.com
$50	T. Rowe Price	800-638-5660	www.troweprice.com
$100	Babson Funds	800-422-2766	www.babsonfunds.com
$100	Dreyfus	800-782-6620	www.dreyfus.com
$100	Highmark Funds	800-433-6884	www.highmarkfunds.com
$100	Neuberger Berman	800-877-9700	www.nbfunds.com

You have a choice when it comes to buying mutual or index funds. You can buy them directly through the fund company itself, or you can open an account at Charles Schwab, Fidelity, Etrade, or any of the other great companies and buy the same no-load fund through them. (Make sure there is no transaction fee involved; there shouldn't be.) Schwab, Fidelity, and Etrade, among others, have pamphlets and computer programs to help you select the best mutual funds for you. There is more good help for you out there than you can imagine.

Some of the great families of funds:

TIAA-CREFF	800-842-2776	WWW.TIAA-CREF.ORG
VANGUARD	800-662-7447	WWW.VANGUARD.COM
T. ROWE PRICE	800-638-5660	WWW.TROWEPRICE.COM
FIDELITY	800-343-3548	WWW.FIDELITY.COM
JANUS	800-525-3713	WWW.JANUS.COM
PIMCO	949-720-6000	WWW.PIMCO.COM

When Do I Sell?

There is no harder question when it comes to the stock market. And there's no single correct answer, because the market never stops going up and down. To answer the question of when to sell, don't worry about what the market is doing. As always, just keep in touch with your inner voice and your time frame.

The answer will vary, depending on your individual circumstances. If you're very lucky, you may never need to use this money or need the income it could generate for your retirement. If that happens to be the case, then the answer may be never. As of the writing of this book, let your beneficiaries inherit it. But be careful, because the tax laws are changing. Currently, when your beneficiaries inherit something, its cost basis for determining gain or loss for tax purposes is what the inheritance was worth the day they inherited it. So if you bought one thousand shares of stock at $10 a share years ago, and over the years the stock splits and the price rises so that you now own eight thousand shares at $40, this means that your $10,000 investment is now worth $320,000. If you sell it, you will owe capital gains taxes on $310,000, the difference between what you bought and sold it for. Now let's assume that instead of selling it, you left it to your beneficiaries; because they inherited it, their cost basis is what the stock was worth when you died: $320,000. If they then sold it for $320,000, they would not owe one penny of capital gains taxes. This tax provision is scheduled to change in 2010.

In all likelihood, however, you're counting on this money for retirement. This means you will one day want or need to switch some or all of your money from growth-oriented investments to an income-generating investment, such as Treasury notes or bills. In any case, you will need to keep a careful watch on that ten-year time horizon.

Let's say that you have had your money diversified among several mutual funds for nine years already, and you know you won't need it for another ten years, if then. As long as those funds are performing as well as or better than other funds that are similar to it, just leave it where it is.

Now let's say you've had your money diversified among several mutual funds for seven years, but this time you know you will probably retire in about three years. At that time you will need this money to start generating income so you can begin to live off the interest that the principal will generate. You will have to make a change. With your eye on your timeline, it is time to start reevaluating right now. Let's say, too, that you had a great run in the market over these seven years, and you've averaged about 15 percent a year on your money.

What do you do? It's terrific that you've done well, but don't try to outsmart the market. You do not have ten years ahead of you in which you can leave your money just to sit there. Take your profits now.

It may turn out that the market suffers a setback, so that if you had ignored your nervousness, you would have been left back at square one. Or the market might skyrocket after you withdraw your money. Who cares? You have made your money. You have listened to your inner voice. You are far better off selling and ceasing to worry than you are letting your fear drain you and make you feel powerless. This is the money you intend to live on for the rest of your life, and you must trust yourself more than you trust others about where to keep the money safe that will keep *you* safe.

Plunging in Deeper?

Once you have invested for a year, you may decide, as thousands of other people have, that yes, you're more than safe on your own. If you find it heady and exhilarating, if it makes you feel both safe and powerful, then by all means plunge in deeper. Watch carefully over what you are creating, keep in mind your time frame, and listen, always, to your inner voice.

If instead, after this first year of investing, you find you're not comfortable with it, and your inner voice says that you would rather have professional help before you plunge in deeper, then again, you must listen to that voice. And you must find the very best help you possibly can.

FINANCIAL ADVISERS

MY STORY

If after I became a broker, any of my clients had ever asked me—and thankfully no one ever did—what I had done for a living before I went to work for Merrill Lynch, I would have told them the truth: Before becoming a broker, I worked as a waitress at the Buttercup Bakery in Berkeley, California. My dream was not to become a broker, but to open a hot tub and sauna place, with a restaurant and haircutting salon built right in: one-stop shopping if you happened to want a meal, a haircut, and a sauna. I would go on and on about this dream to my regular customers, and finally one day a man named Fred Hasbrook gave me a check with a letter that read, "For people like you to have your dreams come true. To be paid back if you can at 0 percent interest in ten years." I was stunned, and even more stunned as word got around and others of my regulars chipped in, too. Believe it or not, I soon had a $50,000 nest egg with which to start my business.

At the suggestion of one of my benefactors, I put the money into an account at Merrill Lynch and was assigned to a broker, a sweet guy whom I'll call Rick. I told him I wanted to keep my money safe, and he had me sign some papers that I didn't even read. Off I went, to have blueprints for my business drawn up. I still have those blueprints.

To make a long story short, that sweet Rick—knowing that the money wasn't mine, knowing that I wanted above all to keep it safe, and knowing that it was being held there so I could open my business—had me investing in these things called options on oil stocks, the most wildly risky and speculative investments I could have been in. I felt funny about this from the beginning, but I didn't know enough, or trust myself enough, to understand why or say no to Rick's grand schemes. In the end, I agreed because I trusted Rick. With his nice office and pin-striped suits, he was the closest I'd ever been to Wall Street or big money. At first we were doing pretty great. In those early weeks we were up $5,000. I couldn't believe it! I had never made so much money without even trying, so I became totally intrigued with this new way to make money and thought that I had better study up on this great new moneymaking discovery.

This was in 1979, before anyone had computers at home, and I was trying to figure out about these options from reading the newspapers every day. I had stock quotes and options quotes pasted up all over my bedroom walls, trying to make sense of them. Finally I began to get the hang of it and understand what we were doing—and how what we were doing was very, very wrong for me. My understanding came too late, I'm afraid. The reversal of oil stocks happened quicker than you could say sauna and hot tub, and I lost it all, all the money I had put in and all the money I had made. Everything. My financial "adviser" had done me in, not to mention what he had done to all those people who had tried to help me.

It took me a long time to get a true understanding of what it takes to handle other people's money. It is not like Monopoly, when after you've finished playing the game you simply take the houses off Park Place, pack up the money that comes with the game, and go on with your day. So much more is at stake.

Rick may have been my broker, and a reckless if not unscrupulous one at that, but I couldn't have been luckier that he was at least with a reputable and nationally recognized firm like Merrill Lynch. Merrill came through in the long run and covered the losses in the account, after I demonstrated that he had misled me about the risks inherent in what we were doing, so in the end I was able to pay back all the money to my investors. I had picked the right firm, at least, if not the right broker at the firm—and both decisions are extremely important if you decide to go with a full-service brokerage firm.

Soon afterward, I joined Merrill Lynch.

Why would Merrill Lynch hire a waitress? They weren't hiring a waitress. What they saw in me was that I would be an excellent saleswoman, and they were right.

At major brokerage firms, the brokers or financial advisers (which is what I became at Merrill Lynch) are mainly commission-based advisers who do not usually come up with the ideas of what you should buy or sell. Most of them take the recommendations of the financial analysts who work for the firm. Your adviser takes these recommendations, checks to see whether they're suited to your needs and financial situation, and tries to sell these investments to you if they (and you) meet those criteria.

My story about Rick isn't meant to frighten you out of asking the help of an adviser, if you feel that's the way to go. Nor is it meant to suggest that all advisers are disreputable, because most do have your best interests at heart and, if the firm itself is reputable and you yourself trust the adviser, you will almost certainly be safe. By turning your money over to someone else, however, you must not give up feeling responsible for it, as I did when I signed those papers. The ultimate responsibility for your money must always remain in your own hands.

WHAT DO FINANCIAL ADVISERS DO?

Many people I speak to tell me one fact and one fact only about their lives: how much they have to invest. This tells me nothing about them and nothing about their financial situation. If someone says she has $10,000 to invest, but also has credit card debt of $8,000 at 18 percent, it may be that her best investment of all would be to pay off that debt first thing. If someone is going to be looking after and investing your money, that person should know everything in your financial picture, including how you feel about risks and what your goals are—the questionnaire I used to send my clients (page 276) will give you an idea of what a concerned and competent adviser will always want to know.

If you've joined the AAII (or can access it from your computer), you will see that there are many different titles and certifications of advisers or planners, some far more qualified than others. Some will just provide you with a financial plan and send you home to carry it out; some will be on your payroll for as long as you want, taking care of your money. You won't want, for example, the adviser you hire to be licensed only to sell you securities. You want to know that your adviser cares enough about managing money to have gone to extra lengths to become a Certified Financial Planner® professional (this is what I am). A Certified Financial Planner® professional has had to pass a series of exams that deal with every aspect of finance, including risk management or insurance, retirement planning, taxes, and estate planning. It usually takes two years to study for and pass these exams, and those who do pass are required to stay up-to-date by taking continuing education courses and to abide by the standards of the Certified Financial Planner Board of Standards, Inc. (the CFP Board; visit their website at www.cfp-board.org).

HOW MUCH DO FINANCIAL ADVISERS CHARGE?

When you go to interview financial advisers, you are considering whether you want to hire each one: You are the boss, regardless of how much they know about money. You are the boss of your money, and when you hire someone to take care of it—just as when you hire a qualified gardener to look after your garden or a qualified child care worker to take care of your child—you are the boss of that person as well.

When I was seeing clients, I set up my own, somewhat unusual, fee schedule with this in mind. When someone—rich, poor, doesn't matter—called my office for an appointment, that prospective client was first sent a letter stating what they were expected to bring along to the appointment and explaining my fee structure. About a week later my secretary almost always would get a call from them saying that the only thing they were having a hard time with was how much I charged. My fee structure dictated that clients must pay me what they thought my services were worth to them. At the end of our session, which ran an average two hours, they decided what my services were worth. My clients were the boss.

Apart from my way, there are a few ways that advisers charge for their services.

FREE CONSULTATION

An adviser who sees you for free is trying to convince you to hand over your money to him to invest for you—and reap the commissions for himself. Since mutual funds, if purchased through an adviser, carry heavy commissions, around 5 percent, most likely mutual funds will make up a hefty part of your portfolio if you go with this adviser. So if you go in to see an adviser for free, so to speak, and hand over $20,000 for him to invest in those loaded funds, then you will have paid $1,000 for that "free" session. The second that you sit down in that office and tell the adviser how much money you have to invest, he knows what it means for him. If you come in with $100,000, he'll get about $5,000. Not bad for an hour or two of work.

FEE-BASED

This is where you simply pay the adviser an hourly fee to tell you what to do with your money. She does not do it for you.

FEES PLUS COMMISSIONS

You pay the adviser a fee to tell you what to do, to create a plan with your money. If you decide you'd like him to implement it for you, he'll also get a commission.

REGISTERED INVESTMENT ADVISERS (RIAS)

Another option is to hire a *registered investment adviser (RIA)*, who will create, in effect, a personal mutual fund for you and serve as the manager of it. RIAs usually require a large minimum to start with, ranging from $50,000 to $5 million, with the average minimum being about $250,000.

An RIA manages your money for you on an ongoing basis, for a fee that is usually a percentage of the money you've given her to manage. This percentage can range from .25 to 3 percent a year, but you should not pay more than 1.5 percent including all commissions. Think about this. The amount you pay is a percentage of the money she is managing: Isn't this a great incentive for her to make your money grow? If you gave her $100,000 initially, and by the end of the year you had $200,000, if you were paying her 1 percent, she'd have made $2,000. (And I hope you would send her an enormous bouquet of flowers as well.) If you lose money, she loses, too. This is an adviser who is truly on the same side of the fence as you and whose compensation is attached to a real incentive to make money for you.

Most RIAs will ask you to sign what is called a *discretionary account trading form*, where you give the RIA permission to trade your account without getting your permission for every transaction. This is absolutely the only time you should even consider doing something like this. You must still make sure that your money is held in a reputable institution like Etrade, Charles Schwab, or Fidelity, for example, and all the RIA has the right to do is buy or sell, not withdraw money except for any fees she is owed.

Not many RIAs buy mutual funds because it does not make sense to pay the RIA 1 percent a year to manage your money and also to pay the full expense ratio of the mutual fund. If you decide to hire an RIA, please find out what she invests in before you sign on.

INTERVIEWING A FINANCIAL ADVISER

If you're in a domestic relationship, you must both go to see the adviser. (I wouldn't see clients who were married or living together unless they came in together.) Before you do, I urge you and your partner to have a talk about what you want to accomplish with the adviser and the fears about money you have and make sure you both have a thorough understanding of where you stand right now. After you've chosen an adviser, you must make all decisions as a team and both be kept up-to-date with what the adviser is doing.

I met so many people, women in particular, who didn't have a clue what to do when their husband or partner died or when they went through a painful separation or divorce. I also saw how bewildered many people became when their parents died, leaving them an inheritance. When you have suffered a loss, you are in a state of grief, and this is not the time to make major financial decisions. Run as fast as you can from an adviser who suggests big changes at this time. My advice is to leave your money in a high-interest-bearing account for between six months and a year, until your inner voice feels okay about doing something with these funds. To be respectful of your money, you must give yourself time to heal.

If you and your partner are interviewing an adviser together, you must both feel comfortable talking to him intimately about your money. The adviser should address you both equally, give you plenty of time, and answer questions and explain fees in a way you can easily understand. You should also be comfortable with the kinds of investments he suggests and understand everything about them when he explains them to you. If he fails to meet any of these criteria, find another adviser.

When you interview anyone for a job, it is up to you to outline your requirements. For example, here are several expectations you should have for a prospective financial adviser:

✴ That she will call you every time she makes a change in your account (unless she is an RIA).

✴ That she will explain in thorough detail why she wants you to make every new transaction.

✴ That she will tell you without your having to ask if she is selling something for you that's not in your retirement account, fully explaining the tax implications.

✴ That she will explain every commission.

✴ That she will never pressure you into doing anything that does not feel right to you.

✴ That she will send you a transaction slip from the brokerage firm that holds your money, telling you what's been bought or sold. This slip must always match transactions you gave permission for.

❧ That she will send you a monthly statement summarizing all that month's transactions, including deposits, withdrawals, and current positions held. This statement must come directly from the brokerage firm that's holding your money, not from your adviser's office.

❧ That she will prepare both quarterly reports and an annual report that will tell you the exact return she is getting on your money, as well as all fees and commissions. The figure on her report must match the report that is generated directly from the brokerage firm. These reports should also show you all the realized gains or losses (all the money you actually made or lost from selling an investment) and all the unrealized gains and losses (investments you own but have not yet sold and thus that have not yet realized a profit or loss). These reports should also include returns of the overall index, so you know whether you're doing better or worse than the index. You want everything on paper.

❧ That she will never ask you to write a check made out to her personally. All the money that is handed over needs to be placed in an institution (E-trade, Schwab, Merrill, or the like), and every check is to be payable to the institution. This is absolutely essential. More than one "adviser" has flown the coop with dozens of clients' money.

❧ That she will return your calls in a timely manner.

❧ That she will always get you the information you request about an investment and find out any answers to questions you have that she doesn't know.

❧ That she will keep you informed about your money, not just call you when she wants to buy or sell something. If a stock has gone down, or is not performing the way she expected it would, you are to hear about it from her, not read about your money first in the newspapers.

You should type up all these requests on a piece of paper and have your adviser sign an agreement to do all the above.

NOW THE ADVISER MUST INTERVIEW YOU

Just as important as what you ask the adviser is what the adviser asks you. Remember: People first, then money.

I learned, in my practice, that I got a better understanding of my clients when I went over the topics on my questionnaire in person with them, rather than having them fill out the answers on their own. Sometimes people had a hard time writing things down or tended to leave things out, so talking through the questions enabled me to find out more about my clients than simply reading through hastily filled out answers. Other advisers feel that this is too time-consuming, but this process is not about saving time. It's about saving—and making—money.

Whether your prospective adviser has you fill out the form or talks you through it, it is absolutely essential that you feel this person wants to get to know you and your money, wants to understand your fears and anxieties about investing, understands how you feel about taking risks, has your best interests at heart. Advisers you interview must spend a lot of time, a couple of hours, getting to know you and your money. They can't simply plug your answers from a questionnaire into a computer and give you a plan—at least not if it is to work well. What needs to be built is a responsible, respectful, and trusting relationship, and you must not settle for less. Following is the questionnaire I used to go over with my clients, outlining the concerns any prospective adviser you interview must address:

CLIENT QUESTIONNAIRE: FINANCIAL WORKSHEET

Name _____   Partner's name _____

Address _____

Phone number _____

Occupation _____   Occupation _____

Retirement date? _____   Retirement date? _____

Will you get a pension? _____   Will you get a pension? _____

Retirement plan _____   Retirement plan _____

Any loans against a   Any loans against a

    retirement plan? _____   retirement plan? _____

Will you get Social Security? ____   Will you get Social Security? ____

Is this your first marriage? _____

If not, what number is it? _____

Is your ex still alive? _____

If you are receiving income from him/her at all, does it stop on

    his/her death? _____

If you want to invest some money, how long do you know,

    without a shadow of a doubt, that you can let it sit without

    touching it? _____

Age _____   Age _____

Health status _____   Health status _____

Medications _____   Medications _____

Parents alive _____   Parents alive _____

Cause and age of death _____   Cause and age of death _____

Divorced/separated _____   Divorced/separated _____

Mother's age/health _____   Mother's age/health _____

Father's age/health _____   Father's age/health _____

Medications _____   Medications _____

Goals

By the time you leave the office today, what is it that you want to
   have learned? (Couples, please list your goals separately.)

Partner A:_____

_____

_____

Partner B: _____

_____

_____

Dreams (to be answered by both people if in a couple)

Do you have any dreams that you would love to see come true? _____

_____

_____

Do you think they will come true?_____

_____

_____

Emotion Quotient

Do you get nervous when you think about investing in stocks?

If you were to buy a stock and it went from $15 a share when you
   bought it and then went down to $10, how would you feel, as
   rated on the scale below?

I'd lose sleep and be sick to my stomach	I'd check the papers daily when investing in stocks	I'd think, That's what happens

   10   9   8   7   6   5   4   3   2   1

Cash Flow

List all sources of income that you have now and that you project to
   have when you retire: _____

_____

_____

Write down two years of expenses so we can see if what you really spend is equal to what you think you spend. (This was discussed in Step 3.) _____

_____

_____

Family
All the following questions apply to both sets of parents:

⊪ Do you have open communication with your parents about their money? _____
⊪ Will you be inheriting any money from your parents? _____
⊪ If your parents need physical/financial help, will you be the one responsible for them? _____
⊪ Are you or any family member willing to move them into your home if they need help? _____
⊪ Do your parents have an LTC insurance policy? _____
⊪ Do your parents have a will or trust and DPAHC? _____
⊪ Are both of your parents citizens of the United States? _____

⊪ Do you/partner have a will? _____
⊪ Do you/partner have a trust? _____
⊪ Do you/partner have a DPAHC? _____
⊪ Do you/partner have an LTC policy? _____
⊪ Are both you and your partner citizens of the United States?

_____
⊪ If not, why not? _____

_____

⊪ Do you/partner have disability insurance? _____
⊪ Do you/partner have errors and omissions or malpractice insurance (if applicable)? _____

❧ What are your deductibles and coverage on your car insurance, house insurance, and health insurance? _____
_____

❧ How long have you/partner worked at your current occupation?
_____

❧ Do you/partner like your current occupation? _____

❧ Do you plan a career change in the foreseeable future? _____

❧ At what age do you/partner want to retire? _____

❧ Has your company downsized in the past 10 years? _____

❧ Children's names: _____

❧ Ages: _____

❧ Are they dependent upon you financially? _____

❧ How long do you anticipate them to be financially dependent?
_____

❧ How long do they anticipate that you will let them be financially dependent? _____

❧ Do you have any children currently on SSI? _____

❧ Do you have any children on Social Security Disability? _____

❧ Do any of your children have (or have a history of) a substance abuse problem? _____

❧ Will you be paying for their college education? _____

❧ Have you started to save for their education? _____

❧ Do they think you will be paying for their college education? ____

❧ Are you willing to sacrifice your retirement security in order to pay for your children's education? _____

❧ Are you opposed to your child having to pay for his or her own education? _____

❧ Have you paid for any of the other children's education at this point in time? _____

❧ Do you talk freely with your children about money? _____

⋈ Do you feel that if you were to die today, they would be capable of handling the money that you are going to leave them? _____

⋈ If not, at what age do you feel you would like them to get this money, if ever? _____

⋈ Do you feel that you want someone else to watch over the money for your children, and if so, till they are how old, if ever? _____

Real Estate

⋈ Do you own a home? _____

⋈ What is the FMV (fair market value) of that home today? _____

⋈ What was the purchase price of this home? _____

⋈ Did you own a home or homes before this one that you sold? ____

⋈ Did you roll your taxable gains (from the sale of your home[s]) into your current home? _____

⋈ If so, what was the purchase price of the first house that you started with? _____

⋈ Have you kept records of all the home improvements that you have made to this home or any other prior homes? _____

⋈ If no records were kept, can you estimate the cost of improvements on all homes to date? _____

⋈ What is the current balance that you owe on the mortgage? _____

⋈ What is the interest rate that you are paying? _____

⋈ Is it a fixed or variable loan? _____

⋈ How many years do you have left until it is paid off? _____

⋈ Do you have any home equity loans or second mortgages on this home? _____

⋈ What is the current balance remaining on that loan? _____

⋈ What is the interest rate of that loan? _____

⋈ Do you plan to keep your current house? _____

⋈ If not, how soon before you sell it? _____

⚜ If you sell it, will you be buying another one? _____

⚜ How much will you want to spend? _____

Do you own any other real estate? If yes, please answer the following
  questions for each piece of property owned:

⚜ What kind of property is it, i.e. apt. building, commercial
  property, rental unit, second home, vacation home, etc.? _____
  _____

⚜ What is the FMV of that piece of real estate? _____

⚜ What was the purchase price? _____

⚜ Did you own other similar real estate that you sold to buy
  this one? _____

⚜ Did you roll your taxable gains into this piece of property? _____

⚜ What was the purchase price of the first property that you
  started with? _____

⚜ What is the current balance that you owe on the mortgage? _____

⚜ What is the interest rate that you are paying? _____

⚜ Is it a fixed or variable loan? _____

⚜ How many years do you have left till it is paid off? _____

⚜ Do you have any equity loans or second mortgages on this
  property? _____

⚜ What is the current balance remaining on that loan? _____

⚜ What is the interest rate of that loan? _____

⚜ Do you plan to keep this property? _____

⚜ If not, how soon before you sell it? _____

⚜ If you sell it, will you be buying another one? _____

⚜ How much will you want to spend? _____

TOTAL EQUITY IN ALL REAL ESTATE OWNED: _____
FMV (fair market value) minus all mortgages and all equity
  loans: _____

Debts

Do you owe any money on a car or car loan? _____

Balance of loan   Car A: _____ Car B: _____ Car C: _____

Interest rate   _____   _____   _____

Years remaining on
    loan?   _____   _____   _____

Do you plan on selling
    any of these cars?   _____   _____   _____

If so, when?   _____   _____   _____

Credit Card Debts (begin with highest interest rate)

Name of Credit Card	Amount Owing	Interest Rate	Yearly Fee
_____	_____	_____	_____
_____	_____	_____	_____
_____	_____	_____	_____
_____	_____	_____	_____

School Loans

_____	_____	_____	_____
_____	_____	_____	_____

Personal Loans

_____	_____	_____	_____

Credit Union Loans

_____	_____	_____	_____
_____	_____	_____	_____

TOTAL CURRENT DEBT: _____

Anticipated Debt

Will you be making any large purchases in the next two years
(buying a new car, a new roof, a computer, taking a vacation, etc.)?
Please list the item needed and the amount you expect to spend.

ITEM   AMOUNT

_____   _____

_____   _____

_____   _____

_____   _____

TOTAL ANTICIPATED DEBT: _____

Add up your current debt and the anticipated debt.

Cash on Hand (available at any time without penalty)

Account Type	Current Balance	Interest Rate	Monthly Income
Savings account	_____	_____	_____
Checking	_____	_____	_____
Money-market funds	_____	_____	_____
Credit unions	_____	_____	_____
Misc.	_____	_____	_____

TOTAL CASH: _____

Cash-Type Investments

Account Type	Current Value	Interest Rate	Maturity Date	Monthly Income
Certificates of deposit	_____	_____	_____	_____
Treasury bills	_____	_____	_____	_____
Misc.	_____	_____	_____	_____

TOTAL CASH-TYPE INVESTMENTS: _____

Other Investments

Account Type	Purchase Price	Current Value	Interest Rate	Maturity Date	Monthly Income
Mutual funds	___	___	___	___	___
Stocks	___	___	___	___	___
Bonds	___	___	___	___	___
Annuities	___	___	___	___	___
Stock options	___	___	___	___	___

TOTAL OTHER INVESTMENTS: _____

Money in Retirement Accounts

Account Type	Current Value	Return	Company Match	Monthly Income
IRA	___	___	___	___
SEP/IRA	___	___	___	___
KEOGH	___	___	___	___
403(b)	___	___	___	___
401(k)	___	___	___	___
TSA	___	___	___	___
MISC.	___	___	___	___

TOTAL RETIREMENT ACCOUNTS: _____

Life Insurance Policies

Name of Company	Owner of Policy	Cash Value	Current Interest Rate	Death Benefit
___	___	___	___	___
___	___	___	___	___
___	___	___	___	___
___	___	___	___	___

TOTAL LIFE INSURANCE CASH VALUE: _____

TOTAL LIFE INSURANCE DEATH BENEFIT: _____

Now add all of the following:
TOTAL EQUITY IN ALL REAL ESTATE OWNED (page 281): _____
TOTAL CASH (page 283): _____
TOTAL CASH-TYPE INVESTMENTS (page 283): _____
TOTAL OTHER INVESTMENTS (opposite): _____
TOTAL RETIREMENT ACCOUNTS (opposite): _____
TOTAL LIFE INSURANCE CASH VALUE (above): _____
EQUALS TOTAL ASSETS: _____
subtract from that
TOTAL CURRENT DEBTS (page 282): _____
EQUALS NET WORTH: _____

TEACH YOUR CHILDREN WELL

You want your children to do the best they can in every way, and you want to give them every advantage you can give them, right? You feed them well, dress them well, teach them everything about the world you know to teach them. You are stunned by how much love you feel for them, and now you understand why parents always say they would step in front of a speeding bus to save their child. You would, too, and of course you are teaching them how not to step into traffic, how not to step into the course of that bus when it's barreling down the street. You want your children to know how to stay safe.

Money, however, is also a safety issue in your children's lives. Just as you, and I, and all of us need money to keep us safe, so will your children need to know all the steps to financial freedom.

Remember how, in the beginning of this book, you went back to your own childhood and began to reconstruct your money memories, to show you how they led to your fears about money today? So, too, are your children becoming imprinted with money memories right now, and it is your responsibility as a parent—or aunt, uncle, godparent, or friend of a child—to give careful thought about how you transmit messages about money to the children in your life.

Over the past few years a small industry has arisen with books, games, and computer programs to teach children about money, which I think is great. If you have a child, buy as many as you can and pull the best ideas and information from them. The advice won't all be the same—that's okay; again, you will follow your inner voice about what and how you want your kids to learn. The best thing about these books and products is that they open up the dialogue about money, a subject that has been treated as a secret for so long. But they're only good as far as they go, because money messages are transmitted as much through the heart as through words you learn in a book. If your kids hear you swear at your stack of bills, if they sense fear, if they're constantly told what you can't afford, that's what they'll learn, even if you go by the books to try to teach them healthier messages.

Today's children will inherit a global economy, a high-tech world, an increasingly competitive universe in which they'll have to make their way. Yet so many parents I see, when I ask them how they teach their children, talk about piggy banks and passbook savings accounts and allowances and how they plan to start saving for their children's college education one of these days. A piggy bank will not exactly teach your children about life in the twenty-first century. It is just another financial symbol relaying the message that to retrieve what you have saved, something has to break. We relay this message many times over to our children, especially when it comes to college funding. In order to send our kids to school, the bank truly has to be broken wide open. You know it, and your kids can feel it, too.

COLLEGE: RUNNING THE NUMBERS

The cost of four-year colleges tends to rise steadily at about 5 percent, while inflation currently seems to be holding steady at about 2 percent. Assuming that your child has seventeen years to go before entering a four-year school that today costs $20,000 a year, for room, board, tuition, and so forth, the total cost of sending your child to college, in today's dollars, will be above $200,000. If it is your plan to pay for a four-year college education for your child, here is what you need to know.

HOW WILL I AFFORD COLLEGE?

If these numbers seem staggering, don't let them be. Try to make decisions today about education tomorrow that will be respectful to you and what you do feel is possible. This is where your inner voice will come into play.

There are alternatives to schools that cost this kind of money. The average state school today is considerably less for residents. In my case, I had to go to a state school while most of my friends went to private schools, because my mom and dad didn't have the money for a private school—big deal. What was great was that I knew what to expect. I knew that I would have to work to get myself through school, and work I did (and have done better [financially speaking] than some of my friends who were given more expensive educations, I might add). So don't feel bad about what you know you can't afford.

Financial freedom is more than just having a lot of money; it's also being proud of what you have and realistic about what you don't have and instilling that pride in your children. It is not being respectful of yourself and your money to go into financial debt forever to pay for an education. Greatness will come to one's life regardless of where one gets an educa-tion, because true greatness starts from within, not from without. True greatness and true education start with the messages that are passed down, the conscious messages and the unconscious ones.

THE SOONER YOU START SAVING, THE BETTER

The best time to start saving is when that baby you know you want to have is still a gleam in your eye—just a few years can make a tremendous difference. Let's say you meet someone and you know that within a year or two you'll be getting married and that shortly after, you're planning on having a child. If you start putting money away right then and there, you'll have to put away less than if you wait.

Let me show you the difference a few years can make. First let's say that your child was just born today and you have projected that you will need $200,000 in seventeen years to pay for his/her college education. You feel you could conservatively average about a 9 percent annual return a year on your money that you would invest to meet this financial obligation. You could either put $40,000 in one lump sum and never have to put in another cent or if you did not have that kind of money, you could start from scratch with investing about $366 a month starting this year and through all the four years they will be attending college.

However, if you were to wait and not start saving until your child was eight years old, you would then have to set aside $54,000 in one lump sum if you could, or if you did not have money to start with, you would need to set aside about $633 a month.

If is far easier to find $366 a month than $633. So start early.

UGMA ACCOUNTS

Many people open what is called a UGMA account—Uniform Gift to Minors Act account. There's a tax break on money contributed to these accounts, but there are also drawbacks. If you are going to start saving for a child's education, I urge you to know all that you can about the ramifications of putting the money in your child's name versus your own name, but here are the main things to be aware of.

When putting money into a UGMA account for your child, you are just the custodian for it until she turns eighteen or twenty-one (account regulations vary by state, so make sure you check), at which time you legally have to turn everything in the account over to your child. There is nothing wrong with this, but you have to keep the following in mind. If Johnny Angel turns out to be Johnny Devil and decides to take this money at that time and not go to college but to buy the latest BMW on the market instead, he can. I've seen it happen. Now, to avoid the above scenario, some may suggest that a UGMA account can be hidden from a minor, but this is a problem for two reasons. First, any minor over age fourteen is expected to sign his or her tax return and thus has a good chance to notice the income from the account. Second and more seriously, if the custodian fails to turn over money that is due to the UGMA beneficiary, he or she breaches the statutory trust terms set by law and is liable for the consequences of that failure, just as a trustee would be, which may include surcharges and other sanctions from a court. So when you put money into a UGMA account, it is your child's, not yours.

Taxation of UGMA Accounts

Most people open a UGMA for the tax break that they do give you; in my opinion, there is nothing wrong with that. But in most cases this tax break is not as great in the end as one may think. Very likely, you'll be investing in good growth-oriented mutual funds or stocks, which you will keep for many years, which in turn will make the tax consequences negligible. But this is how UGMAs are taxed, just so you know.

Assuming the child has no other income and is under age fourteen, the first $750 of investment income falls into the child's zero bracket. The next $750 is taxed at 10 percent, and the rest is taxed at the parents' top bracket. This is the so-called "kiddie tax." If the child is fourteen or over, the parent's tax situation does not come into play at all. All the income is on the child's return and he or she is taxed as an entity unto himself/herself. These numbers are for tax year 2002 and are indexed for inflation. In any case, you should check the Form 1040 instructions for the appropriate number to use for a given tax year. Also note that the IRS regulations require all minors fourteen or older to sign their tax returns. Finally, please note that these tax rules are for income earned by a minor; there is no special treatment for UGMA accounts.

Financial Aid

Another element to keep in mind with UGMA accounts is that it may make it harder for your child to qualify for college financial aid. To determine how much financial aid your child can qualify for, your assets will be taken into consideration. Assets in your child's name will have to be used at the rate of 35 percent. If you have accumulated $50,000 in the UGMA account, your child will have to contribute 35 percent of that, or $17,500, before financial aid could kick in. If the tuition was $15,000, your child wouldn't be able to qualify. But only 6 percent of the parents' assets are taken into consideration, so if instead you kept that $50,000 in your name, just $3,000 of that money will have to go for tuition. This leaves the just-in-case possibility that $12,000 in financial aid could be granted. This is a big difference.

EDUCATIONAL SAVINGS ACCOUNT (FORMERLY THE EDUCATION IRA)

For years, the government has been offering an Education IRA (officially now known as the Coverdell Education Savings Account) as another way to save for a child's education. Tax reform legislation passed in 2001 and taking effect beginning in 2002 has made this a much better way to save. Prior to the new tax law, the largest amount you could save in an Education Savings Account was $500 per year per child; as of 2002, you can now save up to $2,000 per year per child (or, as the IRS terms it, per "beneficiary"). As with the Roth IRA, your contributions are not tax-deductible, but your earnings are tax-free when used for "qualified educational expenses." And starting in 2002, qualified expenses may include not only college and graduate school expenses but also tuition or other costs for grade school and high school and incidental education expenses, such as computers and educational software.

You don't have to be related to a child to contribute to an Education Savings Account, so godparents, friends of the family—anyone—can open an Education Savings Account to help fund a particular child's education. The only restriction here is that the beneficiary, or child, must be under the age of eighteen when contributions are made.

There *are* income limitations in effect for the person making the contribution to an Education Savings Account. For single individuals, eligibility starts to phase out at $95,000 of income and is completely phased out at $110,000 of income. For married couples filing joint returns, as of 2002 the limits are twice those for single individuals. That is, eligibility to contribute starts to phase out at $190,000 of income and is completely phased out at $220,000 of income for married partners filing jointly.

CAUTION: If you are already making contributions to a qualified state tuition program, here's what you need to know about contributing to an Education Savings Account for 2001 and prior. Before 2002, if you contribute to an Education Savings Account in the same year contributions have been made to a qualified state tuition program for the same child, your Education Savings Account contribution will be treated as excess contributions and subject to tax under Section 4973 of the IRS code. In the past, this rule has made it important that all parties interested in providing for the education of a particular child coordinate their efforts, so as not to inadvertently make excess contributions. The law states that excess contributions can be returned with no penalty imposed if the excess-contribution distribution, including any earnings attributable to the excess contribution, is received on or before the due date of the contributor's tax return, including extensions.

For 2002 and later, this rule no longer applies, and Education Savings Account contributions can be made in the same years as contributions to qualified tuition programs are made. In other words, as of 2002, you can save simultaneously in both an Education Savings Account and a qualified tuition program.

Unlike the Roth IRA (as well as the traditional IRA), the Education Savings Account doesn't restrict the source of contributions only to earned income, such as salary and wages. You can contribute money from interest payments, dividends, pension payments, capital gains, etc. This opens the door for grandparents (and possibly children themselves) to make contributions.

There's more good news. Starting in 2002, you can take tax-free distributions from an Education Savings Account and still be eligible to take the HOPE Scholarship or the Lifetime Learning credit, as long as the funds from the Saving Account and the credit are not used to cover the same educational expenses. For example, if a child's tuition is $25,000, and a withdrawal of $15,000 is made from an Education IRA, the excess of $10,000 can be used to claim the HOPE Scholarship or Lifetime Learning credit (see below). But money in an Education Savings Account may make it more difficult for your child to qualify for financial aid.

Please note: Your contributions to an Educational Savings Account do not have any impact on your eligibility to save any amount up to the maximum allowable in a traditional IRA, a Roth IRA, or a combination of the two. In other words, you can save for your child's education in an Education Savings Account and still put money away in an IRA for your own retirement.

Taxation and Regulations

Distributions from an Education Savings Account will not be subject to tax if used for "qualified education expenses." If distributions are not used for qualified education expenses, they will be subject to tax and included in the gross income of the person receiving the distribution. Additionally, if they are not used for qualified education expenses, a 10 percent penalty will usually apply. All funds in an Education Savings Account must be distributed before the time the beneficiary reaches the age of thirty, but the account can be transferred to another beneficiary, without tax or penalty, if the new beneficiary is a member of the family of the old beneficiary.

Because of the many changes made to the Education Savings Account by the 2001 tax reform law—the new higher annual contribution limit, the ability to contribute to the Education Savings Account and also save in 529 plans, the freedom to take distributions from an Education Savings Account and also use the HOPE Scholarship or Lifetime Learning credit in the same year—I have switched from not especially liking the Education Savings Account as an educational savings program to liking it very much indeed. This is an excellent tool to use if you qualify for it.

More Help with College

The Hope Scholarship

The Hope scholarship is there to help with the costs of education for students in the first two years of college (or other eligible post-secondary training). With hope, taxpayers are eligible for a tax credit equal to 100 percent of the first $1,000 of tuition and fees and 50 percent of the second $1,000 (the amounts are indexed for inflation after 2001) for a total maximum credit of $1,500. The credit is available on a per-student basis for net tuition and fees (less grant aid) paid for college enrollment. The credit is phased out for joint filers between $80,000 and $100,000 of income, and for single filers between $40,000 and $50,000 (indexed after 2001). The credit can be claimed in two taxable years (but not beyond the year when the student completes the first two years of college) with respect to any individual enrolled on at least a half-time basis for any portion of the year.

The Lifetime Learning Credit

When the Hope scholarship runs out, the Lifetime Learning credit kicks in. For those beyond the first two years of college, or taking classes part-time to improve or upgrade their job skills, the family will receive a 20 percent tax credit for the first $5,000 of tuition and fees through 2002 (for a total credit of $1,000), and for the first $10,000 thereafter (for a total credit of $2,000). The credit is available for net tuition and fees (less grant aid) paid for post-secondary enrollment. The credit is available on a per-taxpayer (family) basis and is phased out at the same income levels as the Hope scholarship.

529 COLLEGE SAVINGS PLANS

Another way to save for your child's education is by using what is called a 529 plan. Many states have adopted these plans that are open to anyone to use at any accredited college of their choosing.

In a particular 529 plan, regardless of what state you live in or what state your child actually ends up going to school in, you or anyone who wants to can put tens of thousands of dollars, up to $200,000 per account in some states, into one of these savings plans and use this money to pay for the costs at any accredited school of higher education. The costs include not only tuition, but also books, computers, and room and board. What you need to know is that anyone can put money into a 529 plan regardless of the relationship that person has to the benefactor of the plan.

Taxation of 529 Plans

When the earnings of this money are withdrawn from these accounts and used for educational purposes, there is no federal tax due. If the funds are put in a 529 plan within your own state, then when you go to take the money out to pay those school bills, state income taxes will be also avoided on the earnings on the fund. Not only that, but if you contributed to a 529 plan in the state where you live, you may get a tax deduction for your contribution. If you invest in a 529 plan outside of the state in which you reside, you will not get a state tax deduction.

Other benefits include the fact that if you have a 529 plan and your child gets a scholarship, in most cases you can get the 529 plan refunded to you without a penalty. Also, if your child decides not to go to college at all, you can ask to get a refund or else transfer the money to another family member. If you do get a refund under this circumstance, please know that there will be a 10 percent penalty plus taxes due, on the earnings in the account. But the bottom line is that unlike a UGMA account, in a 529 plan, you can take this money back and do whatever you want with it whenever you want. With an UGMA account, the money belongs to the child, who can access it at a state-mandatory age. You can't touch it.

Here are a few more things you should know about 529 plans. When you invest in a 529 plan you are simply putting money in an investment account that someone else is managing. If you do not like the investment performance of your particular 529 plan you can now, as of 2002, transfer your money to another 529 plan. You can make this transfer only once in any twelve-month period. Find out what the 529 plan that you are interested in invests money in, what their investment return has been, and who manages the money. On the other hand, be cognizant of tax benefits. Many people think that it is better to invest in a 529 plan out of state that's been getting better returns than their state's 529 plan. This could be true, but it will depend on whether your state plan and your own state income tax bracket, as well as the returns for the different plans. Run the numbers. This is what you need to take into consideration: any state tax deduction for your contributions as well as your child not having to pay state income taxes on the funds they withdraw to pay for educational expenses. Compare those bottom line numbers to the return the out-of-state 529 plans have been getting. The numbers will tell you which way is the best to go.

For the best up-to-date information on state 529 plans, visit the website www.savingforcollege.com.

Financial Aid/529 Plans

A 529 plan will not hurt your chances to get state financial aid, but it will hurt your chances to get aid from the federal government or from the college. Please note that the money you can obtain in aid from the college or the federal government is far more significant than what the state aid will give you.

Please put your desire to obtain financial aid into the equation before you open a 529 plan or any other plan such as a UGMA account or educational IRA. Please note that you may qualify for financial aid more readily than you think. To qualify for financial aid today, in most cases if you are going to have more than one child in college at the same time, which seems to be the case in many families, you can earn about $100,000 a year and still qualify.

Deduction for Higher Education Expenses

Starting in 2002, taxpayers who meet certain income qualifications can take a tax deduction for higher education expenses. The deduction is limited to $3,000 in 2002 and 2003 and increases to $4,000 in 2004 and 2005. This deduction is available even if you don't itemize deductions on your tax return. The deduction is currently sceduled to expire in 2005.

Here are the income qualifications: Single taxpayers can claim the deduction for 2002 and 2003 if their adjusted gross income does not exceed $65,000. Married taxpayers have to file a joint return to claim the deduction, which they can claim for 2002 and 2003 if their adjusted gross income does not exceed $130,000. For 2004 and 2005, the same income limitations will be enforced to claim the full $4,000 deduction. However, for those years, single taxpayers whose adjusted gross income is more than $65,000 but not more than $80,000, and married taxpayers whose joint adjusted income is more than $130,000 but not more than $160,000, can still take a deduction of up to $2,000 for higher education expenses.

You should note that the deduction is not "phased out" if you exceed the income limitation. You are either entitled to a deduction or you are not. For example in 2002, if you are single and your income is $65,000 and you've paid in excess of $3,000 in qualified higher education expenses, you are entitled to the deduction. If your income goes up by $1, your deduction will be zero.

The deduction for higher education expenses is in lieu of the HOPE Scholarship or the Lifetime Learning credit, so if you are eligible for both benefits, you must choose the one that is most beneficial for you.

If a student has received a distribution from an Education Savings Account, you cannot claim a deduction for the same expenses. If a distribution has been received from a 529 plan, you cannot claim a deduction based upon the income portion of the distribution, but you can claim a deduction for the principal portion of the distribution. For example, if you withdraw $1,000 from a 529 plan to pay for tuition, and the income portion is $150 and the principal portion of the distribution is $850, you can still claim a deduction for the $850 withdrawn from the 529 plan used to pay for tuition. In the case of a distribution from an Education Savings Account, no portion of the distribution can be used to qualify for this deduction.

YOUR CHILDREN'S REAL EDUCATION

College notwithstanding, your children's real education about money will take place all through their childhood, in the way you talk about money, in the way you present what working is all about, in the way they learn what they have a right to hope for in this world.

Children can absorb so much, if you will just trust yourself and open up to them. Play money games with them, using mail-order catalogs and price tags in stores—teach them value. When they're old enough, tell them about your 401(k), your strategies for investing, and what this all means in the context of their young lives. Rather than a traditional passbook savings account, give your children a little money in a mutual fund and let them keep careful watch over it. Talk to your children about how the world presented in advertisements, with a stunning array of things to consume, is different from the real world. Turn the dinner table conversation to the subject of money, and talk to your children about what it means to save for college, for example. Explain what credit cards are, and what you're doing when you go to the bank, and what the cash machine is all about. Talk about what it means to be poor. Talk about what it means to be rich. Talk about charity, and let your children see it in action often. Talk about prices, and values, at the super-market. Talk about mortgages, and debt, and insurance, and how you make choices about money.

By talking to your children about money, you will be talking to them about the way the world really works. And teaching them well.

ON TRUSTING YOURSELF

With this sixth step toward financial freedom, you have now learned to trust yourself more than you trust others. Now, along with that trust, you must watch over all that you have begun to create.

Whether you are managing your money yourself or have handed it over to an adviser, or a combination, you must know exactly how it is doing at all times. Remember, not only must you trust yourself; you must also be respectful of yourself and your money.

You can keep track any way you want, but you must keep track, studying all statements carefully and keeping watch in between. The easiest way to do this is by signing up for an online service like America Online, which will automatically value your portfolio and tell you exactly how much you are up or down every time you punch into it. Make checking your mutual funds and any other investments you own a part of reading the paper every day. It can be a pleasurable part of your day: you are creating wealth.

Your wealth.

With these last three steps we have covered the vital forces behind the doors to financial freedom.

⇥ You must be responsible to those you love.

⇥ You must be respectful of yourself and your money.

⇥ You must trust yourself more than you trust others.

Once you have taken these steps in their entirety, you are blowing the door to financial freedom off its hinges.

You will then be in a position to walk through that door. The next step, the seventh step to financial freedom, guarantees that you do not unintentionally limit what is to be found on the other side.

A NOTE ON STEPS 7, 8, AND 9

When I was a little girl, my grandfather, at the end of his long, hard life, would often say to me, "Suze, listen. They can take your money, they can take your business, they can take your family, they can even take your mind. The one thing they can never take," he would say, "is your heart, and you must grow up valuing your own heart. Love life for what you can give it, Suze, and don't get bitter over what it will take from you."

Who are the people in this life you truly love and cherish? What are the things you value most? What do you think, deep down inside, is the key to your freedom? Do you really think the answer is something as simple as money?

Most people have the goal in mind that they want to be free from their worries about money. That's a perfectly good goal, and that's what the purpose of the first six steps of this book has been: to help you break through the barrier of financial anxieties and put yourself in control of your money.

To me, though, that is just the beginning of financial freedom rather than the end of it. I have come to believe that the pursuit of money for its own sake is a hollow pursuit indeed. So these last three steps to financial freedom are not about money, but about true wealth. About abundance. About my grandfather's lesson that true financial freedom is when you know you are rich, with or without a penny.

The advice in these three short but all-important chapters is radically different from what you will read in any other financial book and unlike what you will hear from any other financial adviser. These last three steps will take you beyond what money can buy, and they will, if you let them, make you rich or, perhaps, remind you that you already are.

STEP 7

BEING OPEN TO RECEIVE
ALL THAT YOU ARE MEANT
TO HAVE

HAVE YOU EVER felt depressed or worried about something important in your life—your work, your relationships? When it happened, did you feel that you had no energy to get through the day, even to carry out your ordinary routines, much less to do challenging tasks in your life or your job? When you feel this way, isn't it true that the phone doesn't ring, the check or callback about a job you've been waiting for doesn't come, even your closest friends seem to vanish for the time being?

Then your mood turns around. You wake up feeling better and stronger one day—maybe there's a reason for it, maybe it just happens. Once your mood turns around, everything else does, too. The phone starts to ring again. The check or callback comes. A friend calls to invite you somewhere nice.

Believe it or not, it works the same way with you and your money. As we've seen, money is a living entity and responds to energy, including yours, and to how you feel about yourself. When you are worrying about money, feeling powerless over your finances and sorry for yourself, money won't want to hang around you, either. On the other hand, when you feel you're in control of your money and have enough to be generous with it, money will naturally flow your way. Strange, perhaps, but still true. You will become that money magnet you want to be.

We all spend a lot of energy fussing over our money, wishing for more income, balancing our checkbooks, wondering whether we'll have enough to pay the bills. But there's a question even more important to ask than "Do I have enough?": Is it possible that you are doing something to prevent more money from coming in? Might you be not only the prisoner, but also the warden in your financial jailhouse?

WHAT I LEARNED FROM THE PARROT SELLER

I was in Mexico once, and there was a merchant at a market who had many parrots for sale. They were just sitting on perches, none of them in cages, none flying away. I was fascinated by the fact that none of them were even trying to escape. I asked the merchant, "Do these birds just love you so much they have no desire to fly away?"

He laughed. "No," he said, "I had to train them to think their perches mean safety and security. When they come to think this, they naturally wrap their claws tightly around the perch and don't want to release it. They keep themselves confined, as if they've forgotten they know how to fly."

Was this hard to do? I asked. "With little birds it's very hard, sometimes even impossible," he said. "It's easy with the large birds."

Suddenly a lightbulb went off in my head. We are, I thought, just like those poor parrots. We have all been taught to clutch our money as tightly as we can, as if our money is the perch of our safety and security. Just like those parrots, we have all forgotten how free we really are—with or without the perch. The more afraid we are, the tighter we hold on, and the more we have trapped ourselves.

When I realized this I asked the merchant how he would go about "unteaching" this behavior. "Easy," he said. "You just show them how to release their grip, and then they can fly as free as they want."

Easy for the parrots, maybe, but how, I wondered, do we go about releasing our own grip on money?

YOUR EXERCISE

Please imagine that you've gone into your kitchen and turned on the faucet. Make a tight fist with both your hands and try to get a sustaining drink of water from that faucet from your fists. You won't be able to.

Now open up your hands, cup them. Put them under the faucet and accept the water flowing freely into your hands. You'll be able to drink to your heart's content. Your thirst will be quenched and the thought "not enough" won't even enter your mind.

It works the same way with our money. If we are grasp what we have so tightly, we are not open to receive notice all that may be trying to flow our way. We m release our grasp.

MY STORY

When I was starting as a commissioned broker, I never really knew for sure if I would make money the next month or not. It was scary. I'd think, Gosh, I had a good month this month, but what about next month? Then I'd freeze in a panic. The more I froze, the more depressed I felt, and sure enough, suddenly there was nothing I felt enthusiastic about buying or selling for my clients. Even when I did try to transact business with them, they could pick up on the lack of enthusiasm in my voice and didn't want to buy from me. It was as if they knew something was wrong. It was uncanny.

I remember being in this terrible funk once, and since I figured my clients would pick up on it anyway, the way I decided to deal with it was to stay home from work one day and escape by watching TV. I happened to catch one of those PBS fund-raising drives. As I continued to watch, I became really moved by the participants' passion, and during one of the pledge breaks, I picked up the phone and pledged $300. Three hundred dollars seemed like quite a hefty amount to me at that time, but somehow I felt that was the right number.

I can't tell you how good I felt when I hung up the phone. I got up, called a few friends, went back to work the next day. Later that week I was in my office, smiling, when Cliff, one of the _____ in the hall, came in and said, "Looks like _____ ts. What happened?" This made me stop _____ nt. I really didn't know at first, but after _____ s before, I realized that my mood had _____ ve the money to PBS.

_____ overty consciousness hit me and I _____ nk, I'd remember that first day. I _____ checkbook and send a check to one charity or another at the time. It was the strangest thing, but I would feel much better right away. Even stranger, as soon as I was feeling spunky again, lots of people would call and want to open a new account with me, or a newspaper article about me would appear and the phone would start ringing off the hook. In every instance, the amount I had given was showered back on me tenfold in no time. More important, with each check I wrote, whether it was for $5 or $500, I felt more powerful. I was able to extinguish the feeling of poverty that had been burning at me. That act, for me, was worth its weight in gold.

It took awhile until it hit me that I had stumbled upon—or perhaps was guided to—the answer to my questions "How does one release one's anxious grasp on money? How does one make oneself open to receive?"

By giving.

I started to test my theory back then with my clients. I went back through many of my files and divided my clients into two groups, one that gave money to charity on a regular monthly basis and one that did not. What I found was that those who donated regularly had an abundance of money, more than they really needed. Most of the others didn't.

I was fascinated by this but couldn't tell if my little study was accurate, because I had no way of knowing whether my more generous clients had more money to begin with; maybe their abundance had nothing to do with what they were giving. Maybe it was a fluke. So I took a different approach. When new clients who weren't doing so well came to see me, I asked those who I thought would be open to it to start donati money each month to a place they'd feel good about givi To new clients who also weren't doing so well but (i ion) wouldn't be open to it, I said nothing. I coul results. The better people felt about themsel they kept their hands open to receive b the more their financial situation improved. It was thrilling. The key was to start respectfully to give money away by making an offering on a regular basis. They had moved toward financial freedom by giving their money to others.

MONEY AND GRACE

In a course I once took in Eastern spiritual tradition, I learned about what is called the dharma of money, which means the "right action" of money. Beyond a shadow of a doubt, I now know the following principle is true: We experience prosperity, true financial freedom, when our actions with respect to money are dharmic, or righteous, actions—that is, actions of generosity, actions of offering.

Money flows through our lives just like water—at times plentiful, at times a trickle. I believe that each one of us is, in effect, a glass, in that we can hold only so much; after that, the water—or the money—just goes down the drain. Some of us are larger glasses, some of us smaller, but we all have the capacity to receive plenty more than we need if we allow it. When you make an offering, the glass will be filled again and again and again. I knew I always felt better right after I made an offering—stronger, worthier, more powerful. And after a while I began to believe that it was no coincidence that after I made an offering more money would always begin to

very strange concept at first; many of question that's always asked when- "But Suze, I know plenty of people erous of spirit as can be, people er give a penny away. How come

THE CHEAPSKATE

People who are cheap are more trapped than any of those parrots on perches. Being cheap has nothing to do with how much money you have. You can be rich and cheap, or poor and generous. Cheap people guard their water glasses and hoard what they have, to make sure nothing flows out. New water always has to flow in to keep the water in the glass fresh and useful; otherwise it grows stagnant, like standing water in a pond. People who are cheap are letting their money stagnate. What they are missing is the serenity that money handled responsibly, generously, and well can bring, and the pleasure.

Ask yourself this: Who is the most generous person you know? Someone who opens up her home to friends, her heart to those in trouble, her wallet judiciously and without resentment? How do you feel toward this person? Do you think this person can feel your love and appreciation coming back to replenish her?

Now ask yourself this question: Is there anyone in your life who you feel is cheap? How do you feel about this person? Do you think he or she can sense the way you feel?

And what about you? Do you think another person would describe you as cheap? Are you constantly worried that people are trying to take advantage of you and your money? Are you unwilling to let money go easily because you're frightened of not having enough? If you have truthfully answered "No" to these questions, no doubt you already give freely, of yourself and your money, and already know freedom in your thoughts, your heart, your soul. If you've hesitated over any of these questions, or found yourself answering "Yes," then by freeing up your money in this step, you will also free up your heart.

THE REASON TO GIVE

You open yourself to receive all that is meant to be yours. Giving not only when you feel poor, but also when you feel rich, lucky, grateful, expansive, vital. Giving to say please, and giving to say thank you. It's the impulse to give that puts you in touch with the best part of yourself—and the principles of abundance that are alive in the world. Yes, we help ourselves when we give, but that is not why we give.

YOUR EXERCISE

Decide on an amount of money that you feel you can give away freely every month. Let your inner voice determine the amount you should make as an offering. True giving comes as an impulse, so the amount need not be cast in stone, and it may vary from month to month. All that matters is that the amount be meaningful to you and that it be given with thought, humility, and gratitude. You must not give less than your inner voice tells you is the meaningful amount, for that is being cheap. That is not the way you want to thank the world and connect with it. Nor must you give more than you can afford, for that is not being responsible to yourself and your money. Your inner voice will dictate the amount each and every month, but each month it must be something.

If you are going to write a check to donate your money, write the check at the beginning of the month and keep it in a special place. Why the beginning of the month? So the act of giving isn't an afterthought. By starting your giving at the beginning of every month, you are making yourself and your offering a real priority, an act that will stay with you throughout the month. If you have so little money that you cannot afford to write a monthly check, make a point of gathering each day whatever spare coins or bills you can, and collect this money in your special place. Watch with respect as your offering accumulates. At the end of the month, and at the end of every month thereafter, please make your offering. Where? Using the following guidelines, choose with your heart—choosing where to give money is one of the great pleasures there is.

WHERE DO I MAKE MY OFFERING?

The action of giving money is different from giving anything else. Because of money's living energy field, it is very hard to give it to another person as a gift in a pure, dharmic way—or to put it in more common terms, with no strings attached. If you give money to an individual, often rather than freeing you, that act can create a whole new set of emotional debts that can wreak havoc on your life the same way financial debt can. Any kind of debt is bondage. This doesn't include giving a present of money for a birthday, wedding, or graduation, but applies only to gifts inspired by a pure impulse to give.

GIVING MONEY TO PARENTS

Studying the teachings of any religion will teach you that you are born with the duty of taking care of your parents, regardless of how well you feel they took care of you. When you give to your parents when they need it, you are truly opening up your hands and releasing your grasp on your money without creating debt. If your parents are in need and you can do this with tremendous humility, so as not to create a reverse bondage, you can give them your offering every month.

GIVING MONEY TO RELATIVES

We do not have the same duty to give to our brothers, sisters, or other family members as we do to our parents. Even though you may love your siblings or other relatives with all your heart, these are different kinds of relationships. When giving to a family member other than a parent, or a person who served in a parental capacity, there is a real danger of this gift of money tainting the purity of your love—thus tainting the purity of your intention. You may be thinking that this doesn't apply to you, given how much you love your brothers and sisters, but I ask you to take heed. I have seen the bitterness such "gifts" can eventually lead to many times in my practice, and I ask you to think very carefully before you give your monthly offering to a family member other than a parent.

For instance, if you happen to have a brother or sister making far more money than you are, do you secretly wish they'd do a little something to help make your own life easier? This is a common thought. But if such a "gift" came, do you really believe that no expectations would be attached? Won't that brother wonder about or care what you did with the money? What if you ran into your sister while you were having dinner at a nice restaurant? Would you freeze with guilt, in case she thought you were spending her gift frivolously? Might your sibling start asking you what you need money for? What if you start doing much better financially? Will you feel the need to give back the money? Will your brother or sister feel you should? If you find yourself answering "Yes" to any of these questions, the gift in question is neither purely given nor purely received. Maybe yours is one of the rare families where you truly do see each other as one. But most of us can't open our hands gracefully to give to or receive from family members in a pure way, so I do not recommend making your monthly offerings to family members.

GIVING MONEY TO FRIENDS

With friends, as with family members (other than children and parents), caregiving is not an inborn dharmic duty, which makes it extremely difficult to give money to friends in an appropriate way. I'm not saying that it can't be done, just that it is extremely difficult.

If you offer something as treasured to you as your money to a needy friend to, say, pay her bills, you have not really done anything to make yourself, or her, more powerful. In fact, you may have created a problem for yourself—because from now on, whenever you see that person, whether you want to or not, you will remember the "gift," and so will your friend. You will remember it in particular if you fall on some harder times somewhere down the road, especially if your friend is doing much better.

Money can forever alter the love in a friendship, so I do not recommend giving your monthly gift to friends.

GIVING MONEY TO A CHARITY

To my mind, the purest gift, the one that truly loosens our cramped clutch on money, is a gift to a charity. With this kind of gift, no debt is created, no bondage. You are faceless to the charity, a name on a donors' data bank. Maybe you're just slipping cash into a donation box, and no one will ever know that you have given it. If you give this way, your gift is pure.

I have found that the most liberating offering of all is one you make to a charity you care deeply about.

YOUR EXERCISE

To see just how powerful money is when it changes hands, try this experiment if you can. Walk up to the first person you see on the street (an ordinary stranger, not a panhandler) and try to hand that person a dollar bill. Note how you feel. How did he look at you? Did he take it? Did he say anything? How much anticipation (or dread) did you feel before giving him the dollar? Were you able to do it at all?

Now take another dollar bill and enter a place of worship. Locate the donation box and place the dollar in it. How did you feel this time? Did you say a prayer as you let that dollar drop? Did you feel better after making your offering? And there was no complicated reaction from the donation box, was there?

Compare how differently you felt after giving each "gift." Most of us feel awkward handing money to a person (and most of us would also feel awkward being the recipient, which should tell you something as well). Remember, the act of giving is meant to open you up, literally to alter how you feel; its power is rooted in your altered state. Most of us, too, feel a serenity when placing the donation in the box, for such a gift to charity is a pure one without the emotional baggage of giving to an individual person.

THOUGHTS OF POVERTY ARE BONDS OF POVERTY

Regardless of how much money you have, it is the natural tendency of the mind to think: I can't give money this month, I don't even have enough to pay the bills. Or: There are so many things that I need, I lack, I want.

This is the exact moment to give, to give an amount that is meaningful but realistic. You must break these thoughts of poverty, for thoughts of poverty are bonds of poverty, for thoughts of poverty are the chains that keep you bound to poverty. Mental chains may be invisible but they imprison you nevertheless. You must and you can break through, overcome, move beyond these mental barriers. You must open your hand. Repeat the new truth you created in Step 3 for strength, think of how much you do have, think of others with far less, and give thanks with your gift.

True financial freedom is a powerful state of mind, a state of being, and it comes from following all nine steps toward financial freedom. When you have reached this seventh step, and feel free to give from what you have and what you are creating, purely and from the heart, you are nearly free. With your offerings you are participating in the flow of wealth, which, I've discovered, is never-ending. It isn't how much you have that creates a sense of freedom. It's how you feel about what you have, or don't have, that either keeps you prisoner or sets you free—which is the eighth step to financial freedom.

STEP 8

UNDERSTANDING THE EBB AND FLOW OF THE MONEY CYCLE

WHEN THE THINGS that occupy us so intensely in the present have receded into the past, we look back at these events, which produce such turmoil and pain, with an entirely different eye. How often have you heard, for example, of someone who is devastated by being fired, only to land a much better job and end up happier? Or of someone whose spouse leaves her, and who decides—one, two, five years later—that it was the best thing that could have happened to her? Or of someone who emerges from a serious illness with a wisdom and appreciation of life that he had never had before? The passage of time always offers a new perspective. "If only I knew then what I know now." Haven't you ever uttered these words? Time can reveal many lessons, but often it takes us too long to listen. The eighth step to financial freedom is about understanding and accepting the natural cycles of money—as it ebbs and flows through our lives, sometimes in harmony, sometimes in discord, much like the cycles of our bodies, our planet—and the constant up-and-down movement of the economy you read about in the newspapers.

It is so important to learn to accept that your own money will also have its ups and downs. No matter how carefully you plan—even if you do every financial thing right—money, like every other living thing, isn't always going to behave in ways you can predict. Sometimes you'll have more than you expected, and at other times, money will flow out and you'll have less than you thought. There may be a time when you have money in the stock market and it goes down dramatically. Or maybe you suddenly inherit a valuable piece of property. Perhaps you are downsized from your job without warning—or given a surprise promotion. I've seen this kind of thing happen with my clients again and again. You think your financial life is rolling along a certain track and boom, you're going in a different direction.

These transitions can be exciting, or often scary, but they are all part of the natural cycles of life—and money. In Step 8, there are two lessons to remember about these natural ups and downs.

First, you must always take the long view of your financial future. If you have taken the steps outlined in this book, the setbacks you may have today or next year will not keep you from financial freedom. In order for you to create what is in your power to create, you must believe that you can and you will.

Second—and for some people this may be more difficult to

do than anything else I have told you so far—you must believe that everything that happens is positive, if you are willing to let it be.

I know some of you are going to say, "Suze, how can it be a positive thing if my husband leaves me and cleans out my bank account?" "How can it be a positive thing if I lose all my savings in a stock market crash?" Please understand, I am not saying such events won't be tragic and painful; I have been through some of them myself, and I know how hard they can be. But I also have learned that they can, if we are open to them, teach us lessons and give us gifts that we would never have found at more comfortable times. Things that seem almost unbearable as they're happening to you can even, in the long run, lead to riches you never imagined.

This is a very simple truth but it has tremendous power. That is how it got its reputation with our grandmothers. If you can believe that somehow everything happens for the best and hold firm to this belief, especially during troubled times or when you undergo what appear to be setbacks in your life, then you will be able to draw the good out of any situation. You will be looking for the benefit, the hidden treasure, and you will be able to profit from even the toughest experience.

I've heard it said that when you first have a dream for yourself, you think it's totally impossible. As time goes on, you'll think it's highly improbable. In the end, you will know it was inevitable all along. Remember to remember your power—everything you've learned with these steps to financial freedom—and put it all into practice every day, because in the grand scheme of life, you'll never really know how things are meant to turn out until they turn out. And when is that? When they turn out as they're meant to turn out, you'll know it.

I learned this from watching the life of my dad.

MY DAD'S STORY

Maybe yes, maybe no.

After his little chicken shack had burned to the ground, my dad was penniless. Because he wasn't properly insured, everything was a total loss, and he had absolutely no money to start up another business. His health was suffering, too; he had gotten emphysema from all the smoke he inhaled in the fire. It was a very hard time in our family. My mom was already working full-time as she always had, and my brothers and I were doing whatever we could to bring in extra money. Still, for a long time after the fire, there was never enough. Everyone was saying how unlucky my dad had been, which started to bother me, so I went right up to him and asked him if he was unlucky. "Maybe yes," he said, "maybe no."

One day I heard him on the phone taking a call. "Really?" he was saying. "How can this be? Are you sure?" And then, "Great! I'll take it!" I walked into the hallway where the phone was and he looked at me and said, "Honey, we are back in business!" I can remember to this day how thrilled he was. A salesman who had been one of my dad's suppliers at the chicken shack told my dad that the meat-packing company was going to give him the start-up money to open a new place, and that they had found the perfect location for him as well. I said, "See, Dad? You are lucky after all, aren't you?" Again he just looked at me and said, "Maybe yes, maybe no."

A few months later, Morry's Deli (named after my dad) opened up on Chicago Avenue in downtown Chicago; my brothers and I worked there every day after school. From the beginning, there was always a line out the door, and this time I knew my dad was really going to make it. Then one day he came home looking forlorn, and said that Northwestern Medical School was expanding and taking over our space, so we would have to find a new location. This can't be, I remember thinking. We were just starting to do so well. Just to check, I said, "I guess we're not so lucky after all, Pops," and he said, "Maybe yes, maybe no."

My dad began looking for a new place. When the word got out that he needed a new location, a landlord back in Hyde Park, where the original chicken shack had been, contacted him and said that he had the perfect spot and that, again, everyone would help with the cost of moving back to Hyde Park. He was so happy—in fact, we were all so happy since, for my brothers and me, it was a whole lot easier getting to Hyde Park than downtown Chicago from where we lived. The day he signed the new lease, I felt I had to set the luck record straight, so I said, "I guess this means our luck has changed for the better, right, Dad?" "Maybe yes, maybe no."

The new store was also a success from the day it opened. I loved it. My brothers and I would race around seeing who could make the sandwiches fastest, especially Dad's corned beef sandwiches, a house specialty. Dad's health was getting worse, but somehow we were able to manage. My brothers Gary and Bobby took turns running the store, and I would work all summer when I was back from school.

Only two years after the store opened, though, we had another fire. It happened at night, at least, so the blessing was that nobody was hurt. This time, I said outright to my dad that I thought he was the unluckiest man in the world, thinking that finally he would agree. "Maybe yes," he said, "maybe no."

It turned out that the fire was caused by an electrical short that had started in the apartments next door. The landlord, knowing that my dad had been doing such great business, put him on notice that he was going to triple the rent after he rebuilt the place. There was no way we could afford it, so, at the age of seventy, with his emphysema getting worse, my dad began looking, once again, for another location. When word got out, a representative from the University of Chicago, who loved my dad (not to mention his food), called up and said they had this place right on campus and would my dad like to open the first private business ever on the university campus? The spot was perfect, right by the bookstore and a hospital where thousands of people worked, and the rent was afford-able. "Wow," my dad said, "I'd love to!" Then he called up his old landlord to say he wasn't moving back in. The landlord was in such shock that he offered him back his spot totally rebuilt, and for less rent than he had been paying before. Now my dad was the one in shock. He took both places.

Soon, with my brother Gary's help, both places were up and running—and successful beyond my father's wildest dreams. For the first time ever, there was enough money—more than enough. My dad knew, too, that my mom would be taken care of after he was gone, and he was so proud that Gary would carry on the family business. I went up to him one day as all this was happening and I said, "You know what, Pops? You are one lucky duck."

This time, to my utter amazement, he said: "Yep, Suze, you got that right."

Not long after that, on June 21, 1981, which was Father's Day, my dad died—in his eyes a lucky man.

My dad's gift was knowing that good luck and bad luck are always in the eyes of the beholder, and always cycling; neither rarely stops for long in any one place. He was able to see past the present situation, whatever it was, to the future. Another thing about Dad's story: Many of the good things would never have happened if the bad events hadn't happened first. If the second fire hadn't happened, and the landlord hadn't tried to raise the rent, Dad would never have found his store at the university nor gotten a better deal at the first store.

YOUR EXERCISE

Please think about your entire financial history. Try to remember all the worst things that have happened to you. Think back to how you felt—tense, afraid, paralyzed, angry, determined to prevail, whatever the emotions were at the time; there may have been several emotions at once. Remember the entire sequence of events. What happened before the crisis to set it off? What was the crisis itself like? How did the crisis resolve itself? What elements of it seemed crucial at the time, and do they still seem important now? How did it change your life? Write down the story if it will help you remember, or pull out any old notes or papers about it, to help you remember how you felt at the time. Here are a few questions to trigger your memories:

⇥ Did you ever not get a job you wanted badly?

⇥ Did you ever quit a job or get fired without knowing where your next penny was coming from?

⇥ Have you ever lost a lot of money on an investment?

⇥ Have you ever had a business deal that you worked hard to put together fall to pieces at the last minute?

⇥ Have you ever had a relationship break up and, in addition to the grief you suffered, found yourself also very worried about money?

⇥ Have you ever had a friendship end over money?

⇥ When and why in your life were you the most frightened about money?

Now, let me ask you this: Have there come any gains from any of these losses? Didn't any of your misfortunes turn out, over time, to be the best thing that could possibly have happened to you? Didn't the gains *come* in ways you could never have predicted? You can turn the same exercise around and do it backward—review events that seemed to you at the time like lucky breaks—and I wouldn't be surprised to discover that these lucky breaks sometimes brought with them problems or heartaches you never expected. Did that mean they weren't really lucky? No—it means they were part of the cycle, and the cycle is natural. Gains and losses aren't flukes, or curses; they are built in, like the doors and windows in a house; and they both have the capacity to bring us closer to the sort of life we long for.

In my own case, I know that my greatest periods of genuine growth came from the not-so-good times. What I got was more than just practical learning, though God knows there was plenty of that and it was very important. Still, it was the times of having nothing that taught me how much I really did have. They taught me to be grateful and to have faith in the natural rhythms of money and life. That inner knowing is the essence of the eighth step.

INNER KNOWING

It is in this eighth step where we must really take the leap and believe that our own inner knowledge and beliefs are what truly create financial freedom. If you want money in your life, then you must welcome it, be open to it, and treat it with respect. Your beliefs and your attitude are what will make you feel rich, feeling free to believe in yourself, knowing that you will take the right actions with your money, no matter how much money you have or do not have today and knowing that everything really does happen for the best.

Next time you feel that bad luck has struck you again, I hope you'll remember my dad's simple phrase—*maybe yes, maybe no*. If you can face your misfortune and ask yourself how you can find the gift, the lesson, in what is upsetting you now, then you are rich despite the setback. And you are only one last step away from true financial freedom.

STEP 9

RECOGNIZING
TRUE WEALTH

NOW IT IS TIME to answer the question, What is true wealth, true financial freedom? This question is the real bottom line of life and each one of us must address it, regardless of the bottom line that shows up each month on our bank statements. Why? Because the quality of our lives does not depend only on how we accumulate, save, and spend our money. True financial freedom lies in defining ourselves by who and what we are, not by what we do or do not have. You are the person you are right now. We cannot measure our self-worth by our net worth.

RUTH'S STORY

I have a friend named Ruth whom I love dearly. Now ninety-four years old, she's the most extraordinary woman I've ever met. She received her Ph.D. in ancient Greek literature from Yale at a time when that was still a rare achievement for a woman, and has spent her life learning, teaching, reading, and living.

She was married for most of her life to Leon, whom she loved deeply. After he died some years ago, she came to me for financial advice. For all her education, she had always left their finances to Leon, and she knew that now she would have to take control herself. After we added all the numbers, she understood that she had far more money than she had imagined she would. She seemed relieved at the news but strangely untouched by it; her money, I would come to learn, has very little to do with who Ruth is.

As our friendship grew, she and I would discuss her finances—and everything else under the sun—every single Wednesday over lunch. There is not a thing that, to this day, I can't talk to Ruth about. She is so wise, so profoundly contented with who she is, that simply being in her presence restores me in a way that's hard to describe in words. I feel that she lives in a state of grace, and that whoever is in her presence is touched by it, too.

In recent years, Ruth grew weaker and she finally decided to give up her apartment. She chose to move into a life-care community, where you deposit a large sum of money, pay a monthly maintenance, and receive whatever nursing or medical care you need. We had invested well over the years, and Ruth had more than enough money to stay in her own house with live-in nursing care, which was what I had thought she would want to do—but her inner voice told her she wanted the home. We packed her books and journals, some souvenirs from her travels, her photographs, her tapes of Leon's lectures, all the things that matter to her, and she moved in.

Ruth to this very day still exudes that state of contentment, of grace, which makes her seem stronger, as if her body weren't beginning to fail her. Her nieces visit her, as do the friends she has still and some of her former students. Not long ago, I asked her how it felt to be growing more frail. "Suze," she said, "my future is so tiny and my past and present are so rich. It surprises me to say this, but I'm not afraid. I'm truly happy and content just as I am." I believed her absolutely.

Ruth's freedom is in the life she has led and the love she knows now. Within herself she knows beyond a shadow of a doubt that she is rich, not just in money, but in the realm of true wealth, where nothing she has can be taken away from her. Though she's in weakening health, at ninety-four, every day she feels rich and free, even strong—and the irony is that her real wealth has nothing to do with her money.

If you today could foresee your last days, if you were on your deathbed right now—and one day you will be, believe me—do you think you would be there wishing you had more money? Or wishing that you were vastly rich in the way my friend Ruth is?

YOUR EXERCISE

Please find a time when you will be alone in your house for *at least* an hour. While everyone is gone, spend that hour inhabiting, really inhabiting, your house. Pretend, for a while, that your house is a store. Walk around, and imagine that you were going to be putting a price tag on every item in this store. You know what you paid, when they were brand-new, for your sofa, refrigerator, washing machine, dining room table, dresser, and three-year-old car. What do you think they would be worth now? Affix the imaginary price tags to these items based on what they would be worth today if your life really were a store.

Now stop to examine the items that really matter to you, the items that resonate with meaning and memories, the items that tug at your heartstrings. Those tools your dad wanted you to have when he died. The funny lamp you and your first lover bought when you fell in love and thought, in those days, that anything was possible. Your small daughter's stuffed animals, all lined up on a shelf. Family photos. A wedding ring. The painting over the mantel that was the first art you ever bought. Your mother's jewelry box and porcelain teapot. Your diary. The scuffed-up desk you've worked at since you were a teenager.

What kind of a price tag would you put on these items? What you're really asking is, What kind of price tag can you put on your *life*?

NINE STEPS: A REVIEW

The world of money, of numbers and stock markets and interest rates and credit cards, seems on the surface about as far as it could be from the world of spirituality, of seeking meaningful answers to the big questions of life. Imagine how it feels to be on a noisy trading floor on Wall Street. Imagine instead how it feels to be alone in a quiet place of worship. But these two worlds must flow in and out of each other, because it takes both money and spiritual understanding to sustain us. Truly speaking, what determines where our money with its awesome power will go, and what it will do for ourselves and others? If we listen, those answers come from the center of our being, from who we really are.

We have learned how powerful a force money is, how it can create fears that will, if we let them, paralyze us in this life. And we have learned how to silence these fears, and put them behind us. We have learned about the dharma of money, the essential right actions that, once we take them, will put our money, and with it, each and every one of us, in step with the natural order of things, on a course with what comes next, and what comes after that. Most important, we have learned an essential lesson about abundance—that abundance is in crucial ways a state of mind. Our money will see us through this life, and even has the power to live on after we are gone, seeing the people we love through their lives, too, and even on into generations we will never know.

Once we have taken care of the people we love, it is worthy to accumulate money, and in this book we have learned how to attract and create great fortunes. With the responsibility of accumulating money, however, comes the equally urgent responsibility of using money wisely, taking satisfaction in what it can do, knowing as well what it can't do. Very rich people who take no pleasure in their money and who never share their bounty will never be financially free. People with much, much less, who do take immense pleasure in what they have so carefully created, will in the end be far freer.

I hope that this book will remind you of the richness and worthiness that have been in your life all along, and I hope, too, that this book will help you to create more wealth, to sustain you and those you love. I would like to think that you've written notes to yourself in it, turned down the pages that were useful to you, and marked passages that you might want to turn to again later. But this book alone will not make you financially free. Money itself cannot make you financially free. Only you can make yourself financially free, and you can do it—and so much more. You have that power.

Now it is time for this book to end, and for your future to begin. Believe these lessons; live them, for financial freedom is within your reach. I wish you abundance, joy, and true wealth—of all kinds.

INDEX

AB tax-planning trusts, 116–132
agent, and power of attorney, 78–79
American Association of Individual
    Investors (AAII), 261
assets, transfer of, 69, 97
attorneys:
    choosing, 72–74
    and probate fees, 72
    and trusts, 65

bypass trusts, 118–131
    and estate taxes, 118, 122,
        123–126
    need for, 126–127
    and probate, 121–122, 123–126
    restrictions on, 121

capital gains taxes, 251–252
charity, 306–315
    dharma of, 311
    exercises in, 310–311, 313–314
    gifts to, 313–315
    and poverty, 314–315
children:
    and college, 287–298
    disinheriting, 128–129
    lessons about money, 286–298

on SSI, 129
    and trusts, 70–71, 129–131
    and UGMAs, 289–291
closed-end funds, 246
cognitive impairment, 105–107
college, cost of, 287–298
compounding interest, 171–175
credit, equity line of, 202
credit cards, 182–196
    average daily balance, 191–192
    and cash advances, 192–193
    fees for, 192–193, 226–227
    grace period of, 192
    hidden, 186–187
    and intelligent debt, 190–194
    and interest charges, 187–190,
        191–194, 196–198
    minimum payments on, 192
    paying off, 196–201
    penalties of, 193
    switching, 190, 193–194
credit shelter trusts, 118–131

daily benefit amount, 109–110
debt, 182–212
    borrowing from 401(k), 199–201
    burden of, 184, 311

debt (*cont.*):
Consumer Credit Counseling
Service (CCCS), 205–212
control of, 194–212
credit card, 183–201
hidden, 186–187
institutional vs. personal, 184
intelligent, 190–194
paying off, 194–203
taking stock of, 195–196
disability, long-term, 113–115
dollar cost averaging, 175–182,
261–262
durable power of attorney for health
care, 75–78

elimination period, 109
equity line of credit, 202
estate taxes:
and bypass trusts, 101–102, 120,
124–128
marital deduction in, 129–130
and revocable living trust, 125
executor of will, 57
expense ratio, 250–251
expenses, *see* spending

fears, 21–33
exercises in, 28–29, 31–32
facing up to, 23–29
new truths about, 29–33
and time for money, 22–23
financial advisers, 266–285
client questionnaire, 276–285
fees of, 227, 269–271
interviewing, 272–275
RIAs, 271–272
roles of, 268–269
financial history, 323–324
financial situation, current, 39–44
529 college savings plans, 295–
298
found money, 212–229
commissions, 227
credit card fees, 226–227

investments, 212–222
IRA fees, 227–228
mortgage payments, 224–226
mutual funds, 227–228
pay phones, 228–229
self-service gas pumps, 228
taxes, 223–224, 229
401(k) plans, 141–142, 143–145
borrowing from, 199–201,
202–205
vs. IRAs, 154
403(b) plans, 145
friends, giving money to, 313
front-end loaded funds, 253

goals, 1–4, 6–7

Health Insurance Counseling and
Advocacy Program, 107
holographic wills, 56
home equity loans, 201–205
home health care clause, 110–113
honesty, 35–50
about current financial situation,
39–44
exercises on, 43–44
and hidden debt, 186–187
hidden expenses and, 39–42
and spending habits, 37–38,
44–45
and trimming expenses, 45–48
Hope Scholarship, 293

index funds, 247–252
individual retirement accounts, *see*
IRAs
inflation rider, 110
inner voice, 234, 324–325
insurance:
life, 79–92
long-term-care, 92–113
long-term disability, 113–116
and Medicaid, 96–97
and mortgage payments, 226
quoting services, 84–85

interest:
  compounding of, 171–175
  and credit cards, 187–190,
    191–196, 196–198
  and money-market accounts,
    215–216
intestate succession, 74–75
investments, 171–175, 212–229
  AAII, 261
  closed-end funds, 246
  compounded interest, 171–175
  dollar cost averaging, 175–182,
    261–262
  financial advisers, 266–285
  and found money, 212–229
  getting started in, 260–262
  index funds, 247–251
  language of, 243–255
  lump sum for, 260–265
  managed funds, 247, 249–252
  money-market accounts,
    214–222, 217–222
  mutual funds, 244–255
  open-end funds, 245–246
  retirement accounts, 139–141
  RIAs, 271–272
  vs. spending, 138–139
IRAs, 156–168
  contributions to, 156–157,
    164–165
  educational, 291–295
  fees for, 228
  guidelines, 164–165
  vs. 401(k) plans, 167
  Roth, 158–168
  and SEPP, 154–155
  and taxes, 167–168
  traditional, 156–168

Keogh plans, 169–170, 170–171

life insurance, 79–92
  amount of, 81–85
  guaranteed earnings of, 88–89
  need for, 80–81, 83

projected earnings of, 88–89
  quoting services, 84–85
  term, 86–92
lifetime learning credit, 295
living wills, 78–79
loans, home equity, 201–205
long-term-care insurance, 92–113
  activities of daily living, 105
  affordability of, 100–102
  bargain of, 98–100
  benefit period of, 108–109
  choosing, 102–103
  cognitive impairment, 105–106
  daily benefit amount, 109
  elimination period of, 108, 109
  home health care clause,
    110–113
  inflation rider, 110
  vs. Medicaid, 96–97
  and medical necessity, 105
  premiums of, 99–100, 108
  qualification for benefits of,
    105–106
  questions about carrier, 103–105
  questions about policy, 105–113
long-term disability insurance,
    113–116

managed funds, 247, 249–252
marital deduction, 129
Medicaid:
  and insurance, 96–97
  and special needs trusts, 129–130
medical necessity, 105
money:
  attracted by respect, 133–135,
    145, 229–230
  distancing people from, 35–36
  found, 212–229
  future value of, 174–175
  giving away, 306–315
  and grace, 308
  healthy environment for, 187, 214
  investing, see investments
  language of, 243–255

money (*cont.*):
  and messages from past, 14–15
  multiplying, 172–174
  outgoing, 37–38, 44–45
  people considered before, 53–54,
    275
  physical contact with, 36
  and poverty, 314–315
  and power, 36, 49
  responsibility for, *see* responsibility
  teaching children about, 286–298
  time and, 22–23, 171–172
  and wealth, 327–330
money cycle, 317–325
  exercise in, 323–324
  and inner voice, 324–325
  long view of, 318–319
  and positive outlook, 319
money-market accounts, 215–222
  choosing, 220–222
  fees, 222
  opening, 219–220
  Treasury, 218
money purchase Keogh plans, 169
mortgage, paying off, 224–226
mutual funds, 244–255
  buying, 261–263
  and capital gains tax, 251–252
  closed-end, 246
  expense ratio of, 250–251
  index, 247–252
  load vs. no-load, 227–228,
    252–255
  managed, 247, 249–252
  open-end, 245–246
  selling, 263–265

net asset value (NAV), 246, 251
non-U.S. citizens trusts, 129
nursing home insurance, *see* long-
  term-care insurance

open-end funds, 245–246
openness, 303–315
  and charity, 306–315

and cheapskates, 309
exercises in, 305, 310, 311,
  313–314
and poverty, 314–315
and security, 304–307

parents, giving money to, 311
past:
  exercises in, 15–19
  as key to future, 9–19
  money messages from, 14–15
pay phones, 228–229
people first, then money, 53–54, 275
positive outlook, 318–319
poverty, and charity, 314–315
power, to use your money, 36, 49
power of attorney for health care,
  durable, 75–79
private mortgage insurance (PMI),
  201–202
probate:
  and bypass trusts, 121–122,
    123–126
  fees, 72
  and revocable living trust, 124
  of will, 57–59, 71–72
profit-sharing Keogh plans,
  169–170
property taxes, 226

rear-end loads [12(b)1 charges],
  253–255
registered investment advisers
  (RIAs), 271–272
relatives, giving money to, 312
respect, 133–230
  and debt, 182–212
  and dollar cost averaging,
    175–182
  exercise in, 135–137
  and found money, 212–229
  and investing, 138–142, 172–175,
    213–222
  money attracted by, 131, 142
  and retirement funds, 137–172

responsibility, 51–132
  and durable power of attorney for
    health care, 75–79
  and life insurance, 79–92
  and long-term-care insurance,
    92–113
  and long-term disability insur-
    ance, 113–116
  to people before money, 53–54
  and tax-planning trusts, 116–131
  and trusts, 60–75
  and what-ifs, 52–53
  and wills, 54–59
retirement accounts, 137–171
  absence of, 155
  basics of, 149–155
  contributions to, 144–145,
    149–151
  and early retirement, 137
  early withdrawal penalties of,
    153, 154–155
  and employment changes,
    153–154
  exercise in, 145
  401(k), 143–145, 149–151, 152,
    153
  403(b), 143
  and investing, 138–155
  IRAs, 153–154, 156–168
  Keogh, 169–171
  qualified employer, 153
  for self-employed, 168–171
  SIMPLE, 149–151, 170–171
  and taxes, 144–145, 152
  and trusts, 68–69
  withdrawals from, 155
return of premium option, 101
revocable living trusts, 60–75
  definitions, 65–68
  and estate taxes, 122–123
  and probate, 123
  setting up, 65–70
  and surviving spouse, 124–126
RIAs (registered investment advisers), 271–272

risks, and dollar cost averaging,
    175–182
Roth IRA, 158–163, 166–168
  advantages of, 166–167
  conversion to, 159–163
  eligibility, 158–159

security, and openness, 304–308
self-employed individuals, retirement
    plans for, 168–171
SEP (simplified employee pension
    plan), 168–169
SEPP (substantially equal periodic
    payments), 154–155
SIMPLE plans, 145, 170–171
Social Security, and retirement,
    145–149
Social Security Income (SSI), 129
special needs trusts, 129–131
spending:
  earning and, 140–142
  hidden expenses, 39–42
  and honesty, 37–38, 48
  vs. investing, 139–140
  trimming of, 45–48
spouses:
  marital deductions for, 129–
    130
  non-U.S. citizens, 129–130
  surviving, 125–126
SSI (Social Security Income), 129
stockbrokers:
  becoming your own, 242–243
  and doubt, 239–240
  and financial advisers, 266–285
  and trust, 231–233, 238–242

taxes:
  capital gains, 251–252
  estate, 117, 122–123, 124–126,
    128
  and IRAs, 156–168
  property, 226
  quarterly payment of, 223–224
  refunds, 229

taxes (*cont.*):
  and retirement funds, 144–145,
    152
tax-planning trusts, 116–129
term life insurance, 86–92
Treasury money-market account, 218
true wealth, 327–330
trust, 231–300
  exercises, 236–238, 241–242
  and feeling your financial pulse,
    234–238
  financial advisers, 266–285
  inner, 234
  and the language of money,
    243–255
  and stockbrokers, 231–233,
    238–240
  testing the waters, 255–265
  of yourself, 257–58
trusts, 60–75
  absence of, 74–75
  and children, 70–72, 129–131
  components of, 66–68

  funding of, 68–70
  and probate, 121–122
  setting up, 65–68
  special needs, 129–131
  tax-planning, 116–131
  vs. wills, 60–62, 71–75

UGMAs (uniform gift to minors
    accounts), 289–291
U.S. Treasury bills, 218

wealth, 327–330
wills, 54–60
  absence of, 74–75
  as backup, 72
  codicils to, 56
  contested, 59
  executor of, 57
  holographic, 56
  living, 78–79
  probate of, 58–59, 71–72
  vs. trusts, 60–61, 71–74

ABOUT THE AUTHOR

SUZE ORMAN is the author of three consecutive *New York Times* bestsellers—*The Road to Wealth*, *The Courage to Be Rich*, and *The 9 Steps to Financial Freedom*—and the national bestseller *You've Earned It, Don't Lose It*. She has written, co-produced, and hosted three PBS pledge shows based on her books, which are among the most successful in the network's history.

Currently a contributing editor to *O: The Oprah Magazine*, Suze Orman is the personal finance editor and hosts special programming titled "Suze Orman's Invest for Success" on CNBC. She appears regularly on QVC as host of her own "Financial Freedom" hour and has a nationally syndicated weekday radio talk show, "The Suze Orman Show." A Certified Financial Planner® professional, she directed the Suze Orman Financial Group from 1987–1997, served as vice president of investments for Prudential Bache Securities from 1983–87, and from 1980–83, was an account executive at Merrill Lynch.

A sought-after speaker, Suze Orman has lectured widely throughout the United States and South Africa. A former financial contributor on NBC News' *Today* and contributor to *Self* magazine, Suze has been featured in such major magazines and newspapers as *Newsweek, People, The New Yorker, Modern Maturity, The New Republic,* and *USA Today*. She has also appeared on *Dateline*, CNN, MSNBC, *Good Morning America, The View,* and numerous times on *Larry King Live* and *The Oprah Winfrey Show*.

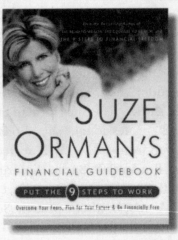